COUNTRY WAYS

COUNTRY WAYS

A Celebration
of
Rural Life

The Reader's Digest Association, Inc.

Pleasantville, New York

Cape Town, Hong Kong, London, Montreal, Sydney

READER'S DIGEST CONDENSED BOOKS

Editor-in-Chief: Barbara J. Morgan

Executive Editor: Tanis H. Erdmann
Senior Managing Editor: Marjorie Palmer
Managing Editors: Jean E. Aptakin, Anne H. Atwater, Thomas Froncek
Senior Staff Editors: Angela H. Plowden-Wardlaw,
Virginia Rice (Rights), Ray Sipherd
Senior Editors: M. Tracy Brigden, Linn Carl,
Joseph P. McGrath, James J. Menick
Associate Editors: Thomas S. Clemmons, Emily Easton, Catharine L. Edmonds,
Alice Jones-Miller, Maureen A. Mackey
Senior Copy Editors: Claire A. Bedolis, Jeane Garment, Jane F. Neighbors
Senior Associate Copy Editors: Maxine Bartow,
Rosalind H. Campbell, Jean S. Friedman
Associate Copy Editors: Ainslie Gilligan, Jeanette Gingold,
Tatiana Ivanow, Marilyn J. Knowlton
Editorial Administrator: Ann M. Dougher
Art Director: William Gregory
Executive Art Editors: Soren Noring, Angelo Perrone
Associate Art Editors, Research: George Calas, Jr., Katherine Kelleher

CB PROJECTS
Executive Editor: Herbert H. Lieberman
Senior Editors: Dana Adkins, Catherine T. Brown, John R. Roberson

CB INTERNATIONAL EDITIONS
Senior Staff Editor: Gary Q. Arpin
Associate Editors: Eva C. Jaunzems, Antonius L. Koster

The following stories appear in condensed form:
"Reverend Black Douglas" and "Cocks Must Crow."

The text and illustration credits that appear
on pages 298–299 are hereby made a part of this copyright page.

Library of Congress Cataloging-in-Publication Data
Country ways. Includes unacc. melodies with chord symbols.
Includes index. 1. Country life—United States.
2. Country life—Literary collections. 3. American literature.
4. Cookery, American. 5. Folk-songs, English—United States.
I. Reader's Digest Association.
S521.5.A2C684   1988   973'.09734   87-23308
ISBN 0-89577-290-6

Printed in the United States of America

CONTENTS

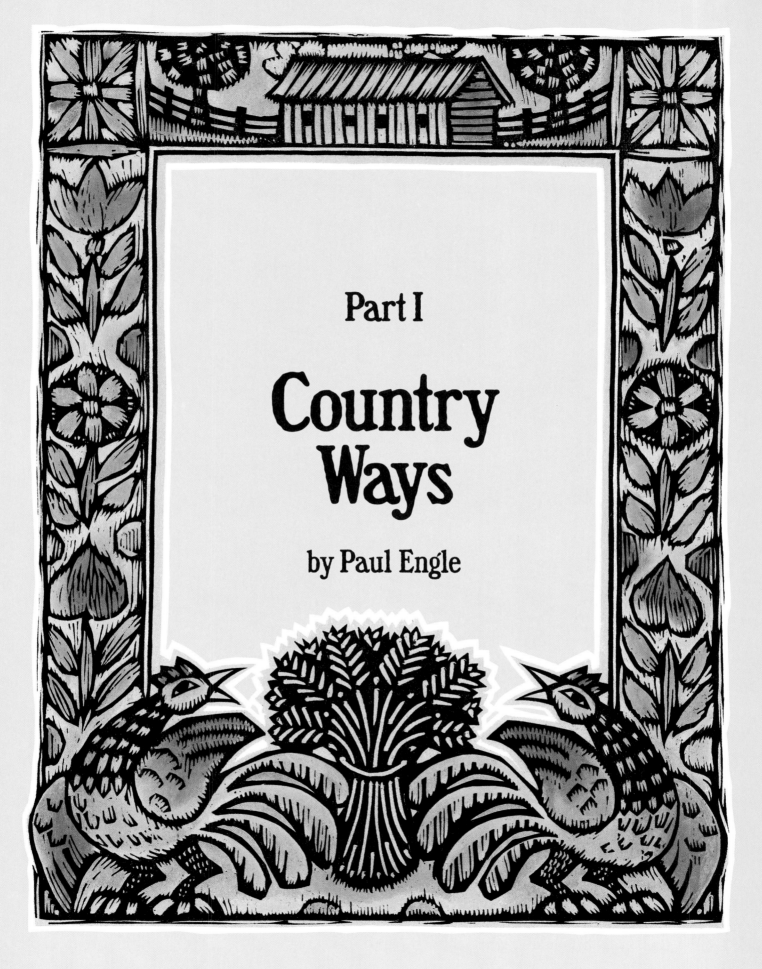

Part I

Country Ways

by Paul Engle

COUNTRY ROADS

Country roads will lead you to another America.

Interstate highways level down hills, remove most curves and all of the corners. Roads in the country keep the flow, the rise and fall of the land, the bends made perhaps a century ago when a horse with wagon turned aside to avoid a tree, a stump, a bog, and no one bothered to straighten out the welcome change from an unswerving roadbed. There is an English poem that describes how "the rolling English drunkard made the rolling English road." Although in Iowa my grandmother would have furiously rejected the notion that any drunkard ever staggered through the dense prairie grass to make a road to her farm, there were turns and twists in our road that suggested that perhaps the first human path was beaten over the low hills by wandering feet not quite certain of their direction and somewhat out of control.

If you have time, drive down an unpaved road in the country, with its covering of gravel or crushed stone. Graders and earthmovers have seldom beaten these roads into submission. They waver as they always did, almost never go through deep cuts, give a feel for the dirt underneath and the ancient contours shaped many thousands of years ago. Another advantage of the unpaved road is that because of its surface, you cannot drive fast. From the interstates, houses, fields and livestock are distant and rapidly disappearing objects. This is also true of the landscape from two-lane concrete highways. From country roads, on the other hand, your speed is slow enough to give a close look at the shapes of farmhouses, at the whole length of fields planted with corn, soybeans, cotton, sugarcane, flax, alfalfa or timothy hay (you have to have the time to tell the difference).

Here is the authentic rural life, whether you are in the red hills of Georgia, the California valleys, the small fields of New England or the great spreads of Texas, or the gently rising and falling fields of the Midwest with their massive reaches of cornstalks. You can watch a farmer plowing, cultivating, picking corn, combining soybeans, cutting cotton or hay. If you wave to him (or her—many farm wives operate machinery today), you will probably get a wave in return, and if one has stopped near the road, you may discover he is happy to quit work for a few minutes and talk. It all goes back to the days when people were few and far apart in the country and any stranger was welcome.

You will find a different sort of traffic on the country roads: farm machinery traveling from one field to another; wagons pulled by tractors (often young girls and boys drive these powerful monsters) taking crops back to bin or barn; pickup trucks loaded with children in the back, eating watermelon in season—or hauling a steer to be butchered, a cow to be bred; a kid riding a black and white pony followed by a dog, tongue out, panting, its paws hurting from the sharp edges of the crushed limestone. In Amish country there will be a vintage black buggy with an enclosed cab, the women and children wearing bonnets, the men with beards and round hats, the horse sometimes wearing blinders to keep it from being distracted or frightened by other horses, dogs—anything moving.

On their Minnesota farm, where three generations of the Benson family live and work, David Benson and his wife, Sally-Anne, head back to the barn with a fresh load of August hay.

If you drive along country roads, you are almost certain to meet rural mail deliverers, leaning out the window on the right from the left-side seat to stuff large metal mailboxes with seed catalogues, first-class letters, the usual advertisements for everything. Today some have right-hand-drive cars to let them move close to the mailboxes on that side. If you stop and talk, you will learn a lot about people along the road, weather, the farm situation, politics, anything you want to discuss. The RFD system (Rural Free Delivery) is one of the most astonishing efforts anywhere in the world, bringing mail to people on farms at far less than the actual cost.

The roadside ditches may be full of wild flowers: sweet williams, violets, wild iris, jack-in-the-pulpit, daisies, red clover strayed from fields. Strangely enough, country roads are wildlife sanctuaries. Pheasants and quail nest in the ditches on each side because of the long grass that offers protection. I have seen a mother quail leading ten little ones along the edge of the road, scuttling them into the ditch as our car passed. Bobolinks nest there, and bluebirds have their favorite hole in a fencepost, to which they return every year. There are red-winged blackbirds flashing their bright colors in the sunlight and letting their liquid-sounding notes flow toward the pond by which they live. Groundhogs often burrow out a den in the ditch side and sit there silently swearing at those who have disturbed them. Rabbits also share the lush grass, wrinkling their noses at passing cars.

Once when I was ten years old, I was driving with my father in the sort of stripped-down buggy that was called a trap. It had only two wheels and was very light; my father used it for fast driving. We were going down a very narrow country road overhung with oak and elm trees when he abruptly pulled up on the reins and stopped the horse.

"Paul, just look at that," he shouted (in all my life with him I never heard him speak softly, not even to my mother), and pointed ahead with the whip. Stretched entirely across the road was the longest bull snake I had ever seen, yellow and black, undulating its slow way to the other side. The horse stamped his feet and snorted, afraid.

"Dad," I said quietly, "why don't you just run over it?" (I never called him Father. He never called me Son.)

We stared at this great, live act of nature—the horse, Tom Engle and I. Finally he said to me, "I hope one day, if I'm ever down on my belly and crawling for a place to hide, somebody will leave me alone and let me git there."

If Eden be on earth at all, 'Tis that which we the country call.

—Henry Vaughan, Poems (1646)

The sounds of country roads are different from those of broad highways. The interstate, of course, has no sounds at all save the whisper of tires on concrete; no birds, no wind tearing at trees, no distant bawling of a calf for its mother, no little pigs grunting as they butt their snouts against the sow, no hushed roar of a distant tractor crossing back and forth over a field, doing in a day more than ten men with horses could have done. The sound of wagon wheels, steel-tired, or of an old car creeping from one farm to the next over a rock or gravel road is rich and satisfying, letting the driver of horse or auto know that he is in contact with the earth itself.

The sound of a horse's hooves striking gravel or concrete is like no other echoing noise in the world. Have you ever driven or ridden over a wood-floored bridge? There is a resonance to the horseshoe striking the vibrating planks that is unlike any other sound. Even the horse seems to enjoy it, ears sharply forward, no urging from bit or whip required to keep it trotting.

(continued on page 17)

Woodcut by Stanley Rice

14

Country Bridges

A bridge occupies a special place in country life, whether it's a simple plank structure spanning a creek, or a beautiful covered bridge rich in history, or a mighty railroad trestle carrying trains with lonesome whistles.

It takes spunk to build a bridge. Spunk to say, "I don't have to take the world just as I find it—I can fell a couple trees across that stream and make it easy to get across." Spunk to get a team together to build a real bridge, lifting beams and sawing planks and driving pilings, maybe standing in cold water awhile before the work is done. But you look at a part of the country that has good bridges, and you know the people who live there have spunk.

Even a small bridge is a country landmark, useful for giving directions or meeting friends. It's a way to get somewhere, from this side to that side. But it's also a place to stop awhile, to watch the water flow by, to wonder where it's been and where it's going. To play a game racing leaf boats from up the bank a ways to the finish at the bridge. To drop a fishing line in the water, and dream about what you might catch.

Towns grow up by bridges. Think how many town names have "bridge" in them: Cambridge, Sturbridge, Bridgeport, Bridgeton, Woodbridge, Southbridge, Iron Bridge, Bridgewater. Towns need sturdy bridges, big enough for a horse and wagon hauling crops to

Stone City, *an oil painting by Grant Wood*

market. It's a shame to build a good bridge and let it rot away, as wood does if unprotected. Back in the Old Country they usually built stone bridges, but not many American country folk got around to that, with so much else to be done clearing land, planting, raising children and all the rest. The sensible idea was to build a bridge with a roof and sides to keep off the rain and sun that harmed the wood. Covered

bridges can last a century or more.

Covered bridges have other advantages. They provide a good place to set up tables for a church supper, or benches for a political rally. And for a boy taking a girl home after dark, they provide the privacy for a little kiss—that's why they are called "kissing bridges."

There was one problem with covered bridges in the old days. In the north country in winter, horses

15

pulled sleighs, not wagons. The roof on the bridge kept the snow off the roadway. So somebody had to shovel snow *onto* the bridge so the sleigh runners could glide across.

No matter how well a team built a bridge, winter tried to knock it down. First it would send ice jams that would grind against the bridge supports. If that didn't work, winter would join forces with spring, providing snow and ice to melt to make a flood. Some years the bridge won the contest, some years it didn't. A sign saying BRIDGE OUT was bad news. It meant long detours and delays. And it was a call for a new test of country spunk.

At first thought, it might seem railroad trestles are not country bridges. It's true they were paid for by big companies in the cities, and built mostly by workers the country folk never saw before or since. They span not just rivers but whole valleys, far far above the level of the water: enormous structures, as impressive as the aqueducts of the Romans. They changed the look of many a country landscape, just as the trains were soon to change much about country life. But the railroad bridges are part of that life, and there have been few finer sights than a locomotive with a plume of steam pulling a long train across a trestle.

When the automobile arrived, country roads with country bridges were not good enough for Hupmobiles and Stutz Bearcats. Motorists wanted "highways," and state governments set up "Departments of Highways" with engineers and surveyors and whole crews that did nothing all year long but work on roads and bridges. They knew how to build bridges of iron, then steel. Often they painted them silver. Some folks thought these new bridges, with all their trusses, were downright ugly. Many of them rattled and clanked fiercely when a car drove over them. But other folks saw a new beauty in a silver bridge reflected in a quiet river, maybe along with some golden leaves on the trees in autumn. A steel bridge seemed like progress. And it is still a bridge, a good landmark, a place for meeting friends, a help to get folks where they're going.

—JRR

16

There are still covered bridges in many states. If you find one, stop and walk through before you drive through, to hear your shoes banging the boards, to feel the sense of being enclosed, to startle the pigeons that roost there, to put yourself back in the nineteenth century. You cannot drive fast on a covered bridge, which will give you a sense of the peace of passage over a stream. Always honk before starting over to alert another car coming from the opposite direction. The bridges are covered not to protect travelers but to keep the wood floor from rotting. A New England carpenter said that the bridges were covered for the same reason our grandmothers wore petticoats— "to protect their underpinning." My father said that covered bridges "spooked" horses because they felt closed in and the echoes of their hooves bounced back at them, louder than in the open.

In winter the country roads used to clang with bells on the harnesses of horses pulling sleighs or bobsleds. Where have all those bells gone? Our roads were loud with them. When people in the country heard winter bells, they always rushed to the window (at least my curious family did) to see who was going so fast and to guess why—a farmer

A road like this was not built for anyone in a hurry. It follows every curve of the stream . . . approaches the covered bridge at a right angle . . . turns abruptly and disappears into the dark mouth of the tunnel.

—Helen Hooven Santmyer, Ohio Town

17

*I cannot conceive
the Spring of lands
that have no Winter.
I take my Winter
gladly, to get Spring
as a keen and fresh
experience.*

—The Odd Farmwife
<u>The Odd Farmhouse</u> (1913)

fallen from the haymow, a wife in labor, a kid desperately ill, a grandpa with a heart attack? Only a family crisis would force a farm family to urge a horse down a snow-filled country road, the white stuff flying up from his hooves, the steel runners hissing. Strings of old sleigh bells can still be found hanging in barns, given a tug now and then by a passing person just to hear them jangle. Our bobsled had hay covering the bottom and buffalo robes against the wind. If Dad felt unusually sympathetic, he would let my brother and me stand on the rear runners, where we could feel their gliding motion and their little bounces over packed snow. Sometimes I was allowed to sit by him on the seat and hold the reins after they had passed through his hands. Even secondhand I could feel the tug and strain of the horse's mouth and the harsh hardness of the steel bit.

There would be sleighs on the back roads, some with landscapes

painted on the sides, some with two seats and pulled by a team, with heavy lap robes for the passengers. Our family had robes made from softened horsehides with the hair still on, and once my father had a heavy winter coat made from the hide of a favorite horse. There was a robe for children made from a black and white spotted pony that I had ridden with a little saddle. He was a gentle creature, with a white blaze down his face and a tiny, rocking canter. I could not bear covering myself with his hide, which I had curried hundreds of times, learning how it twitched when the currycomb hit a sensitive spot. On warm days I had ridden him down the winding country road to visit ponies on other farms, and there was a lot of whinnying back and forth and a few tricky kicks, for many ponies have brittle tempers. That faint whinny coming down the road is another disappeared sound.

18

(continued on page 20)

Burma-Shave Signs

IF YOU
DON'T KNOW
WHOSE SIGNS
THESE ARE
YOU CAN'T HAVE
DRIVEN VERY FAR.

One of the delights of motoring in the middle decades of the twentieth century was reading the jingles posted beside the highways to advertise Burma-Shave brushless shaving cream. Each message was painted on six small wooden signs spaced about a hundred feet apart. On a long trip, everyone in the car looked eagerly for the jingles, and many families would read them in chorus.

Some of the messages promised that Burma-Shave would ensure romantic success:

HIS FACE WAS SMOOTH
AND COOL AS ICE
AND OH LOUISE!
HE SMELLED
SO NICE
BURMA-SHAVE.

or

BEFORE I TRIED IT
THE KISSES
I MISSED
BUT AFTERWARD—BOY!
THE MISSES I KISSED
BURMA-SHAVE.

That was too much sissy love stuff for the kids. They preferred the suggested mayhem of the signs promoting safe driving:

HARDLY A DRIVER
IS NOW ALIVE
WHO PASSED
ON HILLS
AT 75
BURMA-SHAVE.
or
DON'T STICK
YOUR ELBOW
OUT SO FAR
IT MIGHT GO HOME
IN ANOTHER CAR
BURMA-SHAVE.

Burma-Shave was the principal product of the Burma-Vita Company of Minneapolis. It was put on the market in 1925 by company founder Clinton Odell. The signs were the suggestion of his son Allan. With the help of a younger brother, Leonard, Allan painted slogans on scrap lumber, white letters

on a red background, then rented strips of land from farmers for three to twenty-five dollars a year. Leonard dug postholes and put the signs in place. The sales of Burma-Shave began to boom.

Eventually there were more than 7000 sets of signs, in forty-four states. The company put up new jingles each year. They ran a national contest to get the jingles, paying one hundred dollars for those they used. Some years they got more than 50,000 entries. Whether they used the product or not, people loved the signs.

Then came World War II:

"AT EASE," SHE SAID.
"MANEUVERS BEGIN
WHEN YOU GET
THOSE WHISKERS
OFF YOUR CHIN."
BURMA-SHAVE.

The war quickened the pace of American life. Postwar autos were capable of higher speeds, postwar roads were wider. Driving in the fast lane of multilane highways made it hard to read the Burma-Shave signs. Worse, the airplane was attracting many travelers:

'TWOULD BE
MORE FUN
TO GO BY AIR
IF WE COULD PUT
THESE SIGNS UP THERE
BURMA-SHAVE.

But those who traveled country roads still enjoyed the jingles.

In 1963 the Burma-Vita Company was sold to Philip Morris, Inc., and it was decided to discontinue the signs. Rather than leave them to decay, the sign crews went about the country one last time and took down every sign. That was a proper token of respect for an American institution.

—JRR

It is a dog's (good) life on country roads. Every farm has one, two or three, happily sleeping in the shade of an old maple or oak tree in the yard. A passing car is a blessing to them for the chance it gives to demonstrate that they are still alive and still guardians of the home. On one farm we often passed, an ancient dog would shuffle to the edge of the porch, another would run along the end of the yard until he came to the fence, and the third would streak through an open gate and run howling down the road, snapping at the tires as if they were edible. Often the chasing dog would quit at the end of his farm and another dog would take up the pursuit the length of his farm, and so for miles we drove with every size, shape and color of animal, each with a different bark.

Do nothing in great haste, except catching fleas and running from a mad dog.

—The Old Farmer's Almanac (1811)

"Old Blue"—a bluetick hound.

Americans have always been wanderers. Before they could become part of this country, they had to travel to it. Once here, they moved from farm to farm, city to city, state to state (and they still do). In the early years they traveled on terrible jolting, bone-shaking routes where often-springless carriages and wagons constantly became stuck. Country roads today are luxuries compared to those.

Americans also like to have a goal in mind and to reach it, whether it is a job, a profession, or a distant place on the map. Starting out on a vacation, they usually pick a faraway destination and make a schedule to take them there at a definite time on a definite day. That means almost no stopping, except for an occasional historical site. It also leaves little or no time to leave the main highways and turn off onto rural roads, which are one of the great unexplored riches of the country. They not only relate to the past, they *are* the past.

20

(continued on page 23)

Roadside Stands

In late spring the back roads and little byways of America become a veritable bazaar of the homemade and homegrown. Spaced at intervals between cultivated fields, plunked down at the foot of gravel driveways or extending out from a barn, small makeshift stands with terse, mostly hand-printed signs out front invite the passing motorist to pause.

> FRESH GRADE-A EGGS,
> 60¢ A DOZEN
> PURE MAPLE SYRUP
> STRAWBERRIES,
> $3.99 ALL YOU CAN PICK

These are America's roadside stands, a moveable feast of sweet corn; fresh green beans; baskets of tomatoes, plummy red and big as softballs; Jersey white potatoes; wheels of tangy Vermont cheddar; jugs of fresh-pressed cider; jars of honey, jams and jellies.

In an age of giant supermarkets, America still carries on a shameless love affair with these tiny roadside stands that come and go with the seasons and regularly outdo the large chains in both quality and bargain prices.

Nobody knows the name of the enterprising individual who first stacked some fruits and vegetables on a table in front of a farmhouse, thereby creating the first such market. Whoever it was, he or she was undoubtedly a visionary, since the institution is now virtually ubiquitous. It has grown and evolved from the simple stand into the ingenious "Pick-It-Yourself" operations and even bigger, more sophisticated farmers' markets that may feature tours and buggy rides, cider pressing, and corn-shelling competitions as come-ons.

The phenomenon of the roadside

doubtless driving up to farmhouses and inquiring if they couldn't buy butter, eggs, cheese and vegetables, fresher and better than at the corner grocery and for lower prices. Since produce is perishable, prices at such stands have always been highly flexible. What is most plentiful is the cheapest, and an oft-quoted saying of the business is "As the sun goes down, so do the prices."

The number of these roadside markets is estimated at somewhere between ten and twelve thousand scattered throughout the country, with their popularity constantly growing. While there is presently a trend toward bigger and more professional operations, the small mom-and-pop establishments, passed on like a family heirloom from one generation to the next, still hold some inescapable charm for countless people. There is something infinitely reassuring about buying

corn, for instance, from the same small stand year after year. Then, too, customers feel they are returning to a time that was simpler and more gracious. Folks seem friendlier at a roadside stand or a farmers' market. The shopper feels somehow closer to the earth—not surprisingly, when some of that good earth is still clinging to the smooth sides of tomatoes, cucumbers are mercifully unwaxed, and corn silk is wet from the morning dew. Roadside stands make us all feel more in touch with our roots.

—HHL

stand may have first occurred in the second decade of this century, coincidental with the emergence of the automobile industry, when city families lucky enough to own their own car began the custom of taking Sunday drives into the country. Shortly these same city folk were

A cider stand

*There's absolutely
no reason for
being rushed along
with the rush.
Everybody should
be free to go
very slow.*

—Robert Frost

It would be wonderful if, in spite of our urge for planning each day's travel on the millions of trips crisscrossing the United States each year, a day or two could be set aside unplanned. Turn off the big highways with their semitrailers rolling sixteen wheels, steering wheels clutched by tense hands, faces glaring ahead at the mileage signs for the next exit, the next city, the next campground, the next rest stop, the next gas station. Leave all that turbulence of travel and that rigid so-many-miles-a-day schedule and drive down country roads. Your reward will be the powerful and comforting peacefulness of roads winding between fields, of bridges over slowly flowing streams and deep pools where gray catfish the color of the gray water swish their lazy tails, muttering, "Down with hooks." This is the country you will never know until you slow down, turn off, and move at a gentle speed over the gently rolling land.

There will be an occasional roadside market with sweet corn picked a few hours before, squash, green and wax beans, tomatoes bigger than your fist, sun-ripened on the vine, carrots pulled from rich dirt that day, gourds, pumpkins that grew between rows of corn, ready to be carved into the faces of ghosts and relatives. Often the sellers are young girls trying to earn money for their band uniforms at high school. The stand nearest our farm always counted thirteen ears of

23

sweet corn to the dozen. They carried muskmelons (called cantaloupes by the more elegant customers) and watermelons, which they would gladly "plug" for you to prove the succulence inside.

Sometimes there will be little filling stations along the roads, often remnants of settlements long gone. There was one I knew as a kid, called Buffalo Center. It had no buffalo and no center. The filling station and repair garage were in a long-abandoned red brick church. The owner was as eager to talk as to sell you gas. Maybe more so. He had some soda pop, which had obviously been cooling for weeks, and a small tank of minnows as bait for the diminishing number of carp, bass and catfish in the Cedar River a few miles away. He was a candid man, telling you that minnows were really not as good bait for catfish as stinking doughballs, but he couldn't keep them on hand because of the heat.

Country roads have country stores. Many have failed, but there are still those where blue bib overalls hang from the ceiling above cheese that is mild and yellow and sometimes called rat cheese. If you find such a store on a little-traveled road, stop and go in, not because you need anything, but simply to talk to people. Ask what you should visit in the area. There are handsome stone mills that, although not working, may have the original huge millstones and often a dam still in place with a good fishing pool below it. There may be an octagonal barn, or a round barn, or one built on the side of a hill so that you enter at the second level. They will be working places, hay in the mow, cattle outside, feed in the bins, a silo attached (don't enter, for the rich and fermented silage can produce fumes that will knock you out).

Don't look only at the land when you are out on country roads. Look up at the sky, too, and you may see a circling hawk scanning the fields for mice, or autumn flocks of migrating ducks heading south, or honking geese in a great V, their constant noise (what are they talking about to each other at such a height?) often audible on the ground.

Your eyes will change on country roads. On the great highways you stare straight ahead at the endless ribbon of concrete. You do not dare, at high speeds, take your eyes away from that hypnotic gray surface. On country roads your eyes may roam on both sides; they may rest on the peaceful fields. Outside all cities in America there are such comforting roads, taking you past farms where people and animals live in their quiet places.

*You don't
live longer
in the country.
It just seems
that way.*

—from <u>Country Talk</u> by Dick Syatt

THE HOME PLACE

"The home place" is one of the most precise phrases in the English language. Everyone knows that it never refers to a house in any city. It is pure country, meaning not only a dwelling but the garden near it, the barn, the pasture, orchard, fields, fences, animals, machinery. It has always been a place for living as well as working. All through the nineteenth century and most of the twentieth, babies were born on the home place, often in the same bed where their mothers and grandmothers had been born. My mother and father were born on the home places where their families farmed. My brother and sisters were born at home, and I missed hearing the first cry of a child when my own children were delivered in an antiseptic hospital.

The home place was the most concentrated human environment created in the American States. Children led a ranging life that would have been impossible in the little farms of Europe. They rode ponies over the fields and often to school. They climbed trees in the orchard and reached for apples, threw sticks up at the branches of black walnut trees and shook down nuts, carved their initials in fence posts or the wall of the barn or a towering elm tree.

Many farms had creeks running through. Ours did not, but the next farm did. There was a deep hole at a bend. As kids we could swing out on a long wild grapevine and drop into the water. I have swum in the waters of the Mediterranean, the South Pacific, England's Channel coast and Finnish bays, but not one gave me the thrill of flying through the air on a suffocating August day above a creek in Iowa and dropping into the earth-colored water. Small water snakes swam away in dread of our white bodies, and silver perch flipped into the sunlight before diving, as we did, into the deepest darkness of the pool.

27

Springtime: Working in the vegetable garden

Separated from its mother, a spring lamb follows farmer David Benson back to the flock.

Every inch of the home place was worked on, so that a farmer or his wife could in a single day throw down last year's crop from a haymow to the cattle waiting hungry below, then milk the cows who had come fresh, walk through the pasture looking for a stray, plow a cornfield, haul wood from the grove for heating and cooking, split it and stack it, repair harness or hook up a cultivator to a tractor, weed the huge vegetable garden, go out to inspect the brood sows in the farrowing season, look for new lambs in cold early spring. Doing all this often meant covering miles on foot, horseback, by wagon or tractor. Unlike a desk job or a position on an assembly line, where a person might stay within a six-square-foot area all day, there was mobility on the farm. Here was every sort of lifting, pulling, and hammering, for this was home extended over a hundred, two hundred, five hundred acres, all of it needing personal scrutiny and a useful hand. It was a total family affair. The kids had chores to do before school and after. The way of living was a way of working. It was a moving and most human manner of earning food and shelter by a shared effort, such as hardly exists anywhere else—though a miniature example would be the mom-and-pop grocery store.

28

(continued on page 31)

Porches

A door must be open or closed, says a proverb. Country folks don't like that much. They prefer a riddle: When is a door not a door? Answer: When it's a-jar. So they build porches. On a porch you can be inside the house and outside at the same time. That is, you have a roof over your head, to keep off the rain or the sun, and you are close enough to the kitchen for a steady supply of lemonade or iced tea. But you are outdoors where you can be cooled by the breeze, if there is one. You can smell the lilac or the mock orange, hear the crickets, watch the fireflies. You can enjoy a soft summer rain that draws a sort of magical curtain around a porch, emphasizing the boundaries of that special place.

Men enjoy porches for relaxation. Women like the fact that they can take their work to the porch. It's a fine place for shelling peas or butter beans or snapping string beans. And it's one of the best places for doing mending or other handiwork.

On a porch you're in touch with the world—or as much of the world as you know closely. A porch is a sort of lookout. You can see that Milly has been to the dry-goods store to buy material for Amy's graduation dress, or that the Tucker boy is home from boarding school, or that Florence has at last persuaded Agnes to give her her recipe for devil's food cake. If a new family moves in, you know what they look like, and what their sofa and dining room table look like, too. You can gather all that news from a porch, without having to ask anybody anything.

Watching for the mailman is another porch pursuit, particularly for girls of the age of seventeen or thereabouts. Will he bring a postcard from a friend, or an invitation to attend a party or visit a relative for a few days? Will he have a new magazine, or—most exciting of all—a love letter? If a girl spies the mailman as he approaches the mailbox, she can shave several minutes from the hours of suspense and keep her private correspondence private as well.

Children can play on a porch on a rainy day. Or if there's a crawl space they can play *under* a porch

any day, hiding or digging holes in the ground. On a really hot day, they share that space with the family dog, who knows that it is one of the coolest places to be found.

After supper, the whole family can sit on the porch. Neighbors out walking may ask, "How are you?" or—if you invite them several times—may stop to sit a spell. Everybody who knows about porches knows you have to be invited onto a porch just like into a house—the door in the riddle is a-jar, not wide open. An offer of a glass of lemonade may follow. "Don't go to any trouble," says the guest. "I won't,"

says the hostess. And one great thing about company on a porch is that she doesn't. A glass of lemonade is just a glass of lemonade, with no frills, which makes everybody happy.

Later on, when it's time to put the children to bed, an older daughter may have a visit from a boy. If he's a boy the family approves of, everybody else finds reasons to disappear. If he's really lucky, there's a swing on the porch, and the girl sits in it, and after a while he does, too. It's hard to imagine an invention better calculated to foster courtship at just the proper rate than a porch swing.

Some people take pains to dress up their porches. They may paint the ceiling blue to look like the sky or enclose the porch in screening to keep out the bugs. Many buy beautiful wicker rocking chairs with soft cushions, or maybe even a luxurious metal glider to take the place of the swing. Gardeners put plants in pots on porches, where they can fuss over them all summer long. Porches developed to that extent are really a summer version of the living room.

For some people, one porch is not enough. Sleeping porches, usually upstairs on the back of the house, are great for summer nights. Sun porches are rooms inside, full of plants, with lots of windows to let in lots of sun, even in winter—what more highfalutin folks call conservatories. Play porches are similar, full of toys instead of plants.

There was a period when porches were neglected. It was the time when television sets were first spreading across the country. Folks stayed indoors to watch their favorite shows, and called that relaxation. But it wasn't too many years before one summer evening someone said, "Oh, I've seen this one already. I'm going out and sit on the porch."

—JRR

Over 450 pieces of fabric, plus lace, beads and bows, make up this work called Harvest Meal *by Arlette Gosieski.*

The houses were of a wild variety, made from logs, sod, adobe, brick, clapboard. They were hidden in a forest, along a bayou, high on a hill, in a mountain canyon, in a fertile valley, or they were located on an endless empty plain or on a black loam prairie where hundreds of years of tall grass rotting in autumn or burned over in summer had helped to make rich soil that glistened under rain. Some houses on the old home place blurred into the landscape, like the soddies of the Great Plains. Others stood out for miles in the middle of wide plantations, their whiteness and height visible far away. On others, local carpenters had expressed their skill in elaborate scrollwork along the eaves of porches or around windows. Windows were a great luxury, for glass was hard to transport by steamboat, rough railway or oxcart. Many houses, like our small one, were odd-shaped, as rooms were added on for newly arriving kids. They were not insulated, of course; in winter the wind from the north barely slowed on its trip through the house before exiting on the far side.

Our house looked charming on the hill, overlooking the fields. It was a great place to play and to have neighborhood meetings; there was a warm and lively atmosphere in it when all the cousins came home on Thanksgiving and Christmas. The house had no plumbing. In the kitchen were two hand pumps: one for rainwater collected in a cistern, the other for water pumped up from a deep well by our windmill and stored in a reservoir where it kept its coldness and its sweet taste. The well water was very hard because it flowed through

We didn't have much, but we sure had plenty.

—title of recent book about rural women by Sherry Thomas

31

Farm wife Sally-Anne Benson feeds the family cats.

limestone, and big chunks of lime would accumulate in the bottom of our tea kettle. There was a wooden privy fifteen feet from the house, with a quarter moon on the door and a stack of Sears, Roebuck catalogues in a corner. Between privy and house was our woodpile. No lady ever came back to the house without bringing in a chunk of wood for the range to prove the innocent nature of her errand.

The bedrooms were unheated. At temperatures sometimes twenty and thirty below zero, sleeping in them was a test of courage. Mother used to wrap bricks, hot from being in the oven, in old flannel and put them in our beds before we retired. We would move them up and down between the sheets until they were heated and our own body warmth could keep us comfortable. It was spooky to lie in the darkness watching the white breath rise from our mouths like an escaping soul.

One of the happiest aspects of the houses on the old home places was the porch. In open weather we entertained visitors there. It was a quiet place to sit with the family on a summer evening and listen to that reassuring country silence that hung over the land like a blessing after work, an earned blessing. Suddenly whippoorwills would begin their plaintive calls. One below the hill would call, and then one from the grove would answer. It sounded as if they were comforting each other, their soft cries saying, "I'm sad too. It's been a long day. Enjoy the twilight." When elderly relatives visited, we would bring out the stationary rocker from the little-used living room so that they could rock for hours without moving to the dangerous edge of the porch.

Perhaps because of living always some distance from others, the photos and mementos of family members had an intense importance on the home place. In our living room was a photograph of Grandpa in his Civil War cavalry uniform, blue with brass buttons on the jacket, light brown pants with leather facings on the in-

I can recall the gentle squeaking of the white-painted porch swing blending with the soft, soothing harmonies of Mother's hymns, as clearly as if it were yesterday.

—Marilyn Kluger
Country Kitchens Remembered

side, his peaked hat honored by being placed alone on a little table with an elaborately decorated cloth thrown over it. Over his left shoulder was a strap leading across his chest to a scabbard outside his right leg. Carried upright in his left hand was the saber, a reckless length of polished and sharpened steel. He wore not the usual boots, but beaded Sioux Indian moccasins. This handsome man with heavy black beard and head of hair, powerful face and fine eyes, in later years would call to us and to our cousins as we clashed with each other, "Boys. Don't fight." When asked about his Indian encounters, he would say, "We ought to have let those people alone. They just wanted to live their lives in their own country."

On the piano (a lovingly treasured ornament always out of tune) there were photos of family members: baby pictures, some grinning, some scowling, boys in dresses (I wore a dress until I was five, which seemed very adult to me), some frocks tinted pink. Today the photos might be on a TV set because that is the most looked-at object in the living room. There were also the faces of grandmothers, aunts, uncles, even a few cousins. Now there might be a high-school son in football uniform, hands on hips, helmet under one arm. Even in the day of the automobile, rural families live apart and see others much less often than city people, so that the photographs represent a way of silently communicating with people they know. Aunt Tillie (unmarried and a frequent visitor) used to talk to photographs. She was not crazy, just lonely. I once heard her say, "Grandma, you'd just love to ride in Charlie's new car. It even has windows!"

Bibles were important in those houses, for they kept a register of births, deaths and marriages. Our family Bible was kept up-to-date, and I was proud when I could read well enough to find my own name as proof that I really did exist. I was alive in that Book. Years later when I found in a Black Forest town the narrow house where my shoemaking ancestors had lived (carved in the lintel stone above the door was a boot), the first family memento brought out was the ancient Bible. In the midst of many entries was one they pointed out to me—*Jacob Reinheimer. Ausgewandelt nach Amerika. Verschwunden.* ("Emigrated to America. Disappeared.") They were sad that a family member had lost touch with them.

The garden was a center of the summer for Mother and the kids. We helped plant, hoe, weed and harvest. What freshness of food, not only never frozen or shipped, but eaten within half an hour of being picked! Leaf lettuce was cut and at once plunged into cold well water to firm it up after the sun's heat. We shelled peas in a pan, munching some raw, telling from the crispness of the pod that they

Such gardens are not made By singing:—"Oh, how beautiful!" and sitting in the shade.

—Rudyard Kipling
"The Glory of the Garden" (1911)

were tender. Turnips went into many dishes as well as into the big cast-iron pot on the back of the range where there was always a bowl of thick soup waiting for the hungry coming in from barn or field. There were carrots, beets (some pickled for winter), green and wax beans, potatoes to eat directly from the garden when small or to be stored in the root cellar, along with cabbages, carrots and turnips, over winter.

The garden was carefully laid out. At one end were rows of sunflowers, zinnias, marigolds, all tough plants; at the other end, sweet corn and popcorn. In between were the other vegetables. Running along one side was a permanent bed of strawberries and along the other side a permanent bed of asparagus. Almost everything was canned, including sweet corn, which was also dried in the sun. Grandpa refused to touch the dried corn because in the Civil War he had lived on parched corn and could not bear the taste of it.

The root cellar was cut into the wall of the house cellar, which had no light; the floor and walls were of dirt. It was always cool, but the vegetables never froze because they were stored below the frost line. I used to be sent down as a kid to bring up vegetables kept under deep oat straw. It was spooky down there, and even with a kerosene lantern I was scared because the light wavered as my arm moved and the shadows swayed with it. Once I was ordered to go there and sit in

35

Presents'
Birthplaces

Country life does not always have breadth, but it has depth. It is neither artificial nor superficial, but is kept close to the realities.

—Calvin Coolidge

On the road from Plymouth to Boston, just below Penn's Hill, two small cottages nestle side by side. Each is an old New England saltbox, each is made of stout oak beams held tight by wooden pegs, and each, many years ago, bore witness to the American Revolution. But even earlier, their great hearths, the buttery, the borning room, were the hub of life on a small Colonial farmstead. There were forty acres in all, rocky and not very rich ones, and only by main strength were they made to victual the growing family. Yet one day those spare acres at Penn's Hill, and those weathered houses, would give us two U.S. Presidents, John Adams and his son John Quincy—

great statesmen both. Born to the labors of country life, bred on the cider, milk and honey, the biscuit, cheese and ale of New England soil, father and son grew to manhood with dignity, wisdom, and the fighting heart to lead us through a revolution and beyond.

Since then, many men of rustic circumstance have gone on to the American presidency. That man of the people, Andrew Jackson, is thought to be the first President born in a log cabin, and James Garfield the last. But the best-remembered is Abe Lincoln, born in frontier Kentucky when the scream of the pan-

sleepy hamlet in the majestic Hudson Valley. Calvin Coolidge, born in a cottage attached to a Vermont general store, in rooms as bare and plain as the surrounding landscape was craggy and beautiful. And Ulysses S. Grant, born in a little frame house overlooking the mighty Ohio River. Of our more recent Presidents there is Harry Truman, of course, and Lyndon Johnson, one born in the little town of Lamar, Missouri, the other in a farmhouse in rural Texas. By contrast Jimmy Carter, though raised amid farm and field in Georgia, was born in a hospital, and Ronald Reagan in rooms

Lamar, Missouri, birthplace of Harry S Truman

Abraham Lincoln's Nolin's Creek log cabin

ther still filled the night. The boy, a child of hardship, played on an earthen floor and read by the flicker of firelight. The man thus nurtured never lost his backwoods integrity— or his backwoods humor.

There were others, too, who started life as simple country boys in simple country settings: Martin Van Buren, born in the family's long, low clapboard "ordinary," as taverns were then called, in a

above the general store and bank in the small town of Tampico, Illinois.

Such simple beginnings—far from the babble of commerce and industry, and with nature's gifts close at hand—seem to foster something special in a man. And thus if country life is, as Coolidge said, "kept close to the realities," then the countryside has served America and her Presidents well.

—CTB

the dark to meditate on my sins, which must have been many. That clears a child's mind, and even today I can remember the damp, dark smell. "If you don't behave I'll send you down" was the ultimate threat for discipline in our house. It kept order in a lively, often bickering mess of kids.

Of course we had a henhouse, and one of my jobs when I was small was to go out and gather eggs for breakfast. It sounds like fun, but the act itself was tough. Hens can be cross when disturbed. Many times I was pecked on the wrist when trying to get an egg out from under a bad-tempered old biddy. When all of the hens began squawking together, the sound was shattering and scary. Even the roosters joined in, bragging in their male chauvinist way.

It was also my grim duty to run down and capture a couple of young pullets for eating. One early morning when I was about eight years old, I had to learn how to kill. Our method of slaughtering was to tie the hen's legs together, then force its head between two nails in a block of wood and sever the neck with a hatchet. The first time I was told to do this my mother said, "Now Paul, get it the first crack or it'll be an awful mess."

I got it. Watching the bird flopping on the grass afterward, I mourned, "Momma, I won't be able to eat."

She replied, "You'll get hungry during the day, and you'll sit down and grab a drumstick."

I grabbed. I ate.

There is one thing about hens that looks like wisdom—they don't cackle much till they have laid their eggs.

—Josh Billings
The Old Farmer's Almanac (1878)

37

It was the complete immersion of every family member, from Grandpa down to the youngest kid, in the work, play, suffering and joy of the home that made that place forever a deep and moving memory for all of us. There was the cherry tree a cousin fell from and broke his arm, the creek where we all learned to swim, the field where we all first husked corn, the garden where we hauled rich cow manure from the registered Jersey dairy herd and grew the largest tomatoes in the area, the windmill that Aunt Tillie once climbed to the top of and was afraid to climb down. There were the days we all spent working with our father or grandfather, plowing, cultivating, combining. There was the closeness of having generations in the same house.

Retirement or nursing homes did not exist then, and the loved old grandparents were not hustled off to live in isolation. The Amish built "grandpa houses" on the backs of their houses, while the younger generation moved into the main house. There was the little bedroom where our old warrior found his final peace. Grandpa always kept Indian head nickels out of affection for the Indian people, and he gave each of the kids one out of affection for us. How could a strong man with so loving a nature be allowed to leave that farm—part of which

If a person is industrious, and so fortunate as to have a family capable of joining in his labors, and living in the bonds of affection, there can be no doubt that he will prosper.

—James Pickering
Inquiries of an Emigrant (1832)

After a long day "walking beans" (hoeing the soybeans), the Bensons' son, Anton, gets a hug from his mother.

38

Top left: *David Benson brings in ears of field corn for inspection.* Top right: *Grandfather Gus Benson helps decide if the corn is ready for harvest.* Bottom: *Working in the cornfield.*

he received as bounty for his cavalry service—and never put the polished plow down into that soil again? I asked myself that question silently because I did not have the nerve to ask Mother or Dad. Even then I knew there was no answer.

What concerned us on that farm, which was not really a very good one since the beautiful hill had slopes that were too steep and sandy for lush crops, was not only our own intense lives but the living plants and animals that were our care and our livelihood. We watched the first thin corn shoots push through the dirt and become heavy stalks. On sultry summer nights with a hot wind, we saw the oat field sway and glow with thousands of fireflies. We knew the cows and the bull by name and talked to the cows during milking. This we did by hand into a bucket, with an occasional squirt directly into the mouth of a begging cat. We helped dry the newborn calf and wept at the occasional dead one. We were even closer to the horses, for we could ride them out

Grandmother Bertha Benson lends a hand as Sally-Anne—playfully—milks Bluma the cow.

Suckling pigs compete for dinner.

Few animals and indeed few people are quite as shrewd or gifted with such a remarkable natural instinct as a sow.

—Louis Bromfield, "A Hymn to Hawgs"

in the fields, water them, and rub them down when they sweated beneath the grinding August sun.

The whole process of nature was our own natural life. In that way we learned close at hand the remarkable qualities of that maligned and underrated creature, the hog. When sows farrowed we were there, usually carrying the squealing runt to put in a box behind the range to keep warm. When going down the feeder with pails of slop mixed with grain, we knew which clever individuals would eat voraciously as we passed by and then run around the others to be fed again at a lower place on the line. Like people. We shared in the total life of our hogs, from caring for the newborns, to preparing their mash or hog chow, to watching the pork cover their bones, to tending the smokehouse where the hams, bacons, ribs and chops were turned while the fat oozed out and fell on the hickory wood fire.

The friend who told me this story said it was true. He saw a farmer holding up a pig to eat apples from a tree. "What are you doing with that pig?" he asked.

"Feeding him," said the farmer.

"Don't that take a lot of time?" asked my friend.

"What's time to a damn old hog?" the farmer replied and went on feeding apples to his pig.

41

Woodcut by Stanley Rice

In those distant and dramatic days, horses were survival for all farmers. They provided the animal energy to do all of the basic work. If a horse went lame, it was a disaster. Every farmer had his own medicines, salves, ointments, liniments. My mother once mistook a horse drug in a bottle for her own medicine and was found screaming on the floor as it burned her stomach.

Unlike a machine, a horse or mule works just like a person, with bones and muscles and breath and blood. You can tell when an animal is overworked because you know the same feeling when you overwork. You can feel the pull lessen on the reins, you can sense the drive of the legs slackening.

For plowing, planting and reaping there is more than one kind of "horsepower." This page, bottom: a mule. Opposite page, top: a workhorse. Bottom: a combine.

That close and mutually dependent relationship has gone from country life, and it is a human loss. One year a friend of ours down the road bought enough machinery to eliminate the need for his huge team of Percherons.

"Gonna sell 'em for dog food?" my father asked.

"Never," our friend almost shouted. "They worked for me, and now I'm workin' for them."

He turned them out to pasture six months of the year and put them in the barn six months. They were well fed until they died. It was beautiful to see them trotting on their vast legs, with their brown manes waving in the wind, snorting at the tractors that had displaced them.

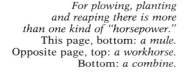

Nobody can look at a horse and tell what he is worth, he is worth to you just how good he is to you and how bad you want him and how well he suits you.

—Will Rogers, from his autobiography

43

One cold autumn day I stood with Uncle Charlie on the old home place while every piece of furniture and machinery, every tool, cow, pig, dish, was auctioned off when he lost the family farm to a second mortgage. The household things looked pathetic outside. Worst was the trucking away of the Jersey cows he had bred over many years. They had won endless blue ribbons at county fairs, so many that his wife made a big blanket of them and his bull wore it in parades around the racetracks of county seat towns where my uncle exhibited his herd. Great-grandpa from Germany broke those fields the first time a plow had ever touched them. It took ten oxen to force the plow through the roots of prairie grass, which ran thirty inches deep.

"It's a good thing Pa ain't here," Charlie said softly as he watched his life being sold off in bits and pieces—tables where four generations had eaten, beds where they had been born and where they had slept all of their lives, the last jars of strawberry preserves, green beans, apple butter. I waited until he went on, "If Pa was here, he'd go in the house and take that old saber down off the wall and cut up a few people."

Last of all Charlie looked across the pasture to the hickory grove where a little tribe of Indians used to camp for a few days late every summer. They appeared silently, and we never knew they were there until dark fell and we could see their campfires. "There'll be some young ears missing out of the cornfield tomorrow," Charlie would say. It was one of the noblest agreements I have ever known. Charlie kept his pride by not telling them to take some ears, and they kept their pride by never asking.

Charlie used to wrestle the leader of the little band each time they came. Uncle was good in the ring, with his curls flopping and his neck thick as a log. He had a great reputation in the county because at a fair one summer he had earned fifty dollars by staying five minutes in the ring with "Strangler" Lewis without being thrown.

Charlie looked a last time across the fields where he had worked seven days a week, twelve hours a day, and put his hand on my shoulder. "Paul, I'd give anything to wrestle the Chief one more time. He was fast on his feet, but he don't come back no more." Charlie clutched my shoulder with his powerful hand and hung on as if he were drowning, as he almost was, in his own tears.

Nor do we go back although we live nearby. It is too long a trip: one way too far, one way too short. As the farmer said when a stranger drove up and asked how far it was to a small town he was trying to find, "Way you're going, 'bout six thousand miles. T'other way, six."

July Hay, *painting by Thomas Hart Benton*

FARMING

It was one of the longest and most dramatic events in human history—the flow of men, women, children, dogs, cats, chickens, horses, cattle, hogs, from the east coast of America to the west, south to the Gulf of Mexico and north to the Canadian border.

Unlike the Spanish soldiers in what became Latin America and the French fur traders in Canada, this was a family matter: husbands and wives, brothers and sisters, babies, adolescents. These people came to work with their hands; what they worked was the soil, and what they made was farms.

It will never happen again, for there is no such open area left in the world, thousands of empty miles over an ever-changing landscape. Nor will there again be so many multitudes of mobile people. The *Mayflower* brought not only men but also women and children as proof that they came to stay. Where they stayed was on the wild land. They settled the rocky New England valleys, the Pennsylvania and New York forests, the Midwest's black loam where the golden crops would flourish, the South's low fields and smoky mountains (often the dirt was red), the desert stretches, the California variety from peak to ocean, north to the forests and plains of Oregon and Washington, into the Wyoming and Montana wilderness. Everywhere they turned the land into new farms or ranches, bringing into emptiness the warm fullness of the family group in which each member worked and knew all that the others did.

> *We are American farmers. . . . Our grandsires freed this virgin continent, plowed it from East to West, and gave it to us. This land is for us and our children to make richer and more fruitful.*
>
> —Farm Journal

Top: *Picking cabbages.* Bottom: *Benson family and friends unloading firewood.* Opposite page: *An Amish woman with her team of horses, pulling a hay baler.*

In his poem on Concord Bridge, Ralph Waldo Emerson, who lived in the town of Concord, wrote the famous lines:

Here once the embattled farmers stood,
And fired the shot heard round the world.

Note that he did not say embattled grocers, lawyers, doctors, railroad men or even soldiers. It was farmers that Paul Revere alerted on his night ride, men fighting just down the road from their own farms. They could handle livestock but they could also handle guns, as the Redcoats soon discovered. They wanted to stand alone on their own feet on their land, to be free as the air they breathed, but they also wanted the whole country to be free from a government across the Atlantic Ocean. When the time came, each farmer gave up his aloneness to stand with the others in that little group by that little bridge over a little river. Perhaps it is right to say that this big nation really began on that day in that small place where farmers stood their ground because it *was* their ground.

It was such men who made farming the greatest American activity, not only before industry came, but even after the factories flourished. They were self-sufficient, making their own houses, the food they ate, much of the clothing they wore. Even today the farmer must be a universal man, not just a plower and a planter, a breeder of hogs, cattle, sheep, chickens, turkeys, a deliverer into this world of calves, colts (not many now), piglets, but also an electrician, a mechanic handling intricate machinery, a carpenter, a veterinarian, painter, roofer, often a user of a calculator or computer.

His wife is also a universal woman, running combines sometimes twelve feet high, handling lambs in freezing weather, canning fruit

The Old Farmer's Almanac

Most Americans know *The Old Farmer's Almanac* as a compendium of wit and wisdom, chock-full of facts concerning the weather, the planets, the stars and tides, and containing poetry, puzzles and anecdotes, advice on farming, cooking and general good health. Very few of us realize, however, that this modest booklet, issued annually without splashy covers and with little advertising to proclaim it, holds the longest unbroken publishing record of any American periodical.

During the course of this nation's history, dozens of different almanacs have been published, but the most popular has been *The Old Farmer's Almanac*. Appearing first in 1793 under the editorship of Robert B. Thomas, the founder of the publication, it filled the void left after the demise of Ben Franklin's *Poor Richard's Almanac*. Now after 196 consecutive issues, it is nothing less than an American institution. As one old-time almanac maker said, "A person without an Almanac is

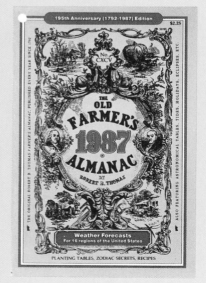

somewhat like a ship without a compass: he never knows what to do or when to do it."

First printed in Boston, *The Farmer's Almanac* ("Old" was officially added to the title in the 1840s) dwelt mostly on matters that concerned rural America, particularly the New England farmer. Even during the most turbulent eras of American history, it paid little heed to war or political strife. Instead it has held forth on a vast range of matters encompassing the human experience. Its tone is often funny and sometimes biting:

"Curiosity is looking over other people's affairs and overlooking our own. [1851]"

It's the practical, flinty old horse sense of the Puritan pilgrim fathers and later the Yankee traders who traversed the countryside. Their lot was not easy, and while their outlook was generally upbeat, they had few illusions about human nature:

"It is with narrow-souled people as with narrow-necked bottles—the less they have in them, the more noise they make in pouring it out. [1803]"

Long before there was a U.S. weather service or a TV weatherman, the American people turned to the *Almanac* to find out what the weather would be tomorrow, next month, or even a year ahead. In 1805, as the result of a printer's error, *The Farmer's Almanac* mistakenly predicted "Rain, Hail, and Snow" for July 13. Imagine the amazement of people when on July 13 in the dead of summer, rain, hail and snow fell just as the *Almanac* said it would. Lots of folks, even today, insist on the infallibility of its forecasts.

There is no limit to the *Almanac's*

erudition. It is ready to hold forth at the drop of a hat on taxes, legislation, matrimony, homemaking, farm plans, carpentry, finance, love and death, not to mention practical home remedies such as how to cure corns or banish freckles. When it comes to bad habits or lax morals, the *Almanac* minces no words:

"The surest way to destroy your own health is to be constantly drinking that of other people. [1860]"

The *Almanac* is no slouch either in the complex area of national economics:

"A recession is a period in which you tighten up your belt. A depression is a time in which you have no belt to tighten. When you have no pants to hold up, it's a panic. [1942]"

The *Almanac* has gone on for nearly two hundred years in its God-fearing, fun-loving, and unabashedly patriotic way. But our enduring affection for it may largely be due to its magnanimous spirit, a spirit as old as the days of the early settlers. Harsh conditions and an often hostile environment compelled them to trust in the principle of good neighbors as the key to a just and harmonious universe. This principle, as reflected in the following quote from the *Almanac*, perhaps comes closest to the heart of this miraculous little publication:

"Is there a sick neighbor whose woodpile is running low, or are there any other things on his premises badly needing attention? Perhaps you can give him a quiet little boost. It takes good neighbors to make a good neighborhood. [1911]"

Long may it wave!

—HHL

50

and vegetables, helping with the tough work in field and barn, cooking the food she has often raised herself in sight of the kitchen window.

In an age of specialized jobs, the husband and wife on a farm must have the widest variety of skills. In spite of mechanization, farming remains a craft. The needs of animals on a six-hundred-acre farm are the same as they were on a fifty-acre farm two hundred years ago. Cattle bawl to be fed or milked—although usually with machines today, seldom by hand. (Indeed, living so far apart, at one time many farm families knew their animals better than they knew their neighbors.)

The life of a farm family was the most human way of life, the work for the day discussed at the breakfast table. The children knew exactly what their father and mother would be doing all day, the whole family having its many different chores. Unlike workers who went to a factory, an office, a desk or a machine, farmers stayed at home, usually in sight of the house. My mother used to ride a pony out to my grandfather in a field, bringing his lunch. As a little girl she knew the hazards, the hard work, the need for going on in every weather.

The kids realized that their lives depended on that vague, far, threatening and always shifting place called the market, where a

*I see
no virtues
where I smell
no sweat.*

—Francis Quarles
Enchiridion (1640)

51

Girls crating cabbages

change up or down of a few cents could make or break a whole year. They, too, were familiar with the tilt of fields, the noises and smells and troubles of animals, the problems that rain or the lack of it, or endless bugs, worms, wind, plant diseases, could bring on any day without warning. It was all chance-taking and prayer. As my grandfather used to say, "The Good Book says, 'Take your troubles to the Lord,' but I wish He'd come down and lend a hand now and then."

Farming was always dangerous, like mining. Animals kicked and bit, tools would cut the flesh. There were roofs and windmills to be climbed, high wagonloads of hay that could tip over, unseen holes in fields, axes that could slip, heavy rocks, wheels, beams to be lifted, horses that could panic and run away, fires of cobs, wood, coal, that could leap out of the firebox on a stove and burn hand or house. If bones were broken, it was a long, slow, painful trip to town in a jolting wagon, driven by wife or child.

One winter while pulling a bobsled from one farm to another, my father's team spooked suddenly and he was thrown forward so that the wide runners slid over him, breaking an arm, some ribs and a leg. He lay there in the snow until a farmer happened to see the team running down the road without a driver. The farmer managed to stop them and drive back the way they had come until he found Dad, helpless and in agony. He picked my father up, put him in the bobsled and drove to our farm, where hours later a doctor came because the same neighbor had gone into town and brought the doctor out in the bobsled. Tom Engle hated hospitals— "They make people sick." He was treated at home.

Farming is still dangerous. Last week a farmer I know turned his tractor over in a ditch and lay pinned under it all night until a passing neighbor found him early next morning. An especially wicked machine is the corn picker, into which a cornstalk will occasionally be drawn along with the ears and get stuck in the revolving rollers. Every year many farmers lose hands and arms, trying to clear the rollers because they consider it a nuisance to turn off the engine and start it again. The National Safety Council has figures proving that among major industry groups, agriculture has one of the highest accidental death rates. But I have never met a farmer who would give up his outdoor-indoor life for any other, however safe, in the city.

Oversee your workmen. . . . If they be boys, separate them; for it is true: one boy is a boy; two boys are a half of a boy; but three boys are no boy at all.

—The Old Farmer's Almanac (1804)

David Benson changes a flat tire on a fully loaded wagon.

Pennsylvania
c.1770

ashes

3'

screen   door

Smoke Houses

The sounds and smells of a farm are unmistakable and often beautiful in their own way. Many farmers have given up chickens because they are a nuisance and because it is so simple to buy eggs in town, but at the crack of dawn roosters can still be heard exulting in their power over rustling, clucking, nervous hens. Much of the old slaughtering of cattle and hogs on the farm is gone. If it is still done, the meat is often taken to a locker plant in town for the hams and bacon to be cured and the rest to be frozen. The wonderful odors of our smokehouse, the fire burning a rich smoke from the hickory growing down in the grove, has all but disappeared. Our noses are deprived of that greasy odor of tangy wood burning and melted fat dripping into the flames.

One of the great smells of the old farm was the swill barrel, a hogshead where all kinds of nourishing objects were thrown for the hogs to eat later. I remember cabbages, corncobs with some grains still clinging, stale bread, old carrots, potato peelings, oats, a little sorghum. They produced a nose-piercing odor. When I put my head into the barrel and inhaled to the bottom of my lungs, the powerful smell sometimes made me dizzy. Uncle Charlie, who lived on the farm all his life, regarded that bitter brew's air as nourishing. "You breathe

Top: Drawings by Eric Sloane.
Bottom: Apple orchard in springtime.

that often enough, Paul, you won't have to eat. Of course, you breathe it too much and you won't be able to eat at all."

The odors of farming were everywhere of every kind, the strong and the subtle. Wild dill grew along our lane and when the summer sun heated it, it gave off a gentle, acrid tang. The fields of late summer field corn had a rank smell when the pollen was at its height and falling on the silk of the ears. In spring apple blossoms not only looked pink, they smelled pink. Windfall apples that the cattle had crushed on the orchard ground fermented to an odor fresher than wine.

There is no Paris perfume as elegant as the fragrance coming from a freshly mowed field of red clover, the crushed blooms and the cut stems caressing the air. Alfalfa has largely replaced it now, but sometimes and unexpectedly it can be smelled across a field at night, and you must stop while the dark breeze brings that sweet odor to the grateful nose.

Our barn, of course, was full of blended smells—fresh oats, timothy hay, horse and cow manure, leather harness and every autumn the neat's-foot oil used to preserve it, to keep it soft. All rose to the haymow where we used to slide at the risk of falling through the hole in the floor. It was through this hole that we threw down hay for the animals with a pitchfork whose wooden handle was polished smooth with decades of rubbing by human hands.

The kitchen was filled with smells no city kitchen ever holds. The cast-iron range gave off a metallic smell when the fire was intense,

Then suddenly, overnight, the orchard would burst into glorious bloom, filling the air with a sweet, tart, innocent fragrance.

—Marilyn Kluger
Country Kitchens Remembered

and on the back of it was the bubbling pot that was our equivalent of the swill barrel. All winter it stayed there. Men coming in cold from chores recognized it the moment the door was opened and would yell "Stew's ready" and take a big bowl. The sour-sweet odor of homemade sauerkraut was often there, enriched by chunks of ham permeated by fumes from our smokehouse. There would be tender slices of beef bubbling in vinegar for sauerbraten, its sharpness cutting the heavy air.

The clothes of farmers who work around animals much of the day are permeated with a musky animal odor. In winter, jackets, overcoats, mittens and scarves would be hung in the kitchen to warm them for the next trip to barn or field. In a few minutes they would begin to steam and add their smell to the cooking smells. Even Aunt Tillie's starch, as she ironed her brother Charlie's shirts with a sadiron heated on the range, gave off a crisp odor. Uncle Charlie's wife always made hot chili sauce, whose fragrance was as red as the tomatoes. Next to it in the air was cinnamon from apple pie. She cooked many things at once when the range was going strong.

No noses ever had it so good, especially on days when bread was baked in the oven for the whole week, including rye with pumpernickel seeds. When spread with home-churned butter (we could see the Jersey cows all white, golden and cream down by the barn) and homemade strawberry jam from our own patch, with cold milk from the same cows, it had a taste like nothing bought at a store.

The eyes of people living on farms are different from the eyes of city people. They look farther in space, across long landscapes of fields, whether their own or belonging to others. They identify distant moving objects as cows, horses, people. They can tell the quality of crops in remote fields by their height and color. They can look at a faraway plowed field and say, "Ed's cornfield looks pretty dry to me." They can spot a hen pheasant silently whirring into a fence corner and comment, "Bet she's got a nest of young ones there. Better not mow it down." They can recognize a dark speck in the sky as a chicken hawk and not a crow.

Because weather absolutely determines good luck or bad to a farmer, he constantly watches for clouds and can predict if they are full of rain

The highest compliment . . . a New England man could give a New England woman: "Thar's one thing I'll say for thet wife o' yourn. . . . My hawgs ain't hed a square meal sence she come on the premises."

—Bertha Damon
A Sense of Humus (1943)

56

(continued on page 58)

Hex Signs

The air is sweet in Pennsylvania Dutch country, the earth rich and good. Look about, and you'll see the gold of ripening grainfields and the green of sun-dappled pastures. Listen, and you'll hear the lowing of dairy herds or the creak and groan of a hay wagon, piled sky high and inching heavily toward a barn. It was here, to this fertile land more than three hundred years ago, that German and Swiss farmers first came to settle. Here they ploughed and planted, built sturdy homes and ample barns—all according to age-old custom. And it is here, today, that their descendants do much the same. For the Pennsylvania Dutch have managed to bring their traditions with them into the present—in the hearty down-home cooking that's made them famous and in many old-time country arts as well. Of these the most engaging is a form of decoration as unusual as it is treasured. To find it, though, you must follow that hay wagon as it lumbers up to the barn.

A huge "Swiss" barn it is, big enough for horses, cattle, feed and grain. Pause for a moment in front and look at the massive double doors. Dutch doors, they're called, the kind you can close at bottom to keep out the chickens and open at top to let in the sun. Now it is above these doors, just under the eaves, that you'll find what you're looking for—the large, round, gaily colored hex signs of the Pennsylvania Dutch.

In Grandmother's day the most familiar hex signs, weathering softly on this barn or that, were simple stars that she called *Schtanna* and daisylike flowers she called *Blumma*. Each was drawn in perfect symmetry and set within a circle of bold, bright colors. Today there are variations on the early designs, with fanciful tulips, hearts or acorns added, or even those whimsical birds, the distelfinks. But just as time has served to embellish the old symbols, so too has it clouded their origins.

And what are those origins, you might wonder. In Pennsylvania Dutch country, even to raise the question is to invite debate. Legend has it that hex signs were once intended to guard against *Hexa*, or witches, those ill-intentioned spirits who might enter a barn through the Dutch doors and plague the animals. More benevolently, the signs might secure the barn against lightning or ensure the fertility of the livestock. But do barn signs really reflect more than a people's love of artful decoration? Do they really echo a belief in magic?

"Balderdash," says one authority on the subject. "No Pennsylvania farmer ever paints designs on his barn to ward off evil spirits."

But turn to another authority, a famous hex-sign artist, and he will provide the counterpoint. "If you believe something hard enough, it will work," he says.

Thus one might be inclined to choose a barn sign with oak leaf and acorn for strength, with a rosette for good fortune or a star for success. But stop and look our artist hard in the eye. Now he might very well revert to the local country idiom and say that hex signs are "just for fancy, just for nice."

—CTB

or are only bright fluff floating through the sky. For thousands of years farmers have learned to look at fields, moving things, changes in light and color, to decide whether dust along the horizon was a harmless wagon, a sinister movement of men, or a cyclone coming to tear the roof off the barn. The farmer can see a cow or mare in the barnyard and tell by her gait how close she is to delivering calf or foal. He will know by the uneasy, circling movement of a sow whether she should be penned up at once before farrowing. He can tell the yield of a distant field of corn by the dark green or light yellow of the leaves, by the density of the stalks and their thickness. He can see a female dog trampling and pushing straw into a circle in a quiet corner of the barn and state firmly, "She's gonna have pups tonight."

Above all, the country eye sees not rows of buildings, brick, wood, stone, metal, glass, but open space. Instead of having to adjust to moving cars, sidewalks of hurrying men, women, children, dogs, it does not have to blink and change focus rapidly. That eye can relax over that space, whether it is a cotton landscape in the South, a corn landscape in the Midwest, orchards of pecans in Georgia, oranges in Florida, apples in Washington, miles of vegetables in California, sugarcane in Louisiana, wheat in Kansas, flax glowing blue in Minnesota, soybeans in Iowa; they all rest the eye in their unmoving assurance that useful things are growing out of the cultivated earth.

The ear also has a different life in the country. How many times in the city do you hear a human voice talking to an automobile? Yet where there are horses there is talk, as simple as "Whoa" or "Back, back," or as varied and complicated as the first calling of a horse's name before entering its stall so it will know you are there and won't kick. There is also the soothing hum in a driver's throat as he tries to settle down a horse that has been frightened.

My father always controlled his horses more by tone of voice than by force of a bit in the mouth because that way he prevented the callusing of the inner edge of the animal's lips that would make it "tough-mouthed." I never heard him speak as gently, as reassuringly to his children as to his horses. With animals he had endless patience, not with his kids. Most of the time around animals he would be making some sound to let them know he was close. One reason was that he was so often alone with them, out in the fields, down in the barn, driving on a country road, and it was a proof of shared companionship.

It was especially important always to let the bull (called by the women in the family "the animal") know you were around him. Uncle

58

A dairy farm

Horse Trading

forelock poll neck withers back loins point of hip rump buttock thigh gaskin cheek muzzle throttle shoulder chest forearm knee cannon hoof fetlock pastern ribs flank stifle hock coronet

Nearly everybody loves to trade. Horse traders just loved to trade more than other folks. They had trading in their blood. Their favorite sport was matching wits with others of their kind. And most of them had a genuine fondness for horses. One horse trader began trading pencils in grade school at about age six. At eight he had fifteen dollars saved and bought his first horse. Another says, "I guess I was just born to like to trade. . . . I'd trade for anything I could get ahold of."

Usually, however, country boys began trading horses at about the age boys today get their first automobiles. In the country young men were working on the farm by then, and fully aware of the excitement that goes with trading: More money was made from an hour of trading talk than from a day of sweaty labor. Admiration was gained for a shrewd trade—or ridicule when the buyer got burned. Also, hundreds of dollars rode on a handshake, and there was a certain code of ethics well understood among horse traders though not immediately apparent to the uninitiated.

An old hand at the game might explain the code this way: "The first rule is you can't go back on a trade. You negotiate terms—an even swap of one horse for another, or a swap plus cash or a hog or something 'to boot.' Once you agree to the terms, you have bought yourself a horse. If the animal turns out to be less than you expected, your best course is to trade him off to someone else.

"The second rule is you shouldn't

misrepresent the animal to the buyer. You can fatten a horse, groom him till he shines, even touch up a few gray hairs the same way you touch up your own. But after that you had best let the prospective buyer judge him for himself. Since most horse traders pride themselves on their knowledge of horseflesh, they spend more time looking at the animal than quizzing you. Asking too many questions makes it seem like they don't know what they are doing. But if a really embarrassing question comes up, you had best reply something like, 'Well, I guess this isn't the horse for you.' Then go look for another buyer."

Not all horse traders were scrupulously honest, however. Some were constantly on the move, leading a string of animals from town to town, trading all the way. According to Will Zoellner, a blacksmith in north Georgia who shod many a hoof, thirty days was about their limit in one place. "A horse trader don't stay long in a town," he said, "because he knows it isn't wise to."

Many were the surprises buyers found in their stables once the horse traders disappeared. The most common was to find that a horse was

older than he looked. Besides dyeing gray hairs, some traders would remove other signs of age. An old horse has hollows over his eyes; these were removed temporarily by injecting air into them with a needle. The length of the teeth is an easy indication of age; it was common practice to file them to make them shorter. A horse that limped would walk well for a while after a shot of novocaine. And some traders even mashed up dynamite in the feed trough, believing it would make old Dobbin frisky as a colt.

The rascals get talked about, but horse traders performed a valuable service in country communities. They knew all the horses and owners in an area, and earned their money by bringing together buyers and sellers. Sometimes a deal required transporting an animal a considerable distance, and the trader did that. A trader might also buy a horse with a problem that he thought he could cure, and often would restore him to a useful life.

"Now I believe in feedin' whatever you have," said one trader. "Buy poor, feed him fat. . . . Ever'body wants a pretty, fat horse."

—JRR

Charlie was once attacked by his Jersey bull when crossing the barn-yard and was thrown over a fence, which saved him because if he had fallen inside the yard he would have been trampled. I was on the safe side of the fence, watching. When Charlie picked himself up he looked at me a moment while getting his breath and then said softly, "Paul, a man's a durn fool not to let a bull know he's there." It was the only profanity I ever heard him use.

Tractors give their own engine noise to the farm today. Now they have cabs that are air-conditioned, radios and tape players and two-way radios connecting the driver with his house so that at noon he can receive a message, "Come an' git it. Food's on." The noises of com-bines, throwing out the harvested grain or beans to a truck, have a deep, rumbling sound. The noise will stop, as the noise of city streets never does. The evening quiet of a farm comes after the corn has been picked, the soybeans brought in, the animals put away in the barn with enough hay and grain to keep them quiet. Then the sudden blessing of silence descends on the farm, as it never can in a city, where human and mechanical restlessness distorts the lovely dark.

Family members gathering for dinner on a farm have an intimate connection with the food because they have raised most of it, from plowing the ground to seeding, cultivating, harvesting. Each of those activities involves its own noise, but at dinner (surprisingly often even today preceded by the saying of grace, because it is obvious that man alone could not provide such abundance) there is only talk about the day's work and the satisfying sounds of jaws breaking up the fibers of home-grown vegetables and meat. I still remember sopping up ham gravy with biscuits and licking it off my fingers with loud smacks.

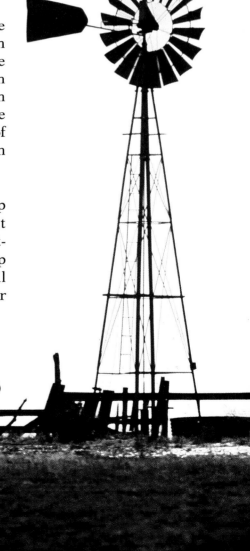

One of the great traditions of farming has always been that of help for any farm in trouble. If word spread around a neighborhood that someone had broken a leg or was seriously ill just at plowing, plant-ing, cultivating or, most of all, at harvest time, a day would be set up for neighbors to help. Along narrow dirt roads that twisted like bull snakes slithering through grass, teams would appear pulling whatever equipment the season demanded.

Family and friends celebrate Heather Benson's twelfth birthday on the Bensons' Minnesota farm.

That spirit goes on strong as ever. When farmers in southeastern states had no hay to feed their livestock because of the searing drought, midwestern farmers sent down both round and rectangular bales in trucks donated by trucking firms, on railcars donated by railroads. The Norfolk Southern Corporation contributed cars to be hooked onto regular trains going to Georgia, Tennessee, Alabama and the Carolinas. A huge sign was put up by an advertising company in Des Moines on behalf of its offices in the South, proclaiming "HAY, THANKS! FROM THE FARMERS OF SOUTH CAROLINA."

National Guard members from Sioux City and Dubuque loaded bales onto an Air Force C-141B at Cedar Rapids Municipal Airport. Said one County Extension agent, appropriately named Oates, of a plea on television by a South Carolina dairy farmer, "It opened the hearts of all these people. . . . No government official ever could get that kind of response."

What was once the greatest single activity of this country, farming, is in big trouble today. Drought, hail, tornados and floods were always a farmer's enemy and always will be, for no amount of hard work and intelligent planning can control them. But now in many parts of the nation, corn, cotton and soybeans are produced in excessive quantities and part of each year's harvest must be put into storage. Many farmers went deeply into debt to buy more land and bigger machinery. Now land prices have dropped so much that the value of a farm may not equal the amount borrowed.

Even that clear, cold, beautiful water coming out of farm wells may now contain so much nitrogen and other chemicals used in fertilizers

A season's harvest stored for the winter

that it is unfit to drink. From the beginning of agriculture the farmer has faced dangers. Today they are often made by man.

Yet there has also always been hope. The work becomes less severe as tractors give a comfortable ride over the land in place of what used to be a harsh hand-to-hand grappling with it. To produce a bushel of corn today takes significantly less time than a few years ago, and is accomplished with much greater ease. The car has brought not only neighbors but towns and cities closer. What used to take a family member riding a horse to alert friends for help after a disaster now needs only a telephone call and a quick response by an automobile driven over a paved road.

When I was a child riding in a wagon or a buggy across the countryside on a mud road, the landscape was dark, save for a rare

kerosene light from a lamp in a farmhouse. When they saw it, my family would ask, "Wonder what's wrong over at the Hamiltons'." Now electricity has brought comfort and illumination. It runs separators that used to work by hand, grinders, power tools, freezers.

In spite of all the current hazards of American farming, it remains among the most productive agriculture in the world. The sun still rises over the long fields and the husband and wife in the country rise with it. The work still goes on all day, but at night the farms no longer fall into darkness. Across the countryside many farmers leave big yard lights on all night, so that one drives from brightness to brightness.

Certainly the old problems of drought and storm are joined by many new risks, but as always the farmer will face them and he will overcome.

The Bensons work late by the lights of a pickup truck, getting their corn stored in a race against the advancing snow.

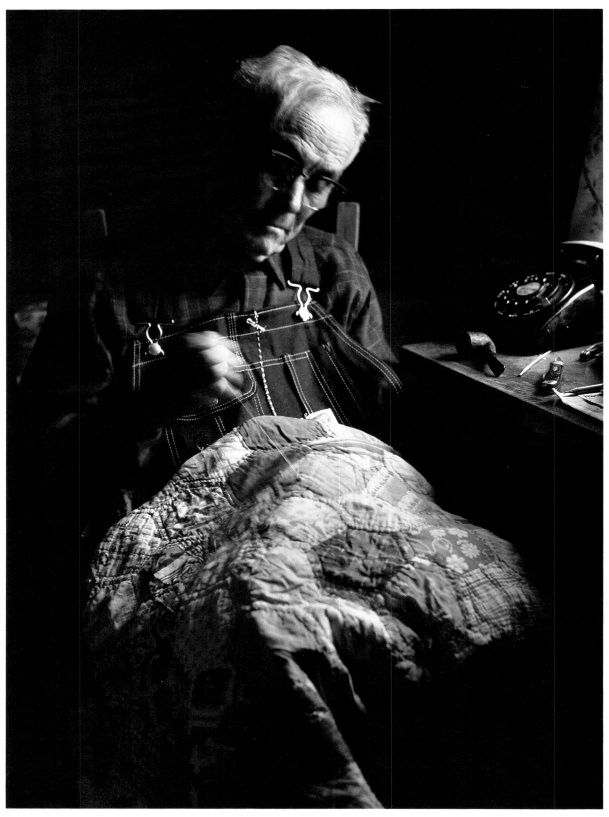

Born in 1891 in a one-room cabin in Tennessee, Alex Stewart (pictured here) became a musical-instrument maker, blacksmith, farmer, moonshiner, miller, quilter, tanner, trapper, wood-carver and herb doctor. Before his death in 1985, he was honored by the National Endowment for the Arts and recognized by the Smithsonian Institution as a master craftsman.

CRAFTS

This was a handmade country.

It is an irony of our history that a nation so industrialized and mechanized today should for most of its first two hundred and fifty years have depended on individuals skilled in working wood, metal, clay, rushes, leather and wool by hand. Every item was an individual thing, with its own variations however slight, as compared to the identical objects later produced on the assembly line.

If you needed a chair to sit on, you made it. First you chopped down a tree. Then you split the wood for legs and back and shaped them with a spokeshave, which was also used for shaping the spokes of a wheel. You fitted the parts together, and for the seat you cut cane, or any available flexible fiber, and wove it into place. The wood could be hickory, oak, ash, maple, walnut or cherry. It was as strong as the hands that had made it and lasted for years beyond the life of the maker. If you wanted a bed you made it too, perhaps from the same tree, or a table, or a cradle that would rock babies for generations to come. Eventually the grain of the wood would glow from the rubbing of all those little hands.

In those early years craftsman's skills were needed for simple survival. If something broke, you fixed it yourself or made a new one. There were few stores where things could be replaced and often no money for replacements. With their practical forms, pieces of furniture, bowls, tin basins, quilts, buggies, wagons—all handmade—had the elegance of plain design. In later years Shaker tables, chairs and benches showed how original and striking great simplicity could be.

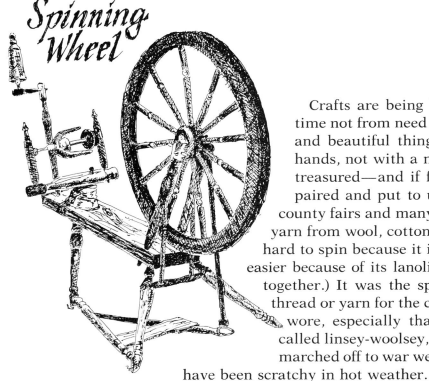

Spinning Wheel

Crafts are being brought to life again today, this time not from need but from the joy of making a new and beautiful thing, the joy of shaping it with the hands, not with a machine. Old spinning wheels are treasured—and if found broken are bought and repaired and put to use. There are demonstrations at county fairs and many are used in homes for producing yarn from wool, cotton or even rabbit fur. (Rabbit fur is hard to spin because it is slippery, whereas wool is much easier because of its lanolin, which makes the strands stick together.) It was the spinning wheel that produced the thread or yarn for the clothes each member of the family wore, especially that early, rough and tough fabric called linsey-woolsey, a mixture of linen and wool. Men marched off to war wearing linsey-woolsey, which must have been scratchy in hot weather.

One of the most curious and useful inventions was a small "visiting wheel," a spinning wheel that women could tie to a horse and take with their work to a neighbor's house. This helped to relieve the loneliness of life on isolated farms. The visiting wheel gave an excuse for talk, for catching up on the news of the neighborhood, the accidents, illnesses, betrothals, children born. The tongues were as busy as the hands, and always in the background the reassuring, steady hum of the turning wheel.

It was all handmade. Sheep for wool were raised on the farm. Flax for linen was planted in a field. In the South cotton was grown in sight of the spinning wheel that would turn it into one-ply or two-ply thread. Before clothes could be worn a long process of spinning, weaving, cutting, sewing, had to take place. This was done by expert hands, trained by mothers and grandmothers and in turn instructing children and grandchildren. That was how country people survived in those days, by learning all of the crafts needed to live life in a harsh environment.

After the yarn had been spun, weaving began. The loom was a frame, usually square or rectangular, on which the warp threads were strung tight. The weft threads were then woven under and over alternate warp threads to make the body of the cloth. The weft could be passed over or under one warp thread or several to make a variety of textures, designs and images. There were many sorts of weaves to use, depending on the number of threads per square inch, on the changes in weft threads in relation to the warp threads, varying the texture from thin to thick to flat to nubbly. The simplest weavings produced percale (of fine cotton thread, used for clothes and sheets), muslin (cotton pillowcases), taffeta (of silk thread). By passing weft threads over and under two or more warp threads, a basket weave was created.

Today the popularity of weaving for the pure pleasure of it has greatly expanded the sorts of things made on looms. Abstract designs are introduced. The old skills are heightened by improved equipment. Now the emphasis is on finding new materials, new designs, experimenting in color and texture.

You can take your time today and not have to work with the haste of long ago. Then the weaving had to be done quickly before it was time to churn the butter, embroider tiny roses on the baby's coverlet and set the bread dough rising. Every farmhouse was a miniature handcrafting factory, turning out one necessity in the morning, two in the afternoon and one in the evening. It was hard, physical and yet aesthetic labor.

"I could weave a yard a day, of the fine thread. . . . Kept my foot a goin', and a throwin' that old-fashioned shuttle all day long."

—Clemmie Pugh, quoted in
A People and Their Quilts

Woman weaving on a loom

69

(continued on page 73)

My grandmother's hands were so callused they scratched my face when she stroked it and sometimes tore threads on the cloth she was weaving. She never complained, for she was happy her hands could be of use to the family, making things that kept us warm and delighted our eyes. Indeed, there was a sense of design in everything she did and it gave us a sense of design in our lives: work, for the morning comes, but make it as handsome as you can.

Hooking rugs is another craft that has been brought back to life. Long ago women used to have hooking bees where patterns and gossip were exchanged. One of the wonderful qualities of an art like this is that textures and designs that had been used many years before keep coming back. I remember one time when my mother's rug-hooking neighborhood group met at our house. As Mother was working out an intricate design the lady opposite her cried out, "That's just what Grandma used to make!"

Nothing was wasted. Hooked and braided rugs utilized every scrap of fabric not being worn or walked on or used to wrap the frail runt in a litter of pigs. When I went to Oxford University as a Rhodes scholar, I took with me a round, three-foot-across braided rug from my grandmother and put it before my fireplace as a symbol of home in Iowa. I recognized in it pieces of Grandpa's overalls so worn with weather and work that the dark blue had almost turned white. There were strips of my sister's stockings, abandoned because they had runs in

"She taught me to splice—which is the hardest thing anybody has to learn. And then we dyed. I carried all the water by pails; I was just exhausted, but I felt, 'Oh, I'm learning to braid.' "

—Jean Will, rug maker, quoted in A Fine Age

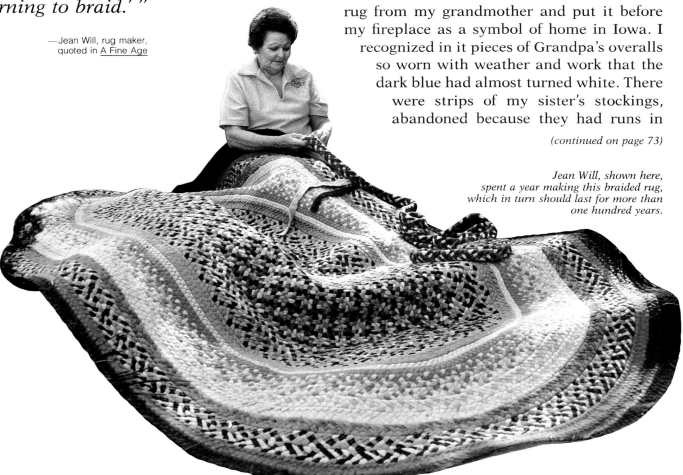

Jean Will, shown here, spent a year making this braided rug, which in turn should last for more than one hundred years.

70

Baskets

A basket is to put things in. Boxes, barrels, buckets, pails, sacks and crocks also serve as containers. But they can't take the place of a good basket. They are too heavy, or they have no handle, or they let their contents get crushed. A basket is usually lightweight and often shaped to carry on your arm or rest on your hip. It is strong—it may last a family for two generations or more—and it is nice to look at.

In pioneer days, country people made their own baskets. Some still do. Others buy from a local man or woman who makes a living making and selling baskets. That's one business you can get into with almost no capital. Your raw materials are free for the taking in the woods, and a pocketknife and an axe are all the equipment that's absolutely required.

Yankee basketmakers prefer wood stripped from the brown ash tree, called "the basket tree." Southerners prefer white oak. Those woods peel apart the best, and last the longest. If they are not available, you can make baskets from many other natural materials: cane, willow, sweet grass, straw, even honeysuckle vine. The prime requirement is that a plant yield strips that can be bent in the weaving process. The word "wicker" designates that sort of flexible material, rather than any specific plant, which explains why so many different baskets are called wicker.

Weaving a basket is a good job for winter days when you can't work outside. That's assuming you have planned ahead and found a good tree and cut it down and brought it home. If it's ash, you may have to soak the log, then pound the living daylights out of it so the growth rings separate and you can pull lengthwise strips, or "splints," from it. Ash or oak, you peel these splints apart and then peel them apart again several times, getting thinner and thinner strips each time. When you finish all this peeling, you've made yourself a good stock of material for weaving a simple basket. A fancier one may call for whittling wood into round ribs to form the skeleton of the basket. Or for boiling catnip leaves to make a green dye for the strips, or hickory bark and walnuts to make a brown dye. With those colors, says Alex Stewart of Hancock County, Tennessee, "You can . . . make one of the purdiest baskets you ever saw."

It takes a lot of patience to create a neat basket from a pile of strips of wood, attaching the rims and arranging the ribs and weaving the filler strips in and out. Twenty hours is not too much to make a good big basket. Not everybody can do it. Those who can have a love of good materials and a natural sense of design.

Such artisans know many shapes, based on intended uses. Or as city folk say, "Form follows function." There are baskets for gathering berries or eggs, or picking cotton, baskets with little legs for rinsing

White oak bushel basket

ments as "Lord, John Rice, if you jest had all the beans that's been picked and carried in out of the gardens and cornfields (that's where the cornfield beans grew) in that old basket, you'd have you something." Or "That ole basket belonged to my sister. . . . I'll never forget she packed her Christmas dinner in that little basket and

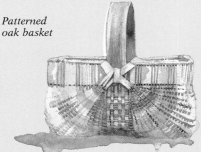

*Patterned
oak basket*

wool, even baskets for storing feathers. Whether round, oval, square or rectangular, each is well proportioned and pleasing to the eye. One shape often seen is called a "gizzard basket" because of its resemblance to a chicken's gizzard. One rarely seen today is a "bed basket," a cradle for a baby.

Such rich variety has developed over a very long history. Some archeologists believe that basketmaking is man's oldest craft, older even than pottery making, and that almost all peoples in all times have

Gizzard basket

Honeysuckle basket

made baskets. The Indians of the Pacific Northwest made what some feel are the most artistic baskets of America. Among later Americans, the members of the religious sect called Shakers made the most esteemed baskets. Museum curators now seek the creations of both those traditions, as well as the best work of many other American makers.

But buying is not always easy. A second-generation basket is a part of the family. John Rice Irwin, founder of the Museum of Appalachia in Tennessee, hears such com-

walked all the way from Caryville—hit took her all day. . . . She died the 9th of March in 1929. So you can see why I wouldn't sell the little basket. . . . I've jest kept it as a sort of a keepsake."

Some artisans making baskets today, especially among the hardy men and women of the Appalachian Mountains, are in their nineties. But there are much younger basketmakers in the country who have

Shaker cheese basket

hundreds of baskets in their futures. Baskets play new roles in modern homes: little baskets hold flowers, middle-sized ones hold magazines, large ones hold ice skates, basketballs and other sports equipment. Those baskets are likely to become members of the family, too.

—JRR

them, of my brother's mackinaw coat, which had originally been sewn by Mother, the thick cloth fighting the needle so that she had to force it through until her fingers bled. There was living red in the pieces braided into my little rug on the floor of the room where I lived in chilly England, and it warmed me in my homesickness to walk barefoot over it. There were also strips from a robin's-egg-blue petticoat that I knew Grandma had worn because I saw a flurry of it one winter day when she fell on the ice. I was startled to find that this laboring farm lady cared enough about beauty to appliqué flowers on an undergarment that she expected no one but her husband to see. But even in places seldom or never seen, she demonstrated a sense of color and form. There were, indeed, strips of cloth in my rug that I could not identify. When I asked my mother what they were from, I was amazed and a little shocked to hear her say that they had once been part of Grandma's corset cover.

One of our joys when we were dirt poor was the luxury of having "candlewick" bedspreads. Candlewicking is a pattern worked into a loose material, usually muslin, with a heavy four-ply cotton thread. French knots, for example, could be used in the design—perhaps as the inside of a flower; padded satin stitches might be used in the border, and outline stitches for the rest. It could also be a simple design of row after row of tufts. When finished, the muslin was soaked in cold water to remove traces of the marker used in making the design and then submerged in very hot water to shrink the cloth. After the fabric had dried, the tufts of cotton thread could be clipped to make them fluffier. They were very popular as bedspreads. I can remember young girls in our area making candlewick bedspreads to put in their hope chests, to be ready when they married.

Years later I discovered that candlewicking was called that because the heavy cotton thread used was the same type as that once used for wicks in candles. Indeed, candle dipping was one of the crafts absolutely necessary in those days, when there was no electricity on farms and kerosene lamps were only beginning to appear. I had the task of clipping the burned end of the lamp wick every night before we lit it. In that dim and smelly light we cooked the food raised in our own fields, the cooking smells triumphing over the kerosene stench. By the inadequate half light of those lamps, crafts were created. A farmer friend who had lost two fingers of his right hand in an accident took up carving. He did it in the evening after the day's hard chores, by the yellowish and flickering glow of a kerosene lamp. He made a slab of cherry wood into a human face, with pain and patience bringing out the grain of the wood into the lines of the face.

Carved wooden clog dancer, a toy popular in Colonial times and reappearing today

"When I whittle, I forget everything; don't nothing bother me."

—John Arnold, wood-carver, quoted in <u>A Fine Age</u>

73

"A lot of the boys liked to go to this basketmaker's place and take lessons. . . . They learned to do . . . not only baskets, but chair seating and making stools."

—Aunt Lola Cannon, quoted in <u>Foxfire 4</u>

Crafts student winding a hearth broom—Berea College, Berea, Kentucky

Often a groom-to-be would make furniture for his future home. Every barn had a workshop with woodworking tools: vises, planes, saws. Seasoning on shelves along the wall were boards from trees on the home place—black walnut, butternut, hickory, cherry, maple and oak. Not every young man was skilled in carpentry, but there was often a relative who could help make the simple but sturdy chairs with wood, cane or rush bottoms, and the chests and the beds needed to set up a couple in housekeeping. The bride was supposed to spend the year making her own clothes, aprons, dresses, knitted stockings, tablecloths, perhaps quilts. There was a joy not only to the marriage, but afterward in living with things handmade by those who used them.

There are many different ways to make a chair seat—the technique shown here involves rolling corn shucks.

74

Grandpa made a marvelous two-thirds-size rocking chair out of black walnut wood from our grove, and gave it to my mother when she married and began to have children. Its great value was a drawer under the seat that could be pulled out when Mother wanted to sew. In the drawer were little pegs for thimbles, spools of thread, trays for snap fasteners, buttons, ribbons, scissors (including one called "pinking"), a tape measure, pincushions for needles as well as pins, rickrack and an egg of slippery glass for darning socks. I would sit on the floor at her feet, fascinated with the steady, slightly creaking rockers moving back and forth, the drawer open at her side, while her nimble fingers sewed a thick wool jacket for me or a pink cotton blouse for my sister. Again, it was not a fun hobby but a needed craft that

Handmade sewing basket

kept us all decent, warm and reasonably clean.

Mother could work in the barn, milk the cows, then come to the house and sew delicate baby clothes or take her heaviest needles and turn old U.S. Army blankets into horse blankets. Remember that stabled animals need food and water twice a day, seven days a week. If there is a blizzard, no matter—you go to the barn and keep those creatures alive and protected, although you would rather rock in your little chair and crochet a yoke for the neck of a blouse. The point is, Mother had all the survival skills needed then, so much greater a variety than one needs now with a car and endless stores from which to buy. Yet that may be one reason why the old, even ancient crafts are being brought back: they have a greater enchantment precisely because they are not demanded by life today. What was a useful object is now a work of art.

75

(continued on page 79)

The Quilter's Art

Quilt making is more than a simple folk art. With roots that run deep in the rural home, it is a proud country tradition—and with good reason. To make a quilt takes special skill, to be sure. But it takes a special turn of mind as well, one that is learned at mother's knee and passed to the next generation with care. To understand, though, you'll have to watch a quilter bent over her fabric in the soft light of the evening. What you'll see there is a trained hand creating patchwork pictures. But take a closer look. What you'll also find is a giving heart at work. Just think of it this way. . . .

Think of the crackling cold that is a New England ice storm or the howling cold that is a prairie blizzard. Either one makes a body want to sink deeper into the bedcovers at night. In Grandmother's day, a country wife would hand-make those bedcovers for her family, and families then were large. Yet cloth might be scarce, and the time for all that sewing—well, once the chores were done, there was mighty little time left. And so Granny learned to work quickly and to make do with the fabric at hand.

If she was thrifty—and most country women were—she kept up her piece bag, gathering into it every last scrap of cloth, homespun or store-bought, she could find. Al-

Quilting on a hoop

most certainly it held bits of cotton or wool left from the clothes she'd sewn. And it might hold rougher stuff too. "Waste not, want not," Granny would say with a shrewd glance at the flour sack that stood in the pantry. Surely it could yield some scraps for her collection.

Yet even a full piece bag rarely held enough of one color or fabric to make a bedcover. Rather the small remnants—this red calico from Baby's dress and that blue flannel from Father's shirt—had to be pieced together somehow to form the top of the quilt. Next a backing was needed, and some bat-

ting, too, to sandwich in between for warmth. Only then could the actual "quilting" begin, that job of stitching the layers together into a comforting, cozy whole.

To hurry things along, Granny might now hold a quilting bee, a party really, when friends gathered round to quilt with her. "Many hands make light work," she'd say, smiling. But even with extra hands now and then, it was a big job. A busy farm wife might be forgiven if she chose to keep the project simple. What difference if she made a Crazy Quilt? By joining the scraps, large and small, just as they came

*Detail of quilt patterns,
clockwise from top:
Double Wedding Ring, Peony,
Star of Bethlehem, Log Cabin*

from the piece bag, she'd save time. And after all, such a quilt would be as warm as any other. But a Crazy Quilt—so named for good reason—was not often her choice. Far more pleasing to the eye were the deftly worked patterns she'd learned as a child. And what wonderful names they had! Tumbling Blocks. Star of Bethlehem. Wild Goose Chase. Rocky Road to Kansas. If one of those took longer to create, so be it. She would find the time. For a quilt was more than a warm bed-cover. It was a token of her thrift and industry. It was a proud bit of family history. It was a spot of beauty in an otherwise plain rural house. Ultimately, it was the work of hand and heart—a loving an-swer to a family's need. And so, using her bright bits of cloth as an artist would use a palette, she'd set to work.

One quilter says she can still see, in her mind's eye, "the light play-ing on the low ceiling and Mama's back bent over her sewing next to the lamp." Another quilter recalls her mother saying "No matter how busy you are there is always time for beauty." And still another puts it this way:

"I see my mother's patchwork quilt
    upon my bed upstairs,
And stitched into each tiny piece
    are all her love and cares."

"Yes, every quilt has a story to tell," Granny would agree. Each of hers, she claimed, was like a magic carpet, taking her back to times past.

A quilter of great age once ex-plained, "It's so much fun to pick up these quilts and see everybody's dresses in it. Oh, here's one of mine when I was sixteen. Mother saved pieces from every dress she ever made for me; when I got older she

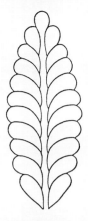

Quilting patterns. Left: *Feather.* Right: *Feathered Wreath.*

gave them to me to make a quilt."

Piecing her own quilt, especially a first quilt, why that was enough to make a girl feel quite grown up. For one thing, it said that Mama now approved her stitchery; for another, that the precious family piece bag, like a book of memories, was open to her too. But how was she to begin?

Well, first she'd settle herself at the window, look through the scraps and sort them, the light tones here, the dark there—just as Mama would do. Then she'd consider. . . . A Nine-Patch pattern, so simple to make, seemed a good first choice. Just a few bright squares in a block, easily arranged. Of course, she loved the star quilts she'd seen

Mama make, their hundreds of tiny jewellike patches pulsing with color. But they were slow to work and—well, better done later, once her eye and hand were surer, once she could make, say, ten fine stitches to the inch. For now, as she began cutting the scraps to size, all she could think was:

"At your sewing do not tarry,
First you quilt and then you marry."

An old adage, it's true, but one that she took to heart. Rural traditions were strong, and tradition had it that before she married, twelve quilts, plus a special bridal quilt, were to be done. Luckily she had only to piece the tops for her hope chest. Later, upon her engage-

ment, neighbors would help finish them off.

The thought was enough to make her smile. There could be more to a quilting bee than just the quilting, she knew. The day would start early, the women bending over the big wooden quilting frame, stitching and talking. And the day would end late, with the sounds of laughter filling the house. For the menfolk would often join them for supper, and music, singing, dancing and games would follow. Oh, it was sure to be a festive day, a day to recall whenever she looked at those quilts. It was a milestone of sorts, too, the start of a lifetime of needlework. All along the way there would be other quilts to make, gifts and tokens of her love: a Friendship Quilt for someone leaving the community; a Freedom Quilt for a boy's coming of age; a tiny crib quilt for the birth of a baby. And if times were hard—as well they might be on a farm—she'd take extra comfort in her craft when a quilt was used to pay a debt. Whether she worked in bright, exuberant colors, soft earth tones, or something in between, her covers would be prized for what they were—products of ingenuity and imagination.

But wait. What if a bedcover had a flaw—like that Honeycomb Quilt right there. The block in the corner, it doesn't quite match the others. Sloppy work, you'd say if you didn't know better. But those attuned to country ways know that God alone is perfect and that one small flaw in an otherwise perfect design is there for a reason—as a sign of the quilter's humility.

"Yes," Granny would say softly, "every quilt is the work of hand and heart. Every one has a story to tell— if only you learn how to read it."

—CTB

"Just move your chair in right here and grab a needle."
Quilting in a group not only makes the work go faster, it's a lot of fun besides.

Even the old-fashioned sampler that used to be done by an ever-conscientious young girl is having a comeback. The moral truths may sound out of date, but the fancy letters never age, and the fancy stitches still produce evidence of the embroidery skills of the maker, which was the original purpose of the work. They were often done by lamplight at night. So clever were many of them, they were passed down from generation to generation. Some were very elaborate, showing Adam and Eve in the garden, outlining the house in which the girl lived, sometimes a cherished household pet, trees, birds like those she could see out the window, religious exhortations. They were usually signed by the embroiderer and sometimes had the name of her teacher, along with the date. The linen was usually homespun from local flax. Some were maps of the area, some had texts from almanacs. Grandma hung hers on the parlor wall. Although a modest lady, she was proud

Cross-stitch sampler

"I've always belonged to some quiltin' club or church bee. When I was raising my kids the club was always my time to get off and get some relief."

—Unidentified woman, quoted in The Quilters

79

*Crewel embroidery
decorating a pillow top*

of her handiwork. On it was carefully stitched the family's grace, translated from Great-grandpa's original German and spoken by the youngest child at dinner:

> Come Lord Jesus, be our guest,
> And share this food that You have blessed.
> Amen!

Sometimes Mother used a loosely twisted yarn for embroidering heavy pillows. She called it "crewel," but I thought she meant "cruel" and was astonished that so gentle a lady could do anything cruel. Many years later when I went to France, I traveled to Normandy to visit the tragically large American cemetery at St. Laurent, a green and beautiful place where the American soldiers who died in the invasion that freed Europe are buried. Then I went on to see the famous Bayeux Tapestry showing the Norman invasion of England. To my astonishment and joy, I found that the embroidery techniques used in that eleventh-century, two-hundred-thirty-one-foot-long and incredibly detailed depiction of an invasion nine hundred years ago were the same as the ones my grandmother and mother used in their creation of humble works for decorating a little farmhouse in Iowa. Both the Bayeux Tapestry and the simple works of my ancestors prove that the human eye and hand can, with sharp needles and good yarn, create a record of human life.

One of the old arts that has made a comeback has been tinsmithing, such an important craft in the nineteenth century, often found in the same family, as fathers taught sons. Now it is no longer a useful trade as much as it is a decorative one. There is a man not far away from us today who toiled much of his life as a sheet-metal worker. For years he has umpired baseball games in the summer and made tin lanterns in his workshop in the winter. People come from miles around to get his lanterns, usually painted green, and hang them outside their houses. He also makes colanders, pails, cookie cutters and canning funnels.

The decorating of tin articles is often called "country painting," and much of it today reproduces the quaint patterns found on old tinware. Today's colors may look brighter because modern paint doesn't fade, but the designs are authentic. One student and teacher of the art today has collected over three thousand patterns found on tin watering cans, little chests, document boxes, pails, trays, sugar bowls, canisters. There are many different kinds of brush strokes used, and some of the makers of early nineteenth-century pieces can be identified by their style. Like other crafts, it is astonishing how elaborate not only the shaping of the object can be, but also its painting. Country painting is one of the most cheerful of the restored arts. When I asked our local tinsmith why he chose that very ordinary-looking material for his products, he said, "Tin is light, it can be turned into any shape, it cuts easily, it doesn't have to be heated like copper, and once it's done you can put any colors and designs on it you can imagine."

Another craft that used to be a

Painted tinware.
Top: *Can for carrying water to washbasins, circa 1870.*
Bottom: *Document box.*

81

Batter jug, salt-glazed stoneware, made in New York or Pennsylvania, 1860–80

necessity and is now an art is the transformation of clay into ceramics. Everywhere potters are shaping elemental dirt into bowls, pots, cups, dishes, plates, flower vases. They are in big cities, in universities, along country roads, out in the suburbs, firing and glazing and creating new forms, new color combinations, even making faces with china teeth on the sides of jugs. There are exhibits in museums where pottery is taken seriously as an art form.

We had a few old pieces at home, but they were fragile and shattered if dropped, which always happened in a busy farm kitchen. Now pottery is returning to our environment. Why? Because the hand is honored more today than the machine, for it can transmit the imagined shape directly from the creative mind. To stand before a wheel turning (throwing) a pot, and then in front of a fired kiln hardening the clay and setting the glaze, hour after hour, to make something that, if you only wanted a useful thing, could be bought quickly and cheaply is to recognize the power of the individual doing and fashioning his own thing.

Now I see that not to have been a little boy sitting on the floor at his mother's feet, wearing clothes she had made, watching her rock and sew, rock and sew, humming or singing, her hands flashing at the tough cloth or the delicate fabric, is not to have lived this lovely and dangerous life to its fullest.

Last summer at a local fair a teenage girl won first prize for her quilt. She also won the hog-calling contest. The country is safe for another year.

"Lot of people will say, 'What do you do when you get that mud up under your fingernails?' I say, 'Work right on. It don't bother me.' "

—Nola Campbell, potter, quoted in Foxfire 9

Churn, salt-glazed stoneware, made in Rochester, New York, 1841–52

82

Brooke Stewart, potter, at work

COUNTRY TOWNS

Everybody knows every body, and sometimes in very familiar ways, because they live so close together.

The kids all go to the same schools, where they are friends (and occasionally enemies) of the other kids.

Adults compete with adults across town for the best garden. It used to be that the first giant tomato was a triumph, not eaten but displayed with a card of honor at the general store.

Even every dog knows every dog, but cats are more independent and prowl their secret ways alone.

There is a sharing unlike anything in a huge city. If someone is sick, neighbors may bring their favorite dishes. Before florists, flowers came from the rows of peonies, zinnias, marigolds, dahlias, picked from the border of the garden, hand tended and hand delivered, always with encouraging remarks: "Tillie, I really believe fresh blooms help a person. I think they fight the flu."

Country towns have the best of all worlds. The townspeople are close to the farms running away to the horizon, but they are spared the ordeal of the quarter-mile lane that has to be plowed before the farm family can rush a sick child to a doctor. The small town is a community in which neighbors are the most important life support. One of the harshest remarks my mother could use to describe a family that stayed aloof from the rest of us was "They don't neighbor much." It was almost like saying "They don't believe in God."

Main Street—Galena, Illinois

85

Volunteer Fire Department
New Durham, New Hampshire

People in those country towns are fierce in their individuality and fierce in their commitment to helping others. One of the most dramatic moments I remember was driving into town and seeing a house on fire. There were people running in and out of the house, rescuing things. I ran in and started to carry out a couch with the help of a stranger. The woman who lived there cried out in a piercing and anguished voice, "Drop it. Go back in and get the baby bed."

I was home. That was my human-sharing territory. She was a strong woman. Weeping, she had to be restrained from running back into the house. She yelled again, "Get the desk in the living room. Grandpa's old letters are in it. Get our wedding pictures on the mantel. Look for the dog."

The volunteer fire department is important to those towns and their survival. When the siren sounds, volunteers drop whatever they are doing: a store clerk holding up a shirt, a druggist about to fill a prescription, a butcher with a chunk of beef. It is a total town effort. In the early days they pulled a hose cart and ran down the street with dogs happily howling behind them. They even used to race other volunteer crews. The heartening thing was that the neighbors were there removing household items before the firemen arrived. They did get the baby bed and the desk out in time, and they did find the terrified dog under the kitchen table.

Just the thought or a plan to go to town on Saturday was the source of great joy and anticipation.

—Roy Webster
Under a Buttermilk Moon

Historically, one of the glories of country towns was the bandstand in the square. In the days before radio, television, records and cassettes, people had to make their own music. One of the first questions asked of a new family moving in was "Can they play anything?" Every Saturday night the band would perform familiar music for brass. The square would be surrounded by wagons and buggies full of parents taking their ease after the day's work, children glad to be there but restless at sitting still, and always babies asleep, now and then startled by a roar from a trombone or a wild roll on a bass drum.

A lot of the bandstand music when I grew up was from the Civil War time, and Grandpa loved it. There was a song scored for band, "Tenting on the Old Camp Ground." Grandpa had done his tenting across Indian Territory in the West, in the sun that burned rider and horse, loaded down with saber, pistol, canteen and carbine, which he pronounced "carbeen." His daughter, my mother, had a little foot-pumped organ. Some evenings Grandpa would say to her, "Eva, play 'Tenting Tonight.'" He would close his eyes and hum along with it as her strong and lovely hands brought the melody out of that thumping and squeaking and puffing instrument.

The band concert was a social occasion, not only a musical event. It brought farmers into town to see their friends, who had probably been born on a farm but had moved in to run a store or a grain elevator. Everybody came to the band concert, because there was nothing else to do in those little places and because it was most people's only chance to hear music other than in church.

Lansing, North Carolina

All around the square, stores were open, especially the drugstore, with its soda fountain and ice-cream cones. Families came to do their weekly shopping before staying on for the band. Indeed, the concert was really a concerted effort, because the entire audience knew all of the players, who were the people they dealt with for the needs of their lives. The family doctor played a clarinet, a veteran played the bugle at opening and closing, a dentist played the snare drum (whose sound, after all, was like his drill). The bass drum was handled by a huge man from the lumberyard, his bass voice howling along with his playing just as Toscanini hummed along with the New York Philharmonic.

Small towns in the old days were animal places. Many families had a barn and kept horses for going out in the country to buy fresh vegetables, dressed chickens, a turkey, for going to church or a funeral or a wedding, for driving to picnics in summer or enjoying that wonderful floating motion of a bobsled in winter. Many also kept a cow or two for family milk. Some kept chickens in coops next to the barn, to the shock of those next door who slept late and couldn't bear the aggressive crowing of roosters early in the morning.

Barber shop—Giddings, Texas

Animals in town had an extra usefulness—it was my happy job to spread their manure on our garden. This was not simply an affair of hauling the stuff and scattering it, for I had to be careful not to let the fresh horse manure touch flowering plants, as it was regarded as "hot" and could burn the roots. I had a special pit in which I aged horse manure until it had reached its real richness and its harshness had leached away.

Ladies with flower gardens consulted me (I was twelve) about the state of my fertilizer, and in its prime I hauled it in a wagon and distributed it with great delicacy under the rosebushes. I have never been so honored as in those innocent days when wives of men I knew as powerful in the community would stop me on my afternoon paper route and ask, "Paul, I saw you delivering old horse manure to Millie next door. Do you have any left? I'm starting a new bed of dahlias and phlox, and I need some. Can you come tomorrow?" I was a little businessman in a little town, but I had my identity as I could not have had it anywhere else.

88

(continued on page 91)

Town Squares

Every town needs a town square. Why is that? The past is full of answers.

A New Englander will tell you his town common was once a little patch of pasture for the townspeople's cows. A politician will say Rome had its forum, where the citizens came to hear speeches. A preacher will remember the various accounts in the Bible of people meeting at a town well. A sergeant will remind you of the fortified town enclosed by a stockade with a drill field at the center. A Louisianian will mention the French tradition of late-afternoon promenades around the square by young men and women desiring to see and be seen.

The square in a small American town combines all those benefits—benefits for man and beast—and more. Basic requirements used to be a place to hitch the horses—usually a hitching bar—a pump and a watering trough. Later the trough was replaced by a stone fountain, sometimes with water on three levels, for men, horses and dogs. And still later the hitching bar gave way to a row of parking spaces.

Every square needs a place for people to sit and talk. A fence rail will do, but a bench is more comfortable. "Watching all the girls go by" is always fun. A leisurely game of checkers or dominoes may pass the hours for some. But the universal activity is talk. The Liars' Bench was an institution in some towns, where men sat and told tales of things they had never done but wished they had. Tales about the War. Which war? Well, many a town square still has a cannon left over from the Civil War, kept as a sort of conversation piece. Many also have a statue in bronze of an individual the town wants to honor, or one erected

IN MEMORY OF THE
TOWN'S BRAVE SONS
WHO FOUGHT . . .

Milford, New Hampshire

Plaistow, New Hampshire

The statue in the square is central to the annual Memorial Day parade. Before or after the marching, someone places a wreath at its foot. Someone else may make a speech. More speeches mark the Fourth of July. Many towns have a beautiful white bandstand in the town square, and people bring picnics to an Independence Day concert of marches by John Philip Sousa, followed by fireworks.

If a town is the county seat, it is home to the courthouse. The courthouse is often the most impressive building on the square, representing the majesty of government. Court days are exciting days, with much coming and going of lawyers,

plaintiffs, defendants, witnesses and spectators.

Rivaling the courthouse in size is the church on the square—sometimes several churches. Church bells announce services on Sunday in the morning and again in the evening, and perhaps prayer meeting on Wednesday evening. Historically, during at least one week in the year there were also services every night, constituting what was sometimes called a protracted meeting, or more commonly, a revival.

Throughout the year the square witnesses the milestone events of births, marriages, deaths. To the courthouse come young couples seeking marriage licenses, well-

loved doctors filing birth certificates, lawyers probating wills. To the church come families and friends for the corresponding weddings, baptisms, funerals.

The town clock is often a feature of the courthouse or the church or both. It is huge, visible from far away, sometimes with four faces on a square tower. Clockwork that size is not easy to keep in good repair, but it is a point of civic pride to have a town clock that actually tells time.

Some towns reserved the square for public buildings; others allowed commerce there. If allowed, the most important commercial building on the square is the bank, built with massive walls to reassure depositors. Then there is the drugstore, where once the pharmacist filled prescriptions while other members of his family dispensed lemonade and carbonated soft drinks and ice cream from a marble soda fountain. In times past a sort of informal town council may have met at the drugstore, as at midmorning each day prominent citizens strolled over for a little refreshment, then sat and chatted about local affairs.

What of the present? Is it still true every town needs a town square? It still needs a place for people to come together in formal and informal ways. Today teenagers may promenade in autos rather than on foot, but they still need to see and be seen. The drugstore may have been replaced by a coffee shop as the gathering place for chats on local affairs, but the interactions of people continue much the same. Perhaps that shows clearest in a recent definition of today's enclosed, air-conditioned shopping mall: "a town square with a roof over it."

—JRR

It was all more personal there. The doctor knew everyone; every person was his patient, as there was no other doctor. Usually he had spent his whole life in the town, had delivered all of the children and often later delivered their children. It was a time when people were born at home and died at home. The doctor made house calls night and day with his satchel full of miracles—by today's standard desperately inadequate. His horse was crucial to his career. It took him in a buggy in summer and in a sleigh in winter. He had to be a professional with an instinct because his scientific knowledge was limited. One told me when he came to our house outside a small town, "When I enter a sickroom, my nose tells me the nature of the disease." It wasn't as good as a laboratory test, but most times it worked.

Often a country doctor was paid in produce. For removing an inflamed appendix, he received a quarter of a beef steer. For delivering a baby, he might be given half a pig. In winter he would be asked, "Doc, can you wait till summer?" Then a pair of dressed chickens would arrive, or a basket of vegetables, or sweet corn, or apples. His standard cure for a pain in the gut was a steaming hot poultice of oatmeal, the same stuff he ate for breakfast. In a house where the family had seldom gone beyond high school and usually not beyond grade school, his mere presence healed.

The small-town doctor also knew everything about everybody. He knew all of the problems in all of the houses, including the intimate complications that would have shocked the community had they become public knowledge. There is a story in John Baskin's book *New Burlington* of a young girl who had come back from a big city pregnant and without a husband. She asked her mother in the doctor's office, "Could it have happened in my sleep and I didn't know?" To this the mother replied, "No, it couldn't. That's the wakenest thing that is!"

After a midnight house call, at the end of a long day of handling human crises—setting the leg of a farmer who had fallen from a haymow, diagnosing pneumonia when he knew there were no adequate drugs for it, putting chamomile ointment on poison ivy blisters, comforting a father who told him, "Wife's poorly, kids all got the croup, and the cat don't look good"—the doctor would wearily crawl into his buggy, gently slap the reins, and go to sleep while the horse pulled him home, stamping its feet when they arrived outside the barn.

There was a warm feeling of community in those towns. Most people on a street knew when the doctor had visited a neighbor and arrived soon after he left, bringing soup or fresh-baked bread or a casserole of home-smoked ham with new potatoes in milk. When a

If your town has a good doctor, encourage him in every way to stay —especially by paying his bill promptly.

—The Old Farmer's Almanac (1943)

Town Hall—Ridgefield, Connecticut

Doctor and Doll, *painting by Norman Rockwell*

baby was born, there would be a shower of useful presents. (What an accurate word, "shower," as if the gifts fell from heaven and not from the hands of friends who had just spent an hour over a stove fueled with wood or coal.)

Pain in a little wooden house on a town corner was soon felt in homes on other streets. Friends would rush next door to share sympathy or would telephone. In the time of the party line word would spread instantly from the first call by way of eight or ten others on the line, who in turn called another number and eight or ten would answer. Soon most people in town knew what was happening in that small room several streets away and knew who was suffering.

That sense of belonging to each other endures today. A small-town doctor still treats patients whom he knows, seldom a stranger. The pharmacist still knows from the prescriptions he fills what ailments a family has. There is still a deep concern among townspeople for how the local high school football team will do (or won't do), what the new band uniforms will look like, whether the new water tower will be finished before winter. The people in small towns belong to each other.

A high school band at the Beulah County Fair—Beulah, North Dakota

It is easy to walk fast in a city—among strangers who don't stop you—but in a country town walking is slow because you know and stop to talk to almost everyone you meet. The conversation itself is not important for little world-shaking news is communicated on a small-town street, but it is important that you take the time to say hello to a friend and discuss anything from the first sprouts of corn in a garden to the case of the oldest resident who is dying. If you don't stop, you might be called uppity,

and that is one of the severe sins, only a little below the carnal ones.

In America's past, every country town had two social centers. One was the town hall (or the courthouse if it was the county seat). The other was the general store. The courthouse and the town hall were limited to definite duties, like paying taxes, registering to vote and recording marriages, births and divorces. People might sit on the front steps and talk a while, but mostly they were places where you did some necessary business and then went back to home or work.

The store was where you bought things for the whole family. It was wisely called "general," because you could generally get any item needed there. The storekeeper, usually with black sateen sleevelets over his shirt from cuff to elbow, was not merely a merchant but a counselor, the person in town best informed on all its residents, their problems and joys. He was often also the postmaster, town clerk, psychiatrist, prescriber of nostrums and, above all, the source of news before it appeared in the local newspaper. One Saturday afternoon I saw a farm worker hand his weekly check to our storekeeper and heard him say, "Joe, I might get a little out of order tonight and come in for my check. No matter what names I call you, don't give it to me. Because on Sunday I'll be sorry . . . and so will you."

There wasn't much money floating around in small towns then, so there was a lot of bartering for stuff a farm or garden could not raise. The result was that many storekeepers "carried" their customers. I often overheard a customer, after purchasing groceries and dry goods, tell Joe to "write it down." Joe, whose position in the town was only a little below that of priest or minister, wrote it down and did a little praying that he would one day be paid. He was paid too—after harvest and before Christmas, unless the family had a disaster.

The old concept of the cracker-barrel philosopher was accurate. Many things came in barrels, because an order had to last a long time: sugar, vinegar, rice, molasses, coffee, flour, candy. The barrel was as useful to the store as the cash register and scales, for it provided a place for husbands to sit and gossip (men are worse gossips than women are supposed to be) while their wives shopped. This was no quick-order or fast-food joint. Shopping was a time for talking as well as buying. It was as much a social event as it was a business occasion. There was almost no need that could not be satisfied. Within the space of a small building you could buy a shotgun, dishes, shoe blacking, soap, ham and bacon, poultry feed, china, crockery, pots and pans, shotgun shells and sauerkraut.

Along the counter where cloth was sold in the ladies' department, there were two brass tacks exactly one yard apart for measuring, which may account for the expression "getting down to brass tacks." One department, referred to as notions, contained small items like thread, thimbles, buttons, needles, rickrack (do

A courthouse attracts loafers as molasses does flies.

—Helen Hooven Santmyer
Ohio Town

Courthouse—Silverton, Colorado

Country store conversation
Cosby, Tennessee

any of the young today know what that zigzag decoration is called?). In the men's department there were overalls with multitudes of pockets and a noose on one leg to hold a hammer. In addition there were suspenders, red flannel underwear (we knew husbands who bought small sizes without admitting they were for their wives), shoes, boots, and gloves made of cloth, cowhide or goatskin (these stank when wet).

One of the most popular areas was the patent medicine counter. How many were really patented? There was a strong liniment recommended for man or beast. Hostetter's Celebrated Stomach Bitters was in most houses; given the heavy nature of food then, there was surely a lot of stomach discomfort needing bitter relief. "Female Tonics" were big sellers in those days before obstetrics and gynecology had reached their present brilliance. While clerking in a store after school when I was a grim adolescent, I actually had women customers who would write out the name "Lydia E. Pinkham's Vegetable Compound" on a piece of paper and hand it to me because they were too shy to speak the words.

We had a neighbor who was a strong speaker in favor of temperance. One day when my mother and I were in her house, she said, "I've got to go to my temperance society meeting now, but I've got to take my tonic to get my strength up." She took a half tumbler and tossed it off enthusiastically. Years later I discovered that those female tonics often contained a very high level of alcohol, so that in her innocence

96

(continued on page 99)

The Little Red Schoolhouse

West Lane Schoolhouse (1756)—Ridgefield, Connecticut

Traditionally the little red schoolhouse is pictured as a rectangular wood-frame building, but the one-room, one-teacher schoolhouse could just as well have been brick or stone, octagonal or even designed along the lines of a church, including a cupola or belfry. And it was more likely to be white with red or green trim than it was to be red.

From the colonial era well into the twentieth century, the country schoolhouse was the heart and soul of American education. Mandated by a uniquely American concept, that of a guaranteed free public education for all, these institutions emerged from a law of 1647 setting forth provisions to build "petty" schools, which were to become the forerunner of the grammar school. Reading, writing and arithmetic were of secondary importance in these early schools. The primary focus was on the reading of Scripture and rudimentary Latin.

As late as 1913 there were 212,000 one-room schools operating in the United States. Only about 835 of them remain in use today. Teaching in such institutions was no slight undertaking. Often a single teacher had the responsibility of educating as many as thirty children in eight different grades. This meant that he or she had to prepare eight different sets of lesson plans for each school day and keep the other students quiet and occupied while working with each small group.

The typical one-room schoolhouse was just that: a single room, which in earliest times was no doubt fashioned from a makeshift outbuilding—an old barn, a chicken coop, a wagon shed. By the 1920s, however, all these buildings were basically of similar design, since by that time construction specifications were formulated by state laws and by state and federal education departments. The interiors of these single rooms were notably austere, sometimes consisting of only two rows of school desks separated by an aisle, boys on one side, girls on the other. At the front was a teacher's desk. In the middle of the room was a stove, generally of the potbelly variety, to heat the building in frigid weather. Often there was a cloakroom in which students could hang their outer garments and leave their lunch pails till noontime came.

During frontier times these little one-room schoolhouses inevitably became the focus of community activity, not merely a place of learn-

Desks—West Lane Schoolhouse

97

ing. Adults came together there to vote, to thrash out civic problems common to all, and for social occasions, such as suppers and dances.

Named mostly for states, cities, national heroes, such as presidents and generals, as well as the physical characteristics of specific locales, the schools had such colorful names as the Apple Pie School, in Kansas, the Puckerbrush School, in Iowa, and the Poison Spider School, in Wyoming. The dreams of the early settlers were reflected in schools named Beulah and Excelsior, and animals familiar to them in such names as Possum Hollow and Poor Puss.

In his autobiography Mark Twain recounts vividly his first day as a young student in such an institution:

"The country schoolhouse was three miles from my uncle's farm. It stood in a clearing in the woods and would hold about twenty-five boys and girls. We attended the school with more or less regularity once or twice a week, in summer, walking to it in the cool of the morning by the forest paths, and back in the gloaming at the end of the day. All the pupils brought their dinners in baskets—corn dodger, buttermilk, and other good things—and sat in the shade of the trees at noon and ate them. It is the part of my education which I look back upon with the most satisfaction. My first visit to the school was when I was seven. A strapping girl of fifteen, in the customary sunbonnet and calico dress, asked me if I 'used tobacco'—meaning did I chew it. I said no. It roused her scorn. She reported me to all the crowd, and said: 'Here is a boy seven years old who can't chew tobacco.'"

Today most children attend school in large modern buildings with auditoriums and cafeterias. The little red schoolhouse, like many worthy institutions of the past, has waned.

Occasionally along the back roads of America you may still come across a one-room school, dilapidated and fallen to ruin from disuse. For anyone old enough to recall them, these abandoned wrecks reverberate with ghosts—the ghosts of all those laughing youths who sat at the desks, played snap-the-whip in the school yards and passed through the portals to go off and make their way in the world.

—HHL

Last Day of School, *painting by John Falter*

Penny candy counter—Evans Market, Lancaster, New Hampshire

our dear lady probably went off to attack the demon rum while loaded with the same.

The store was full of odors. There was a red coffee grinder, which released that dark aroma into an air already filled with the smells of vinegar, cheese, smoked meat, roasted peanuts, pickles, dried fish. Once when a store went out of business, the owner gave my mother its spice chest with row after row of wooden drawers, some still full. Even when Mother had used all of the remaining spices, the box, two and a half feet square, still retained its spicy smell. Out of sentiment I kept it long after my mother died. Twenty years later I could still sniff it and bring back the scent of that store and with it the image of Mother carefully measuring out the cloves, bay leaves, oregano, several red, white and black peppers.

That was tobacco time. No cigarettes, but lots of cigars in boxes with remarkably underdressed women on the inside of their lids. For some reason cigars were named after racehorses, presidents and Cleopatra. There was also a little machine for slicing plug tobacco, like Horse Shoe—so called because it looked like the bottom of a horse's hoof? Chewing tobacco often came in long, hard lengths wrapped in thick lead foil, and during the First World War we saved the foil as a patriotic duty.

In those days you could walk into a general store naked (but few did!) and come out completely clothed, well fed, smelling of perfume

A country merchant advertised various commodities for sale and gave notice that he would take in payment all kinds of country produce except promises.

—The Old Farmer's Almanac (1804)

99

*The talk
in a country store
is known to be good
—sage, amusing,
colorful and rich in
its perception of
human nature.*

—John Kenneth Galbraith
The Scotch

Whittlers—Fort Ransom, North Dakota

or tobacco according to your choice, having mailed a letter to a relative. It was not a general, but a universal, store. The remarkable thing was that it existed in country towns full of fierce individuals who at the same time had a strong sense of community feeling and of responsibility for each other. It was like the days of the frontier, when people were moving west for their own private reasons, but at night the wagons were circled and the men (even the women) kept their rifles ready because there were wolves and Indians outside and

they could survive only by being together. There was an old saying that breaking the land also broke women and horses. But by working together in a competitive decency, those country towns did not break.

The hand that planted the seed in a backyard garden brought the flower to the sick person who had the garden next door.

It is called survival.

It is called country town.

It is called love.

GATHERINGS

They were fierce individuals, those country people, wanting to do things their own way in their own time, yet they had a fierce need to gather together on every possible occasion. It was lonesome out on the farms.

Marriages, funerals, births, grave illnesses, accidents, church suppers, fairs, harvesting with shared equipment, holidays, anything was a cherished excuse for a meeting.

When travel was by horse, there were no surprise visits—the top of a buggy, the curved dashboard of a sleigh or the wide body of a wagon could be seen coming from far away, giving time to put something in the oven, stir up the stew, even bake a pie. It was expected that anyone making the effort to come a distance should be fed. My ancient aunt Rose (her round cheeks the same red as the flower) used to say, "It seems like a body gets hungry just going anyplace."

If there was a marriage or funeral on a farm, you could tell who was coming and what they were driving long before they arrived. Always the food came with them, for those occasions heighten the appetite. After the funeral sermon,

103

Church picnic—Poplar Grove Baptist Church,
Watauga County, North Carolina

during which the deceased was nurtured with words just as the mourners would be nurtured with the fruits of the fields, and the trip from the graveyard, it took perhaps fifteen minutes for the people dressed in their dark, stiff and seldom-used Sunday best to glance at each other until one was bold enough to say what was in everyone's mind: "Might as well get out the grub." Instantly the table shook under the weight of massive amounts of potatoes, kraut, vegetables, home-baked bread, cookies with hickory nuts, butternuts or black walnuts inside, apple pies reeking of cinnamon, angel food cake lovingly held in the hands when carried on those rough roads so that it would not "fall." Eating was a proper part of the whole sad ritual, for it was a form of prayer—the length of praying and the length of eating were acts of decent respect for the dead.

People gathered close to each other because they were living so far apart. There was no telephone to let them hear the voice of neighbor or relative, no television on which they could see people's faces, no automobile to take them quickly across the county or the state, and only a slow postal service to bring them letters. This meant that for human comfort they had to go to other places, or they saw and talked with no one except for immediate family. That gave all personal contact an enormous value, a reassurance that people cared about them.

Aunt Rose indicated her view in a remark to my mother that I, being eight years old and loving to listen to adults talking confidentially, overheard while pretending to read a mail-order catalogue. She and her family lived on a desolate farm in the northwest woods of Minnesota, ten miles to another farm. The soil was gravel outwash from glaciers, with no humus for growing real crops. Her husband, Herm, said he took a hammer to the garden so he could tap whatever he dug up to see if it was a potato or a stone.

Rose was a violent prohibitionist. Although not one drop of the demon rum was allowed in the house, she howled against it every day as if it were one of the sinister black bears in the woods that had shambled toward the house, threatening to blow it down or kill the cattle.

On that drear day while I was sitting on the floor trying to look innocent (I'm still trying after seventy-eight years!), Rose said to my mother, "Eva, I'm ashamed to talk this way, but sometimes when Herm is gone all day and I've had to chase the deer out of the barnyard because they eat the feed for the livestock and the wolves are howling in the timber, I declare if there was whiskey around I'd be tempted

When all the food had been placed on the tables, an unspoken signal would ripple down the line and we would all stand quietly while the minister spoke a grace of thanksgiving.

—Edna Lewis
The Taste of Country Cooking

104

to touch it. 'Course I don't, and afterward I pray for forgiveness."

Then her face brightened and she almost shouted, "There's a church supper tomorrow night. Let's all go."

Church suppers gave people time to talk, to exchange news about crops, weather, family joys and tragedies, and to eat six kinds of pies and cakes compared to the one kind they would get at home. Of course all of the food had to be blessed before it was touched (Aunt Tillie said it tasted better that way).

> Lord, again You have been good.
> Thank You for abundant food.
> We turn to You our grateful face,
> In worship of Your saving grace.

Tillie used to complain if the preacher gave a short blessing. "Takes a long prayer for a body to build up a real appetite," she would say.

Gatherings had a very human purpose. In that time of houses separated by long distances, young men and women had trouble getting together. Church suppers and all the other social gatherings—barn raisings, auctions, box socials, school events, group threshings—were the only times they could meet openly, even if it was under the

Country Fair, *painting by Grandma Moses*

suspicious gaze of many eyes. Compared to the ease with which young persons today can escape the presence of their parents, there must have been a special excitement in meeting so rarely and so publicly. Perhaps one reason that young people married early in those days was that marriage was a way to get some privacy.

The raising of a new barn was usually a community project, bringing together many men and women in the area, especially those with special skills. Men were not only farmers, they also were amateur carpenters, stoneworkers (later mixers of cement), painters, men handy with their hands. From miles away men with their tools and women with their pans and ingredients would gather at the site and work all day for the sake of others. Strongly individualistic, they were even stronger when working together.

This was equally true of the women in the area of their own responsibility, the kitchen. Jobs were shared. Some would be assigned

106

(continued on page 109)

Country Fairs

There's an old country saying that goes, "Give to the land and it will give back." A Vermont farmer would add, "Here we turn grass into milk and corn into hogs." And so it is with a sense of destiny fulfilled that each year we celebrate this bounty with one gay, grand and gaudy burst of energy called the country fair.

Sometimes a high-flown phrase like "agricultural exposition" creeps into the name of a fair, but when it does, folks tend to ignore it. And so much the better, for there are large fairs and small fairs, state fairs and local fairs, all across the land. But big or small, a fair is a fair, and the spirit is the same. Often there's a brass band blaring, old-time fiddlers fiddling away and the tootle of a calliope calling children to the carousel. The Ferris wheel has its music, too, as it coaxes squeals from merry riders. Hawkers add their voices to the din—"Taffy apples! Taffy apples! Homemade candy here!"—while pitchmen with other wares to sell urge us to hurry, hurry, step right up and spend a dollar or two.

The throngs of visitors, both town and country folk, love it all. In large family groups they come, arriving early, staying late, and hoping to savor all the entertainments and every one of the exhibits. In fact, the heart of a country fair is not really in the rides and the games and the music, delightful as these are. It's in the exhibits—in the huge barns and sheds and tents topped with colored pennants, where a farm family's gardening and breeding, dairy and poultry skills are judged and rewarded. Let's mingle with the eager crowds streaming through those buildings and see how it's done.

Inside a stock barn you'll find that the carnival atmosphere recedes. In its place is the smell of fresh straw and of animals groomed to a fare-thee-well. "Clean as clergy," a farm boy would say. The sounds in the barn are softer, too. From the hog pens comes the snuffle and grunt of satisfied porkers. All the breeds are here—Durocs, Yorkshires, Chester Whites—and all the colors, from white to red to very black. But it's the name tags that catch the eye. There's Blubber and Bumper, Blossom, Daisy and Lulu.

Notice Daffodil there, so plump she looks like the hog that got into the honeypot. Pointing to her, the boy in overalls is saying to a visitor, "Yes, sir, she's a Poland China. She

Lebanon, Tennessee

was only a handful at birth, two and a half pounds. Now she weighs over two hundred. Well behaved, too. I'm hoping she'll do all right in the judging tomorrow."

Now let's move on to the dairy barns, to the rows of stalls, each

Watermelon Festival—Hope, Arkansas

with its black-and-white Holstein or its fawn-colored Jersey or spotted Guernsey. There's an air of excitement here, for the judging is over and ribbons now hang proudly above some of the stalls. There are blue ribbons and red ribbons for first place and second place, and the prizewinners, pleased as punch, are happy to talk with visitors. In fact, one dairyman is saying to a wide-eyed city child, "Did you know that milk is measured in pounds?"

The child, nearly dwarfed by the flank of a huge Holstein, shakes her head.

"Well, a good milch cow may give more than sixteen thousand pounds a year."

As if to agree, the Holstein emits a long, lowing *moo-ooo*, and everyone laughs.

Outside again, the fairgoers now must make a choice. Some drift off to the left to see the gabbling, squawking occupants of the poultry

shed. Some move ahead to an enclosure with a big KEEP OUT sign—as though the snorting, pawing bull within it were not enough to hold the curious at bay. But most go to the right, to the sheep-showing ring, where boys and girls, some quite young, are putting the final touches on their leggy Suffolk lambs. The animals, with fleecy white coats and black faces and stockings, have been washed and trimmed, and once the judges arrive, the Fitting and Showmanship trials will begin. What counts here is effort—what the child has managed to accomplish with the animal.

There is so much still to see and do at the fair that one wonders where to turn next. In the great halls are displays of field and orchard produce that never fail to amaze: cornstalks looking tall as chimney stacks, apples so big that one of them would make a pie. On display, too, is the bounty of garden and home kitchen, all ranked in rows of gleaming mason jars. Walking past the pickles and preserves, a hungry family finds itself even hungrier, and for them there are specialty foods sizzling on grills, along with the traditional corn on the cob, homemade sausage, hand-pulled taffy. Then, to soothe the teary child whose cotton candy was snatched from his hand by a mischievous goat, there are gingersnaps at a stand nearby. But the day is getting late now, and a comfortable, quiet weariness slowly replaces the chatter and excitement of the morning. Reluctantly families gather for the journey home. The fair is nearly over for this year, but it won't be too long before people, young and old, begin to think about next year's country fair.

—CTB

to preparing and cooking thirty pounds of potatoes, some to roasting forty pounds of beef, some to hams, some to great vessels of baked and green beans, some to corn on the cob if it was the right season. A hundred ears were eaten within minutes of being picked, husked and cooked while the kernels were still sweet. Butter was fresh-churned— many pounds of it were brought in jars by the families with the most dairy cows. Red beet pickles were always the special dish of one family, rhubarb pies of another, pudding with raisins and nuts of yet another. Pies were filled with every sort of fruit, most of it picked from trees in the orchard that day. It was my impression as a little boy that the endless pies, the same every year, were old friends and if left alone would speak to each other.

I loved those barn raisings because of the bustle of many men sawing, hammering, nailing at the same time, watching how fast the barn was roofed when twenty-four strong and skillful hands were pounding together. My favorite place, however, was the kitchen. The noise of the pounding was diffused through the open air, but the food preparation was done in a small, enclosed space. Besides the clatter of knives, pans, lids on an iron range, glasses and plates, there was that great fascination of women talking, saying things they would not have spoken had men been present. I must have looked harmless (little did they know!), for the rich gossip I heard was wonderful as a look at the reality and complexity of relations between men and women.

"Carrie's having trouble again with Ed, the old fool."

"Bob Smith and Susan Smith are sparkin' and want to get married, but their parents say no, because they have the same name—but they ain't related. It's a cryin' shame."

"That useless boy of Emma's is back home. No wonder he's no good, with that smelly goat of a father, always disappearing and lying he has to go look for the sheep. I know what kinda sheep he's after."

The men were hungry after working all day, often on high ladders. They came pouring back from the barn to the washbasins filled with cold well water that were scattered along outdoor tables. They were full of jokes:

"Jim, that hammer of yours mostly drives bent nails."

"There's barn swallows out in the trees. Just can't wait until we get done so they can move in."

"Joe, that older girl of yours is a real looker. Better not let her out in the rain."

"Frank Cook's tryin' to have all the kids his Josie can manufacture so's he can save money on hired men."

Heel and toe
*   and away we go!*
Tune up the fiddle
*   and rosin up*
*   the bow.*

—Della T. Lutes, <u>Home Grown</u>

When supper was over, there would be the sharp scrape of a bow on a fiddle from the barn, singing of the dance to follow. The young men and women were the first to leave for the barn, trying to look discreet as they stole a few private moments together before the dance began. Looking back, I believe that the parents deliberately stayed behind to let them have that rarest of all gatherings in that time, a boy and a girl alone together. The warm twilight descended on a useful barn raised by a whole neighborhood, the arches of its haymow as graceful as the curves of the young ladies who were walking toward it with a stride that was almost dancing.

The dance on the barn floor was for all ages and the culmination of the day. Sometimes, when there was a shortage, men wore a handkerchief on an arm to pretend they were women. A square dance was traditional, which meant a caller as well as a fiddler, but usually the evening ended with waltzes. The old songs were known by everyone: "Oh Dem Golden Slippers," "Buffalo Gals," "Arkansas Traveller," "Devil's Dream."

How wonderful that a building united people who above all did not want to live too close together. Every morning Uncle Herm stepped outside his little house in the Minnesota wilderness and breathed deeply several times, stretching his arms. Of the chill air he said, "It's strong stuff, but it's mine." Yet when the time came to gather in the whole neighborhood, they all came and worked for a fellow farmer.

Auctions were also ingatherings of people, many of whom came not to bid but only to share an exciting event with friends not seen in a long time. Horse auctions were the best, of course, because there were live animals being trotted up and down, examined in leg and tooth. Country people depended on the horse entirely, and buying one was a crucial necessity, for a bad judgment could cripple a farm. This accounted for the intensity of the bidding, the auctioneer chanting the numbers in a special high voice whose tone was never used for any other purpose save hypnotizing someone into raising his bid ("I'mbidattwohundredwho'llmakeittwofiftyI'vegottwofiftywho'llgimmethreehundred") until the animal was sold. A mare with a foal at her side was always a lovely attraction, as the little creature trotted hard to keep up with its mother, rubbing its head against her flank and nickering in fear if they were separated.

Sometimes household furniture, farm tools, even dolls would be auctioned. There was often to-and-fro banter between buyer and auctioneer.

Buyer: "Is that band saw guaranteed for life?"

*Swing your partners
one and all,
Swing that
lady in the
checkered shawl,
Gents, hands
in your pockets,
back to the wall,
Take a chaw
of terbacker
and balance all.
Quit that hugging,
ain't you
a-shamed,
Promenade,
Oh, Promenade!*

111

Lubbock Club lamb sale—Fairgrounds, Lubbock, Texas

Auctioneer: "Your life, the saw's life or your wife's?"
Buyer: "I won't buy anything ain't guaranteed."
Auctioneer: "Nothin' guaranteed for life, not even life."

Toughest was the auction when a farm was lost, where often a baby crib would be sold by the man who had been born in it. Even last summer's canned fruit and vegetables would be sold in front of the woman who for weeks had sweated over the blazing range, making them. Some of her neighbors looked at her guiltily when they bid, as if it were stealing. A small boy howled when his toy electric train was sold to another family with a small boy. Crops of oats, corn, hay, were auctioned right in the barn where the farmer had stored them at harvest. But there were kind acts too—when a family was about to lose the farm that was their home and their life, farmers would gather in a group, talk fast, bid one dollar and threaten anyone who bid the real price. And give it back to the owner.

112

(continued on page 115)

Rural Cemeteries

How do you go about finding the heart of a place that time and history have roared past? You find the cemeteries, of course. Graveyards, after all, reflect the customs, beliefs and social structure of the time and place in which they are set. Nowhere is this so true as in the tiny rural graveyards of countless American towns and hamlets, where many of the occupants—dating back for centuries—were related or at least knew each other. It is in these small final resting grounds that the chronicles of families and towns, and even the triumphs and tragedies of a nation, may be read.

"Died of wounds received at Shiloh," an epitaph seemingly simple, so eloquently understates the anguish and grief of a nation divided. Rows of headstones graced by small American flags, marking the places where the veterans of this nation's wars lie, may say even more. A diminutive moss-covered tablet with a crude angel's head or possibly the outline of a child's shoe graven on it, the name and pitifully brief span of life recorded there along with the words "Consumption," "Diphtheria," or "Scarlet Fever," tells all at a glance.

Some epitaphs become virtual biographies of the deceased, listing their accomplishments and details of their professions. From reading the Milford, Connecticut, tombstone of Rev. Bezaleel Pinneo, who died in 1849 at the age of eighty, we learn that:

> During his ministry
> He enjoyed 7 revivals,
> Admitted 716 members,
> Baptized 1,117 and
> Buried 1,126 of his flock.

Blacksmith Joseph Hill, on the other hand, was buried in 1826 at age sixty-five in Norton, Massachusetts, with these words on his stone:

> My sledge and hammer
>   be reclined
> My bellows too
>   have lost their wind;
> My fire's extinguished,
>   forge decay'd
> And in the dust
>   my vise is laid.
> My iron's spent,
>   my coals are gone,
> The last nail's drove,
>   my work is done.

Zion Hill Church Cemetery—Wilton, Connecticut

A black husband and wife lie side by side in Jaffrey, New Hampshire, under the following inscriptions:

> Sacred to the Memory of
> Amos Fortune
> who was born free in Africa
> a slave in America, he purchased
> liberty, professed Christianity,
> lived reputably & died hopefully,
> Nov. 17 1801 AEt. 91.

> Sacred to the Memory of Violate,
> by sale the slave of
> Amos Fortune,
> by marriage his wife, by her
> fidelity his friend and solace,
> She died his Widow
> Sept. 13 1802 AEt. 73.

113

These and epitaphs like "Darling, we miss thee" and "Meet me in Heaven" tell of a love that endures beyond this earth, whereas two identical stones in a Long Island cemetery suggest a different story. There a husband and wife lie side by side. The inscription on her stone reads "Rest in Peace." On his is "No Comment."

And for succinctness Lorenzo Sabine's epitaph in Eastport, Maine, is hard to surpass. It is simply the word "Transplanted."

But graveyards are not, as commonly believed, primarily for the dead; they are for the living. They provide a sense of continuity with the past as well as a perspective with which to contemplate the future. We are closest to our forefathers when treading on the ground in which they are buried. On national holidays such as Memorial Day and the Fourth of July, small rural cemeteries have long provided the setting for social events and celebrations. The living come to commune with the dear departed, to meet old friends, to beautify grave sites with plants and flowers, to confirm genealogical data concerning their ancestors.

Many rural communities set aside a Saturday in spring for graveyard working. Local townspeople gather to tidy the graves by hoeing, raking, and providing a general spring cleanup. The work is carried out by men, women and children alike. A noon meal is served, and the general mood of the crowd is frolicsome and happy. Chatting and gossiping, people move amid the tombstones. The laughter of children, pretending to be working but more likely up to mischief, rings through the trees. The air is full of the fragrance of new-bloomed lilac. The earth is green with renewal after the long, ice-bound sleep of winter. Grandparents and grandchildren, fathers and mothers, uncles, aunts and cousins, the old and young alike, all gather here to affirm the continuity of the race. The little fence-enclosed cemetery of a small town has a charm and serenity unique unto itself.

The eighteenth-century British statesman and orator Edmund Burke seemed to summarize it best when he said, "I would rather sleep in the southern corner of a little country churchyard than in the tomb of the Capulets."

—HHL

All-Day Dinner on the Grounds of the Grove Level Baptist Church, *painting by Mattie Lou O'Kelley*

County fairs were in those earlier days the greatest gatherings of all. People came from other counties, even from other states. There was something for everyone, from slides for the little kids to outrageous twirling rides and the Ferris wheel for teenagers (and for the many who remained teenagers in mind all of their lives) to horse races—which the women liked as much as the men, because they too had grown up with horses. There were competitions for the top hogs, beef steers, dairy cows, bulls, chickens and, above all, roosters, who spent the day swearing at each other from the security of their cages. Always there was the amphitheater show with its trained dog acts, clowns, a tug-of-war between rival towns held on the racetrack and, of course, the dancing girls.

"I declare," Aunt Tillie said, "they wear less every year."

"Maybe one day they'll get down to nothing," Uncle Charlie replied, half as an act of courage and half in hope.

It was a place and time for exchanging news, so important to people who lived in isolation much of the time. Entire families would get together for a picnic in the outfield, beyond the baseball diamond, and share their food. A lot of the talk was about the relatives of each family. Sometimes when a name was mentioned, there would be an embarrassed silence and quick glances from one person to another because all knew the crime or the silliness of the absent cousin.

At the food exhibits some fairgoers would follow the judges down the rows of jams, jellies, breads, cookies, jars of precisely arranged beans, trays of fresh vegetables. The judges were often the same year after year, so some of the food entered was designed with the well-known preferences of a specific person in mind. There was cunning as well as taste in the competition. Next-door neighbors would glare at each other when the judge lingered too long over one's entry. Tillie

115

The County Agricultural Agent, *painting by Norman Rockwell*

always watched the judge's eyes. "If he closes them when he's tasting your stuff," she whispered, "you're gonna win."

Since 1926 the 4-H boys and girls have been one of the remarkable gatherings at the fairs. The whole idea of an organization of rural and small-town kids devoted to the four concepts of Head, Heart, Hands and Health is an American invention. All year they work at their varied projects—raising beef steers, designing and sewing dresses, doing experiments on feeding sheep and cattle, keeping careful records of amount fed each day, rate of gain, and even, in the case of beef cattle and hogs, recording the depth of back fat. The animal that wins is auctioned off—often bought by a local restaurant for publicity's sake. Led away to slaughter, it may be followed by the tears of the young person who had raised it from a calf, washed it down with a hose, put curls in the hair on its flanks, shampooed its tail and braided it with ribbons, taught it to lead with halter and rope.

It is very difficult to watch these well-mannered, decently dressed, obviously bright young persons in action without feeling that the country is in good shape. Today 4-H is so popular that some big state fairs have had to build special dormitories to house the members. Often whole families are included in the activities. The father may enter a pen of pigs or a twelve-hundred-pound steer, the mother crocheted or embroidered work, a son his bawling calf, a daughter her dairy heifer or a dress, another son his five-gaited saddle horse, another daughter her pen of lambs. There is an intensity of concentration by every member of the family unlike anything else in our lives, and it is a wholesome and heartening sight.

There are many other kinds of gatherings. The church has traditionally been one of the liveliest centers for rural communities. In the early days people regularly attended church—out of faith, of course, but also as an expression of how much trust they had in each other and how much need. Working alone in the open country, they cherished any occasion that brought them into a common place. Their children were baptized there, weddings were solemnized there, funerals took place in the church, which became the center for some of the most fervent and earnest hours of their lives. Even the revival meetings— when a traveling preacher was brought in from outside, often to give his usually higher-key addresses in a tent because a small church could not hold the crowds—were social occasions. One could hear the sermon far off, as if the minister were chosen as much for volume of sound as for elegance of doctrine.

Another gathering was the annual visit of the threshers. There were still a few steam outfits going from farm to farm when I was growing up. You could hear their deep boom coming before you could see the metal monster itself. As in Grant Wood's painting *Dinner for Threshers*, the threshing crew often were neighbors added to the men who owned and ran the rig, so that sometimes as many as sixteen men had to be fed. This meant early morning and even day-before cooking by the women.

It was in many ways the most exciting day of the year for children.

Abide with me!
Fast falls
  the eventide,
The darkness
  deepens—
Lord, with me abide!

—Henry F. Lyte
from the hymn "Abide With Me"

Tent revival meeting

It began with the bustle, clamor, clashing of pots and pans and went on for hours as the bundles were brought from the fields in wagons and forked into the machine at one side while from the other the oats or wheat was hauled away. It was dirty, sweaty, loud work, and it produced a harvest of appetites as well as of grain. A ten-gallon crock of sauerkraut disappeared in ten minutes. Although the men washed faces and hands before eating, there was always chaff left in their hair and on their clothes. The women waited to have their dinner until after the workers were fed, which might have looked unkind, but Aunt Rose used to say when I asked if she minded waiting, "Paul, I tried a little of every dish all morning. Had to, in order to make sure it was decent grub."

There were box socials, usually at church, where young ladies prepared their best dishes and young men bid on them. There was a lot of scheming, and a girl would put a special mark on hers so that her fellow would go up in the bidding until he bought it and could eat with her. As with most matters in those days, it was all very human. There was usually hymn singing after supper. Even the children knew "The Old Rugged Cross," "Stand Up, Stand Up for Jesus," "Abide With Me." (I didn't know what "abide" meant, but it sounded a little like a game, maybe hide-and-seek, and I was all for it.) Phrases haunt my memory still: "Help of the helpless," "Fast falls the eventide."

Dinner for Threshers,
painting by Grant Wood

So those country people led their lives, strong men, women, children (and countless dogs) made stronger by gathering together. Once when Uncle Herm turned his team into the long lane leading to his house, the wolves almost brought down one of the horses—which would have meant my uncle's death. He began cracking his whip. Aunt Rose heard it, and grabbing his deer rifle and a handful of cartridges, ran out to the lane. She planted herself there and began picking off wolves. After some had been hit, the others ran away into the timber, their howls vibrating in the bitter winter air over frozen ground and snow. If she had missed, she and Herm would have died, along with the invaluable team of horses. It never occurred to her not to run out and stand up to wild animals. That was her man driving that team.

When my father asked Aunt Rose how she was able to aim so straight, she said with a soft violence in her voice, "Don't drink."

So they endured.

So they survived.

So with their bare hands they created a country out of love for each other and the people around them, whom they saw too seldom. If told that, they would have been embarrassed. They would have denied it. But deep down they knew it was true, that it kept them going on with their lives so equally full of dreams and dangers.

Today, deep down, we also know it was true.

For several days before the threshers' arrival, every able body was put to work baking, gathering and preparing fruits and vegetables . . . setting up extra tables, and cleaning house.

—Marilyn Kluger
Country Kitchens Remembered

Part II

Down-Home Cooking

COMPANY'S COMING

by Celestine Sibley

My mother grew up on her grandparents' farm in south Georgia at the turn of the century, when extra labor, hired for cotton chopping or at harvest time, was paid "a dollar a day and dinner."

What was generally referred to as "cash money" was important, of course, but the dinner was the real remuneration because the cooks in the family set themselves to outdo every other cook in the settlement with the variety and bounty of the food. One summer, my mother remembered, her grandparents lucked into what was rare in the country in the summertime—fifty pounds of ice. Sometimes when this happened, there was lemonade; and if the windfall threatened to melt too fast, they hurried to make what was the rarest and most memorable of treats, peach ice cream.

This time my great-grandmother decided on iced tea. It must have been a new thing because the workers had never tasted it before, and for one little boy who had come to work with his father, it was unalloyed delight. Holding his glass up to catch the light, he turned it between his hands in awe.

"Look, Pa!" he cried. "Ain't it purty and don't it rattle?"

Not all country cooking is pretty. But the stir of company coming has ever created its own kind of rattle in a country house: the tintinnabulation of pots and skillets, of shelled peas plinking into a pan, of eggbeaters whirring, of crockery saucer pounding country steak to tenderness, of spoon clinking against bowl as cake batter is beaten.

In the days when farm life was fairly lonely, lacking the diversion of radio, television and easy transportation, the arrival of *anybody* was

123

The arrival of anybody was cause for what my mother always called "putting on the big pot and the little pot, too."

cause for what my mother always called "putting on the big pot and the little pot, too." When no guest was imminent, the home folks might throw a "frolic." I have heard my great-aunts tell of taking down the beds and putting them outdoors to make room for dancing; there were always pickers and singers, and before the evening was over everybody sang such old-time ballads as "Finger Ring," "Barbara Allen" and "May the Circle Be Unbroken." Sometimes the scarcity of provisions made a frolic all the more needful. They cooked what they had, often no more than a pot of beans and an iron skillet of corn bread.

But a work gathering, a cane grinding or a hog killing, which always drew a convocation of friends and neighbors when the temperature dropped in winter and the wind was right, warranted a grander spread. Pork loin, surrounded by sweet potatoes, roasted in the oven while the urgent business of cooking cane juice or butchering went on in the yard. Those who came to help were given a portion of syrup or meat to take home, of course, but the hostess felt an obligation to feed them well as they worked—hot biscuits, corn bread, summer-canned vegetables, a choice of apple or peach turnovers, fried nut brown and silvered with a dusting of sugar, and jellies and preserves and pickles.

The arrival of a peddler or a preacher or, best of all, a Bible salesman was a time of great excitement in the country before paved roads and automobiles made company commonplace. The girls were sent to make the beds up fresh with held-back-for-company sheets. The boys were dispatched to the chicken yard to catch, in a scuffle of squawking and flying feathers, frying-size pullets for supper. The man of the family brought a ham out of the smokehouse and maybe, if the situation was right, a jug of moonshine or cider or muscadine wine. The woman, mindful of the fact that travelers are always faint with hunger, moved with all speed to start the vegetables simmering, to bring up the milk and butter from the springhouse and put together a pudding or a cake or a dish of stewed fruit. I never saw an electric mixer or a food processor that could produce a cake as fast as a country woman with unexpected company hovering on the threshold.

Bible salesmen were thrice-honored guests because, historically, they were young men working their way through college. If there were marriageable girls in the family, a handsome college boy could be practically heaven-sent. But even if romance was not a consideration, there was the honor of having an "educated" visitor under the roof, for country people revered learning and listened eagerly to those who had been places and talked knowledgeably of what was going on in the outside world. Sometimes, surfeited with fried chicken and maybe spareribs and rice and five kinds of vegetables and sweet potato pone and butter cake, the young college man would be asked to "give us a reading from the Good Book." The family would gather 'round on the front porch in the long summer twilight to listen to words that may have been more familiar to them than to their visitor but were ever new, ever exalting.

In the absence of visitors there were reliable seasonal fetes that tested the prowess of cooks and were a showcase for the expertise of the better ones. The box social demonstrated not only the culinary but the artistic attainments of the women in a family. The object of the party-sale was to raise money for some worthy cause, school or church. It also paired off young people, enabling the shy and the tongue-tied to get together with the sanction of school and church and under the benign eyes of their elders, for the decorated boxes containing the food were auctioned off and the buyer of a box got to sit and eat supper with the young woman who brought it. Ostensibly the young woman herself turned an ordinary shoe box into an art object and filled it with a delicious meal cooked by her own hands.

In my case my mother was the entrepreneur who produced both box and supper. I was twelve years old and bound for the gala of the season at the two-room schoolhouse in Creola, Alabama. I had read Edna Ferber's Pulitzer Prize–winning novel *So Big*, and I remembered how her heroine, Selina, had been the laughingstock of a midwestern community because she brought a daintily decorated box with food so delicate and effete it was but a sissy morsel, vanquished in one gulp by the husky hearty eater who was accustomed to gargantuan farm fare.

Don't worry, said my mother, looking over the chicken yard for a likely candidate for my box. For some reason she was out of Rhode Island Red fryers, down, in fact, to Boob McNutt, a gawky game rooster named for a funny-paper character. My mother hated Boob for the clumsy way he loped over the yard, wings outstretched, squawking fatuously at her best laying hens. She was glad of an excuse to get rid of him and the box social was it.

She killed and cooked Boob and placed the supposedly choice pieces of drumstick, second joint and white meat beside the carefully wrapped deviled eggs, the ham sandwiches and the chocolate layer cake in my box. She had worked hard on that container, stitching up blue and white crepe paper ruffles and gluing them across the top and along the sides.

The auctioneer, a glib neighbor, could raise no more than 25 cents for my box. It went to a seventh-grade boy named H. B., whom I kind of liked. (An older girl's box, chastely wrapped in butcher paper from the store and ornamented with a single wilting rose, brought $5.)

H. B. was so uncomfortable about sitting with me he hung his buttocks over the desk seat halfway into the aisle. Then he bit into a drumstick, which was so tough and rubbery that when he pulled it away from his mouth, it snapped back.

"Poor Boob," I said mournfully.

"You're the boob!" cried H. B. "I want my quarter back!"

It was the ultimate humiliation for a twelve-year-old girl, but my mother, whose sense of humor outweighed pride in her culinary skill, laughed so heartily that the other cooks in the crowd, some of them of peerless Pennsylvania, Minnesota and Illinois origin, laughed too. The box social was remembered as one of the merriest we ever had. (But not by me.)

Tailgate picnics are, I suppose, technically country eat-meets, but when I've attended one, I always go back in memory to the cemetery "workings" of my childhood. Now there was a social event of special spirit and style. In northwest Florida a couple of times a year families with relatives buried in churchyards evocatively called Old Salem or New Hope or Shiloh would gather to rake and burn leaves and prune the shrubbery, right toppling headstones and weed around their graves. It was a time of sociability for the grown-ups, who spoke cheerfully of events in the settlement, read once more the markers on the graves and talked fondly, sometimes humorously, of the departed. Teenage romances flowered there because when the work was done, young couples developed a thirst that sent them to the nearby spring down in the woods. Sometimes they disappeared into thickets on the pretext of picking whatever wild fruit was in season—huckleberries in summer, mayhaws and persimmons in fall.

For a child the main event was the lunch, which was, in picnic parlance, "spread together." Here the women set out on makeshift deal tables their specialties: creamed fresh corn and candied sweet potatoes, sliced roast beef and pork, chicken in every conceivable way—baked, fried, in salad, in dumplings—ham under a glaze of mustard and honey, green beans flavored with smoked bacon, tender young squash seasoned with onions and butter, three or four kinds of potato salad, biscuits, cold but still light and flaky, corn bread enriched by those morsels of crisp pork called cracklings. I never went to a country outing to which somebody, bless her, had not brought a banana pudding, and you could absolutely count on gingerbread, chocolate layer cake, apple pie, blueberry or blackberry cobbler and—the triumph of any gathering—a sour cream pound cake. For a late afternoon refreshment, just before the workers hitched up to go home, there were watermelons cooling in tubs of spring water.

126

Cemetery workings are fading away since the advent of mausoleums and "perpetual care" cemeteries, but the habit of feasting in the old country churchyards still prevails. Homecomings and Decoration Days bring back wandering members or their descendants to little white clapboard meetinghouses to put in a day of singing and praying and to decorate the graves of their forebears. They spread dinner together under the old oak or elm trees, where cicadas, called July flies, saw out a song of summertime. Where there was once a washtub full of lemonade there may now be coolers of soft drinks. Where mules and horses and oxen stamped and swished their tails at flies in the shade there are now automobiles. But the fellowship, the spirit and the food are intact.

Perhaps because food is won by hard, backbreaking labor in the country—and in time of drought or pestilence or war it was scarce to the point of nonexistence—the preparation and eating of a good meal amount to a celebration. When I was a little girl, I watched in youthful finickiness an old great-aunt make a breakfast of cold collard greens and corn pone.

"Ugh! How can you eat that stuff?" I cried. "And for breakfast . . . ugh!"

She smiled serenely.

"Child, if you had lived during the bad days after the Civil War," she said, "you would be glad to eat what you can get when you can get it."

She finished her breakfast with obvious enjoyment, and years later there were to be times when a dish of cold collards and a piece of hoecake tasted mighty good to me.

The sharing of bread and salt, ancient symbol of hospitality, is sacred to the country-bred. I once saw a poor mountaineer (and him, as my Great-Aunt Babe would have said, "without a dust of meal or a drap of whiskey in the house") dip up a gourdful of clear cold water from his spring and extend it to a stranger. He did so with the pride and pleasure that must have accompanied such an offer to a thirsty wayfarer crossing the desert in biblical times.

"Hit's sweet water," he said.

There were to be times when a dish of cold collards and a piece of hoecake tasted mighty good to me.

127

The recipes in this section were chosen for their charming history and frequent appearances on country tables. Old recipes such as these were passed down from generation to generation. They often varied with the region of the country and with the season and availability of ingredients. In short, a particular recipe may not be just the way your mother or grandmother cooked that dish, but we hope seeing it here may evoke some pleasant memories nonetheless.

A word of warning: These dishes are not for the calorie- or cholesterol-conscious. They were created originally to satisfy the hunger produced by the hard, physical, dawn-to-dusk labor of farming. As Roy Webster describes in his book, *Under a Buttermilk Moon*, about an Arkansas boyhood:

Just an ordinary day started out with breakfast, not a ⅝-ounce box of cereal, but a real meal. I'm talking about home-cured bacon, more than a couple of slices too, eggs, at least two, a glass or two of Maude's milk that tested five or six percent butterfat, biscuits usually, but sometimes a few slices of homemade light bread loaded with pure home-churned butter and toasted in the hot oven of a wood-burning range, then smeared with a quarter of an inch of homemade strawberry preserves. When you got up from the table you were fortified—not for all day— just 'til noon.

Then there'd be dinner, not lunch. In the spring and early summer, it would be a big kettle of navy beans that had been soaked overnight, then cooked all morning with a big ham hock the size of your two fists. . . . There was a big bowl of wild greens that . . . had been picked the day before, washed, blanched, seasoned with bacon rinds, then simmered on the back of the stove 'til dinnertime. A batch of stone-ground corn bread baked in too large a pan so it would be thin and crusty. About 20 or 30 minutes of this and you were fortified again—'til chore time.

For supper, not dinner, it would be a kettle of black-eyed peas seasoned with bacon fryings, and corn on the cob with melted butter running down between the kernels, and a slice or two of country-cured ham. For dessert, a cobbler with a golden brown crust, dished out into an oatmeal bowl and covered with thick folds of hand-skimmed cream. . . .

Did we overeat? Lands no. Following a team of quick-stepping horses between the two handles of a walking plow solved the calorie problem— you did well to last a half day.

BREADS

ANGEL BISCUITS

Nothing says "country cooking" quite like homemade biscuits. Baked to just the right shade of golden brown and spread with butter or with some good pan gravy poured over them, they are unbeatable. But biscuits have to be served hot. Celestine Sibley, who hails from Georgia, has written: "In this, the hot bread belt, it is considered unpardonable to serve a guest a cold biscuit. There's an old story . . . of the northern visitor who spent months in the South and never got to taste biscuits because every time he would reach for one his hostesses would cry, 'Let me get you a hot one!' and snatch them away."

Here are two recipes: the first for "riz" biscuits as heavenly as their name, the second for old-fashioned buttermilk biscuits.

1 package (2½ teaspoons) active dry yeast
1 cup warm buttermilk (or use 1 tablespoon distilled white vinegar plus enough warm milk to equal 1 cup)
½ teaspoon baking soda
2½ cups flour
2 tablespoons sugar
½ teaspoon salt
½ cup lard or solid vegetable shortening
About 2 tablespoons melted butter or margarine

In a bowl, dissolve the yeast in the warm buttermilk. Stir in the baking soda.

In a large bowl, stir together the flour, sugar, and salt. Cut in the lard or shortening with a pastry cutter or two knives until the mixture is like coarse meal. Add yeast mixture and stir well.

Turn the dough out onto a floured surface and roll out to about ½ inch thick. Brush with the melted butter or margarine. Cut into 2- to 2½-inch rounds with a biscuit cutter and place almost touching, buttered side down, on a greased baking sheet. Brush the tops with butter. Cover lightly with plastic wrap and let rise in a warm, draft-free spot for 1 hour.

Bake the biscuits in a 425° F. oven until lightly browned, about 25 minutes. Serve immediately with butter or gravy. Makes about 20 biscuits.

Miss Mary's Down-Home Cooking

BUTTERMILK BISCUITS

In New Southern Cooking *there is a story about how cooking teacher Shirley Corriher learned to make buttermilk biscuits. She recalls: "My grandmother made the best biscuits in the world every day, and I would always stand right by her side watching. . . . I would use her big wooden biscuit bowl, the same flour, the same shortening, and the same buttermilk. Nanny's biscuits were light, feathery, delicate, moist. Mine were a nasty dry hard mess. I would cry out in frustration, 'Nanny, what did I do wrong?' She would wrap her arms around me and hug me and say, 'Why, Shirley, honey, you just forgot to add a touch of grace.'"*

2 cups all-purpose flour, plus more as needed
¼ teaspoon baking soda
1 tablespoon baking powder
1 teaspoon salt
6 tablespoons lard or solid vegetable shortening
¾ cup buttermilk

Sift the dry ingredients into a roomy bowl. Cut in the shortening with a pastry blender or a fork until the mixture has the texture of coarse meal. Add the buttermilk and mix with your hand, lightly but thoroughly. Add a little more flour if the dough is too sticky. Knead for 1 minute. Wrap in wax paper or foil and refrigerate until well chilled, at least 20 minutes.

Preheat the oven to 450° F.

Roll the dough out ½ inch thick on a lightly floured surface or pastry cloth. (Always roll from the center out for tender, crisp biscuits.) Cut the dough into the desired size biscuits.

Place the biscuits on a dark baking sheet and bake until golden brown, 10 to 12 minutes. Makes 25 to 30 biscuits.

Note: If some dough is left over, it

129

is wiser to bake the biscuits and freeze them, as the buttermilk dough will not keep over 10 to 12 hours.

The Heritage of Southern Cooking

SPOON BREAD

Spoon breads, also called batter breads, are descendants of the Indians' cornmeal porridges. Some spoon breads are soufflé-like. Nika Hazelton calls the version below "a delicate, pudding-like spoon bread." But everyone seems to agree that the best spoon breads are made with stone-ground cornmeal, which has a more floury, less gritty texture than ordinary meal.

1 cup stone-ground or other white or yellow cornmeal
1 cup boiling water
1 cup buttermilk and 1 cup milk, or 2 cups milk
1 teaspoon salt
1½ teaspoons baking powder
½ teaspoon baking soda (omit if all milk is used)
3 eggs, well beaten
3 tablespoons melted butter

Put the cornmeal into a bowl. Pour in boiling water, stirring as you pour to avoid lumping. Cool, stirring frequently to keep smooth. If you use buttermilk and milk, combine in another bowl and stir in

salt, baking powder, and baking soda. (If you are using all milk, omit baking soda.) Stir into cooled cornmeal, beating until smooth. Beat in beaten eggs and mix thoroughly. Blend in melted butter. Generously butter a 1½-quart baking dish. Turn batter into baking dish. Bake in a preheated moderate oven (375° F.) for about 40 to 50 minutes or until well set and golden brown. Serve from baking dish. Makes 4 to 6 servings.

American Home Cooking

SKILLET CORN BREAD

The Colonial American ancestor of this is "spider corn bread," named for the pan in which it was baked— an iron frying pan with three legs that was placed right over the hot coals.

Some people make corn bread with yellow meal; others swear by white. Some like sugar in their corn bread; others abhor it. This recipe calls for no sugar and white meal.

Should you have leftovers, you might try "Cornbread in a Glass" from White Trash Cooking *for a light evening supper or snack: "Pour buttermilk in a big ice-tea glass filled with toasted cornbread. Let the bread soak up the buttermilk and then eat it with a long ice-tea spoon."*

1 cup buttermilk
½ teaspoon baking soda
1¾ cups white stone-ground corn-meal
½ teaspoon baking soda
1 teaspoon salt
1 egg, beaten
2 to 3 tablespoons butter or bacon fat

Put the buttermilk and soda into a bowl and mix well. Sift into it the

cornmeal, baking soda, and salt and beat until smooth. Beat in beaten egg. Heat 2 to 3 tablespoons butter or bacon fat in a heavy 10-inch frying pan and swish it around to coat bottom and sides of frying pan. Pour any remaining butter into the batter and blend. Pour batter into the hot frying pan. Bake in a preheated moderate oven (375° F.) for about 30 to 40 minutes or until set and shrinking from sides of frying pan. Serve hot in wedges, with butter and molasses or sorghum molasses. Makes 4 to 6 servings.

American Home Cooking

CRACKLING BREAD

Edna Lewis, whose recipe for crackling bread is given below, says: "One of my favorite foods that we always had after hog killing was crackling bread. When the lard was rendered and strained, little defatted pieces were left which we called cracklings. Cut into small pieces and mixed into cornmeal batter they made a bread which was deliciously crispy and chewy."

For those who don't have any hogs at hand, here's Edna Lewis's advice on making cracklings today.

CRACKLINGS:

Cracklings are the crispy bits strained from pork fat after it is rendered. The fat is usually from the loin, and it can be found cut in strips in the large supermarkets and butcher shops throughout the year (2 pounds will yield 2 cups of cracklings).

To prepare the fat for rendering, cut away any lean bits or skin because they will become hard and spoil your cracklings. Wipe each piece off in case there is any residue left from the butcher's block. Cut the fat into ½-inch pieces. Cook in a heavy-bottomed saucepan or iron skillet with ¼ cup of water to avoid the fat sticking in the beginning. Start on medium heat, watch closely, and stir often at first until the fat begins to melt. Lower the heat and let the fat separate slowly. The pieces of fat will begin to float. The defatted, browned pieces will go to the bottom and shrink to half their original size. Strain the fat away; it is excellent lard for making bread and frying. Leave the defatted pieces to cool. When ready to use, cut into ¼-inch pieces.

BREAD:

2 cups water-ground white cornmeal
½ teaspoon salt
½ teaspoon baking soda
½ teaspoon baking powder
1 cup cracklings, cut in ¼-inch
  pieces
2 tablespoons butter
1 cup buttermilk

Sift together meal, salt, soda, and baking powder into a mixing bowl. Sprinkle the cracklings over the meal mixture and stir well. Put the butter into a baking pan, about 9 x 10 inches, and set it in a warm oven. Pour the buttermilk into the meal mixture, stirring vigorously. This is a stiffer dough than other meal batters. Remove the pan from the oven, tilting it back and forth to butter the whole surface. Pour the excess butter into the meal batter and return the pan to the oven to keep it hot while you finish stirring the batter. Remove the pan from the oven and spoon in the meal batter, spreading it evenly over the pan with the back of the spoon. Bake for 25 to 30 minutes at 400° F. Cut into squares and serve hot. Serves 4 to 5.
The Taste of Country Cooking

BOSTON BROWN BREAD

This steamed bread dates back to Puritan times. Jane and Michael Stern have unearthed an old rhymed recipe for it:

Three cups of corn meal,
One of rye flour;
Three cups of sweet milk,
One cup of sour;
A cup of molasses
To render it sweet,
Two teaspoons of soda
Will make it complete.

This was written in the days before graham flour was used. Here's a recipe more widely accepted these days:

1 cup rye flour
1 cup cornmeal
1 cup graham flour
¾ teaspoon baking soda
1 teaspoon salt
¾ cup molasses
2 cups buttermilk
1 cup chopped raisins
  (optional)

Sift all dry ingredients together, add molasses, buttermilk, raisins. Divide batter and place in two buttered 1-quart pudding molds or three buttered 1-pound coffee cans, filling them about three-fourths full. Molds must be covered tightly, with buttered lids tied and taped so the bread won't force the cover off on rising. Place molds in a pan filled with enough boiling water to reach halfway up the mold and steam for 3 hours, keeping water at the halfway mark. Serve piping hot with butter and baked beans.
The American Heritage Cookbook

FLANNEL CAKES

The authors of The American Heritage Cookbook *say the following about this well-loved dish: "Stacks of these griddle cakes were consumed in the old lumbering camps, where they were known both as Flannel Cakes (possibly in honor of the layers of flannel shirts worn by the lumberjacks or because the griddle cakes tasted like flannel) and as Strings of Flats, or Flatcars, presumably for the railroad flatcars that took the lumber to market."*

1 cup sifted all-purpose flour
1 tablespoon baking powder
½ teaspoon salt
2 tablespoons sugar
2 eggs
1 cup milk
2 tablespoons melted butter

131

Sift flour, baking powder, salt, and sugar into a mixing bowl. In a separate container, beat eggs until light, then stir in milk and melted butter. With as few strokes as possible blend egg mixture in with the dry ingredients. Pour batter onto a hot, greased griddle (griddle is hot enough when a few drops of water tested on it sizzle) and cook until both sides are nicely browned. Serve at once with butter and warm maple syrup or honey.

The American Heritage Cookbook

SOURDOUGH BREAD

The American Heritage Cookbook gives the following history of this dish: "Sourdough may be the oldest of all breads, dating as far back as 4000 B.C., but—according to one theory—it was unknown in America until Columbus landed with a sourdough starter in the hold of his ship. . . . The bread became identified with America because of the Alaskan sourdoughs—prospectors who carried sourdough starter pots strapped to their packs so they could make a batch of bread whenever they felt the need, without walking fifty miles to the nearest town for a bit of yeast."

SOURDOUGH STARTER:
2 cups lukewarm water
1 package active dry yeast or
  1 yeast cake
2 cups all-purpose flour
½ teaspoon salt

Mix the ingredients in a medium-sized crock. Cover loosely with cheesecloth and place in a warm spot in the kitchen. Every day, for 4 days, add ½ cup lukewarm water and ½ cup flour to feed the starter. At the end of 4 to 6 days, it should begin to give off a sour smell. If you do not plan to use the starter or part of it immediately, add a little more flour and lukewarm water and store in the refrigerator. It should be fed every week by adding additional water and flour. When using the starter take out 1 or 2 cups and be certain to replace them with equal amounts of lukewarm water and flour. Be careful not to let fat or egg get into the starter.

BREAD:
1 cup lukewarm water or potato
  water
1 tablespoon sugar
1 to 2 tablespoons melted butter,
  bacon fat, or lard
1 tablespoon or more salt
1 cup sourdough starter
¼ teaspoon baking soda
4½ cups (about) all-purpose flour
Melted butter or margarine

In a mixing bowl, stir together the lukewarm water or potato water, sugar, fat and salt. Measure the starter, mix in the soda, and stir into the water mixture. Gradually beat in the flour to make a very stiff dough. Turn out onto a floured surface and knead in about ½ cup more flour to make a smooth, satiny dough. Put back into the bowl, brush the top of the dough with melted butter or margarine. Cover with a cloth, wax paper, or foil, and

let stand in a warm place until double in bulk. Again turn out on a lightly floured surface. Cut the dough in half and shape into two loaves. Let stand in a warm place until the loaves are double in bulk. Carefully place in a preheated 375° F. oven and bake about 40 minutes, or until the loaves shrink from the sides of the pan. Turn on a rack to cool.

James Beard's American Cookery

BLUEBERRY MUFFINS

2 cups sifted all-purpose flour
3 tablespoons sugar
3 teaspoons baking powder
1 teaspoon salt
⅞ cup milk
¼ cup vegetable oil
2 tablespoons maple syrup
1 egg, lightly beaten
1 cup fresh blueberries, washed and
  patted dry, *or* 1 10-ounce package
  frozen blueberries, thawed and
  drained very dry

Sift flour, sugar, baking powder and salt into a mixing bowl; combine milk with vegetable oil, maple syrup and egg. Make a well in the center of the dry ingredients, pour in combined liquid ingredients all at once and mix lightly, just enough to dampen dry ingredients. Don't overmix or muffins will be tough—no matter if the batter is lumpy. Quickly fold in blueberries.

Spoon into well-greased muffin-pan cups, filling each about three-fourths full. Bake in a hot oven (400° F.) for 20 to 25 minutes or until muffins are nicely browned and have pulled from sides of muffin-pan cups. Serve hot with plenty of butter and, if you like, drizzlings of maple syrup. Makes 12 muffins.

The Grass Roots Cookbook

MAIN DISHES

CHICKEN AND DUMPLINGS

In rural America chicken and dumplings was often served for Sunday dinner. Edna Lewis, who grew up in Virginia, says that at her house, "No winter meal was complete without a fat, old Barred rock hen saved for a cold day, stewed and served piping hot with dumplings made of a rich biscuit dough."

1 5- to 6-pound stewing chicken, cut up, or 2 broiler-fryers, cut up
3 celery ribs with leaves
2 carrots, pared and sliced
1 small onion, cut up
3 sprigs parsley
2 teaspoons salt
¼ teaspoon pepper
1 bay leaf

In a large kettle, add enough water to cover the chicken pieces. Add vegetables and seasonings. Cover and bring to a boil. Simmer for 2½ hours or until meat is tender.

Prepare "Slick" Dumplings or Fluffy Dumplings, and cook with the stewed chicken as directed.

Remove dumplings and chicken to a platter and keep warm. Strain the broth in which the chicken and dumplings were cooked. Prepare gravy, using the following recipe. Serves 6 to 8.

CHICKEN GRAVY:
1 quart strained chicken broth
¼ cup flour
1 cup cold water
1 teaspoon salt
¼ teaspoon pepper

Heat the broth in a saucepan. Combine the flour and cold water; gradually add to the broth, mixing well. Cook, stirring constantly, until the mixture thickens. Add the salt and pepper, and pour over the chicken and dumplings.

"SLICK" DUMPLINGS:
3 cups flour
1 teaspoon salt
2 cups boiling chicken broth

Sift together the flour and salt. Pour the boiling broth into the flour and stir until well blended. Place dough on floured board and roll out to about ⅛-inch thickness. Cut into 1-inch squares, and drop into boiling chicken and broth. Cook until tender, about 15 minutes.

133

FLUFFY DUMPLINGS:

1 cup flour
½ teaspoon salt
1½ teaspoons baking powder
½ cup milk
2 tablespoons melted shortening

Sift together flour, salt, and baking powder. Stir in milk and melted shortening to make a soft dough. Drop dumplings by spoonfuls into gently boiling broth. Cover tightly and steam, without lifting cover, for 12 to 15 minutes.
Country Kitchens Remembered

BARBECUED SPARERIBS

There are many different kinds of barbecue sauces. The following sauce hails from Texas; and while some might say that a barbecue true to its name has to be cooked outside over a pit fire made with hickory logs, this recipe can be made right in your oven.

2 tablespoons butter
1 cup minced onion
1 large garlic clove, minced
½ cup tomato ketchup or chili
   sauce or half of each
Grated rind of 1 lemon
Juice of 1 lemon
2 tablespoons Worcestershire sauce
⅔ cup water
½ teaspoon dry mustard or to taste
½ teaspoon salt
½ teaspoon freshly ground pepper
Dash of Tabasco
1 to 2 tablespoons brown sugar
3 pounds meaty spareribs

Combine all ingredients except the spareribs in a heavy saucepan. Bring to boiling point, lower heat, and simmer without a cover for about 5 minutes or covered for 10 minutes. Trim all excess fat from spareribs. Cool sauce a little before

using. Place the spareribs in a baking pan and cover with the sauce. Cook in a preheated moderate oven (350° F.) for about 2 hours, basting occasionally with pan liquid. Serve hot or cold. Makes 4 to 6 servings.
American Home Cooking

NEW ENGLAND BAKED BEANS

In Puritan times Sabbath began on Saturday at sundown and ended at sundown on Sunday. The perfect answer to what to serve the family for Saturday night supper and Sunday breakfast, when work was forbidden, was Boston baked beans. A pot of these could be cooked in a brick oven alongside their natural accompaniments of Boston brown bread and Indian pudding and started hours ahead of time. As written in Mary J. Lincoln's Boston Cook Book *(1883): "Who can say that each dish was not the better for such close companionship during the long hours between the finishing of Saturday's baking and the Sunday morning meal?"*

1 quart pea or navy beans
½ pound fat salt pork
2 teaspoons salt
1 tablespoon brown sugar
¼ cup dark molasses
½ teaspoon dry mustard
½ teaspoon Worcestershire sauce
Boiling water

Wash and soak beans in cold water overnight; drain, cover with fresh water and cook slowly until skins break. To test: take a few beans on tip of spoon and blow on them gently; if skins break and curl back, they are sufficiently cooked. Turn beans into bean pot. Pour boiling water over pork, scrape rind until white, score in ½-inch strips and press into top of beans, leaving only rind exposed. Mix salt, brown sugar, molasses, mustard and Worcestershire sauce; add 1 cup boiling water and pour over beans. Add additional water to cover beans, if necessary. Cover and bake in slow oven (250° to 300° F.) for 6 to 8 hours, adding additional water to keep beans just covered; uncover during last ½ hour to brown pork and beans. One small onion may be placed in bottom of bean pot. Makes 6 to 8 servings.
America's Cook Book

CHICKEN GUMBO

In American Home Cooking, *Nika Hazelton states: "Gumbos . . . are truly and originally American dishes, and wonderful ones at that. They are usually associated with the Creole cookery of New Orleans and the rest of Louisiana, but they are also made in other states of the Deep South. These highly flavored dishes . . . are thickened with either okra or filé powder. Okra gave gumbo its name, which is the African word for that* vegetable. . . . Filé powder is made from dried powdered sassafras leaves, discovered as a thickener by the local Choctaw Indians."

2 tablespoons butter
1 chicken, 3 to 3½ pounds, cut into pieces
1½ to 2 pounds ham slices, cut into 1-inch cubes
1 onion, chopped
½ pod hot red pepper, seeded
1 sprig thyme or parsley, chopped
6 large tomatoes, peeled and chopped
1 quart (1 pound) okra, sliced
3 quarts boiling water
1 bay leaf
Salt and cayenne pepper to taste

Heat the butter in a heavy kettle or Dutch oven, add the chicken and ham and cook, covered, about 10 minutes.

Add the onion, red pepper, thyme and solid part of the tomatoes, reserving the juice. Simmer a few minutes, stirring often.

Add the okra and simmer, stirring, until brown.

Add the reserved tomato juice, the boiling water and bay leaf. Season with salt and cayenne and simmer, covered, about 1 hour.

Serve with rice. Makes 8 to 10 servings.
The New York Times Cookbook

HAM STEAK AND RED-EYE GRAVY

In her book A Place Called Sweet Apple, *Celestine Sibley says: "Just recently I read in that marvelous volume* Bull Cook and Authentic Historical Recipes and Practices *that red-eye gravy was given its name by General Andrew Jackson. It seems that Old Hickory had a cook who, as*

we say, 'took whiskey' and as a result was often red-eyed at breakfast time. The general is supposed to have told him to bring him some ham with gravy 'as red as your eyes.' Overhearing it, soldiers took up the name, as soldiers will, and it has come down through the years to designate the hot meat juice, which is left in the skillet after frying ham."

1 center slice country ham, about ⅜ inch thick
1 cup water
Black coffee (optional)

If the ham is salty, soak the slice in water for 30 minutes to 1 hour. Drain and pat dry.

Cook the slice in a heavy skillet slowly, until tender, about 20 minutes. Set aside on a warm platter.

Add 1 cup water to the skillet and cook, stirring to loosen all the browned particles and pieces of "red" meat. Boil 2 minutes. Add tablespoon or two of coffee to darken further if desired. Makes 3 servings.
The New York Times Heritage Cookbook

SOUTHERN FRIED CHICKEN

Ben Robertson in Red Hills and Cotton *spoke for many others when he said: "I don't think I ever had all the fried chicken I could eat until I was twenty-one years of age. I never got*

enough because I like the thigh and the gizzard, and half the others also preferred those pieces. We never expected ever even to taste the liver— the older men were served the liver."

1 frying chicken, 3 to 3½ pounds
1 teaspoon salt, plus more to taste
Freshly ground black pepper to taste
1 cup all-purpose flour
Lard or solid vegetable shortening for frying

Cut the chicken into comfortable serving pieces (breast in half, thigh and leg separated). Rinse the pieces and dry them well with paper towels. Season the chicken with salt and pepper.

Mix 1 teaspoon salt into the flour and coat the chicken by rolling the pieces firmly in the flour or by tossing them in the flour in a plastic bag. Before frying, shake the pieces to rid them of any excess flour.

Heat enough lard or shortening to come to a depth of 1½ inches in a heavy black iron pan. When the fat is piping hot but not smoking, add the largest pieces first. Do not crowd. Cover the pan and fry over medium-high heat for 8 minutes.

After the chicken has browned on one side, turn it to brown the other side. Keep the fat at a medium-high temperature but remove the cover. (You will have to watch the chicken as it cooks.) The total cooking time for tender chicken will be about 20 minutes. Drain on paper towels. Serves 4.

FRIED CHICKEN GRAVY:
2 tablespoons drippings from fried chicken
3 tablespoons all-purpose flour
1½ cups milk
Salt and freshly ground white pepper to taste

135

Pour off all the fat from the pan except about 2 tablespoons, leaving the golden brown crunchy bits. Add the flour and blend over rather low heat. Add the milk and cook, stirring constantly, until the gravy has thickened. Add salt and lots of pepper to taste. Serve over hot biscuits.
The Heritage of Southern Cooking

BRUNSWICK COUNTY STEW

John and Marie Roberson, from whose Famous American Recipes *the following recipe comes, say: "Here is a savory, rich stew that originated in Brunswick County, Virginia, as a hearty meal for all-day outdoor gatherings—political, religious, or just plain neighborly. It was first made with squirrel (which was very plentiful) and chicken."*

1 5-pound chicken
1 pound lean veal or beef
2 large potatoes
4 cups whole kernel corn
1 large onion, diced
4 cups lima beans
2 8-ounce cans tomato sauce or 2 cups cooked tomatoes
1 teaspoon salt
¼ teaspoon pepper
Few dashes of Tabasco sauce
¼ teaspoon Worcestershire sauce
4 tablespoons butter or margarine

Simmer chicken and veal or beef together in water to cover until chicken is ready to fall from the bones. Cool and shred chicken and veal, discarding skin and fat. Put meat back into broth, skimmed of excess fat, and continue to simmer. Dice potatoes and cook with corn, onions and beans in tomato sauce. When potatoes are tender, combine vegetables with meat and chicken. The mixture will be thin like soup. Simmer

for several hours to thicken. Season with remaining ingredients; add butter or margarine.

The secret of Brunswick Stew is the long period of simmering which makes for a thorough blending of flavors and a rich, thick stew. Makes 10 to 12 servings.
Famous American Recipes

NEW ENGLAND BOILED DINNER

1 6-pound corned beef brisket, trimmed of excess fat
10 cups (2½ quarts) cold water
12 medium-sized carrots, peeled and cut in 2-inch chunks
16 new potatoes of uniform size, peeled
24 small white onions of uniform size, peeled
1 medium-sized cabbage, cut in 12 slim wedges (do not remove central core or cabbage wedges will fall apart)
Pepper to season
Salt to season (if needed; you may not need salt as corned beef is salty)
10 small to medium-sized beets, scrubbed, boiled in their skins until fork-tender, then peeled

Note: The beets will take about 1 to 1½ hours to cook; time them carefully so that they are ready to

serve at the same time as the boiled dinner.

Place corned beef in a very large heavy kettle, add water and bring to a simmer; skim off as much scum as possible, adjust heat so that water ripples gently, cover kettle and simmer brisket about 45 to 55 minutes per pound until fork-tender— 4½ to 5½ hours in all.

About 1½ hours before brisket is tender, skim as much fat from kettle liquid as possible. Add carrots, re-cover and continue simmering; after ½ hour, add potatoes, re-cover and simmer ½ hour. Add onions, pushing them down into kettle, re-cover and simmer 10 minutes. Add cabbage wedges, submerging them gently in kettle liquid, re-cover and simmer 15 to 20 minutes or until crisp-tender. Taste kettle liquid for seasoning, add pepper to taste and, if needed, salt.

Remove brisket from kettle, slice thin across the grain and arrange on a heated large, deep platter. Wreathe with kettle vegetables, lifting them out with a slotted spoon. Add clusters of beets and serve. Makes 8 to 10 servings.
The Grass Roots Cookbook

CHICKEN-FRIED BEEFSTEAK AND MILK GRAVY

Marilyn Kluger in her book Country Kitchens Remembered *writes evocatively about this dish:*

There is no set recipe for these two standbys in the country kitchens I remember, but there were methods that I can describe.

Beefsteaks were cut thin, less than ½ inch thick, and pounded to break down the connective tissue and tenderize them. Even choice cuts were treated this way. A wooden mallet with "teeth" carved in it, a wooden potato masher, or the side of a heavy plate could be used to pound the meat. Mother used the handle of our trusty "butcher knife." The steak was then coated in flour, fried like chicken in lard, and seasoned with salt and pepper.

. . . Chicken-fried steak and fried chicken were not truly farm-style without milk gravy made with the pan drippings. Remove the meat from the pan. Sift flour into the sizzling-hot fat, while stirring constantly. Stir and cook the flour over medium-high heat for a minute or two, but only long enough to very slightly "tan" the flour mixture. If it is browned too much, the gravy will be dark and taste scorched. While stirring the flour-fat mixture vigorously, pour the milk in quickly in a large stream. Turn the heat down and continue stirring while the mixture thickens. Season to taste with salt and pepper.

Gravy was not something for which a country cook had measurements . . . [but] as a rule, approximately equal amounts of flour and pan drippings are needed. One-fourth cup drippings and ¼ cup flour to 3 or 4 cups of milk makes enough gravy for moderate servings for a family of four.

Milk gravy was spooned over mashed potatoes, over meat, over fried green tomatoes, biscuits, or plain bread. There were times when supper was simply milk gravy and biscuits. . . . [Milk gravy] was coun-

trified but delicious, and absolutely essential when three abundant daily meals were a necessity.
Country Kitchens Remembered

RED FLANNEL HASH

If you happen to have any leftovers from your New England Boiled Dinner (page 136), here's a good way to use them up.

6 medium-sized whole beets, cooked
4 medium-sized potatoes, cooked
1½ cups chopped cooked corned beef
½ teaspoon salt
⅛ teaspoon pepper
4 tablespoons butter or drippings
1 tablespoon water
2 tablespoons cream

Coarsely chop beets and potatoes. Mix with corned beef, salt and pepper. Melt butter or drippings in a heavy skillet. Add meat mixture and sprinkle with water. Cook over medium heat about 20 to 25 minutes or until the hash has a browned crust on the bottom. Pour over the cream and cook 5 minutes longer. Fold over as for an omelet. Serve hot with corn bread. Makes 4 servings.
Famous American Recipes

MARYLAND CRAB CAKES

"Most people use eggs in their crab cakes," says Mary Seymour (Mrs. Charles Seymour of Talbot County, Maryland), whose recipe follows, "but I don't like to. It's another meat to me, plus if you don't use a lot of mayonnaise or something in the mixture to loosen it up, the eggs dry the crab out and make it tough. The mixture should be juicy and soft but still

thick enough to hold together. You should shape it just enough to stick the cakes together, but try not to handle it too much or the crab will pack down too tight."

1 pound lump or backfin crabmeat, picked over for bits of shell and cartilage, then flaked with a fork
1 tablespoon minced parsley
1 tablespoon grated onion
1 tablespoon prepared spicy brown mustard
1½ slices white bread, broken into small pieces and soaked in ⅓ cup milk (do not squeeze the milk out of the bread after soaking)
½ teaspoon Worcestershire sauce
½ teaspoon salt
Pinch of pepper
3 to 4 tablespoons butter (for browning the crab cakes)

Mix together all ingredients except the butter, shape into 8 cakes about 1 inch thick, then cover loosely and chill in the refrigerator 1 hour.

Melt 3 tablespoons of the butter in a very large heavy skillet and when it begins to sizzle gently, add crab cakes and brown about 4 to 5 minutes on a side. Handle the crab cakes gently, turning with a pan-

137

cake turner—they're soft and fragile and may fall apart if treated with a heavy hand. If needed, add the additional tablespoon of butter to keep crab cakes from sticking. Serve skillet-hot. Makes 4 servings.
The Grass Roots Cookbook

PICKLED PIGS' FEET

8 pigs' feet
1 quart vinegar
6 whole cloves
2 bay leaves
1 stick cinnamon
2 tablespoons salt
¼ teaspoon pepper
¼ cup brown sugar
1 onion, sliced

Clean the feet, making sure the toes and dewclaws are removed and also the glandular tissue between the toes, the hair and any dirt.

Cover with boiling water and simmer until tender, 2½ to 3 hours. In a large enamel pan combine vinegar, cloves, bay leaves, stick of cinnamon, salt, pepper, brown sugar and onion. Simmer 1 hour. Strain liquid to remove spices. Add 2 to 4 cups liquid in which pigs' feet have been cooked. Pour over feet and chill 2 days, if possible.

138 *Old Fashioned Recipe Book*

SCRAPPLE

The Pennsylvania Dutch called it "ponhaws" and traditionally it was one way to use up scraps of pork left over after slaughtering a hog.

1½ pounds pork shoulder
¼ pound pork liver
1 cup yellow cornmeal
2 teaspoons salt
¼ cup onions, chopped fine
Dash of ground cloves
¼ teaspoon dried thyme
1 teaspoon dried sage
1 teaspoon dried marjoram
½ teaspoon freshly ground pepper

Combine pork shoulder and liver in a saucepan with 1 quart water and cook, over a moderate heat, for 1 hour. Drain, reserving the broth. Discard all bones and chop meat fine. Blend cornmeal, salt, 1 cup water, and 2 cups of the broth in a saucepan. Cook, stirring constantly, until thick. Stir in meat, onions, all the spices and herbs. Cover and simmer gently for about 1 hour over a very low heat. Pour into a 9 x 5 x 3-inch loaf pan and chill until firm. Cut into slices about ½ to ¾ inch thick, dust lightly with flour, and fry in a little heated shortening over a moderate heat until crisp on both sides. Serve at once.
The American Heritage Cookbook

NEW ENGLAND CLAM CHOWDER

The authors of The American Heritage Cookbook *tell us: "Every New Englander worth his salty independence has his own version of what is essential to Clam Chowder. The most notable heresy is Manhattan Clam Chowder, which calls for water rather than milk—and tomatoes!*

Down Easters are so nettled over the Tomato Question that the Maine legislature once introduced a bill to outlaw forever the mixing of clams and tomatoes."

1 quart clams
1 cup water
4 slices salt pork, cut into small pieces
1 medium-to-large onion, thinly sliced
3 cups potatoes, peeled and diced
1 tablespoon salt
½ teaspoon freshly ground pepper
2 cups boiling water
1 quart scalded milk
8 soda crackers, soaked in milk
1 tablespoon flour
1 tablespoon butter

Scrub the clams. Place them in a large kettle with 1 cup water, cover, and cook over medium-high heat till they open. Remove the clams, strain the liquid, and chop the clams. Try out the salt pork in a skillet, and when crisp, transfer to absorbent paper. Pour off all but 2 tablespoons fat from the skillet and sauté the onion slices lightly for 4 to 5 minutes, turning them with a wooden spatula several times. Parboil the potatoes 5 minutes in salted water to cover. Arrange the onions in the bottom of a heavy saucepan and top with a layer of half the potatoes. Add the salt pork pieces, then the chopped clams, then another layer of potatoes and salt and pepper. Add the boiling water and cook 10 minutes. Add the scalded milk and bring to a boil. Add the soaked crackers and liquid the clams cooked in. Finally add the flour and butter kneaded together. Bring to the boiling point and correct the seasoning. Serve in hot chowder bowls.

Note: If you are using canned

minced clams, add the broth to the chowder as above, but do not add the clams till the very last minute. If you are using tiny, tender clams, add some minced tougher clams earlier, and reserve 1½ to 2 cups of the tender clams to add at the very last minute.
James Beard's American Cookery

CHILI CON CARNE

James Beard, whose recipe follows, calls it: "A famous dish, Texan by adoption, that probably arouses more heated controversy about the proper style of preparation than anything I know. Some chop the beef into cubes, others grind it. Some like tomatoes, others abhor them. Almost everyone agrees that a true chili con carne is without beans, although it is perfectly all right to serve kidney beans with the chili."

4 tablespoons beef fat
2 large onions, chopped
½ pound beef kidney fat (suet), finely chopped
3 pounds top round or rump, cut into small dice or ground
2 cloves garlic
1 tablespoon salt
3 tablespoons chili powder, or more to taste
1 tablespoon cumin seeds
Dash of Tabasco
2 quarts beef broth, or boiling water mixed with bouillon cubes

Melt beef fat in a large skillet and sauté onions for 5 minutes until translucent. Add beef kidney fat. Let this cook slowly until the suet is all rendered and the onion practically melted into the fat. Add beef, garlic, and salt. Let the meat brown well and blend with the fat and the onion. Add chili powder, cumin, and Tabasco. Cover with boiling beef stock (or boiling water mixed with bouillon cubes). Simmer over low flame, covered, for about 2½ hours, stirring occasionally. Taste for seasoning—add more salt or chili powder if necessary. Makes 6 servings.
The New James Beard

POTATO PANCAKES AND APPLESAUCE

This can be served as a side dish and often is. However, with the addition of applesauce and a few slices of bacon it makes a good main dish.

3 large potatoes
2 eggs, well beaten
2 tablespoons milk
3 tablespoons flour
¼ teaspoon baking powder
1 teaspoon salt
1 tablespoon grated onion
¼ teaspoon pepper

Pare potatoes, cover with cold water, and let stand several hours. Pour off water, grate potatoes into cold water to prevent discoloration; then drain potatoes well. Add eggs, mix well. Stir in remaining ingredients. Drop mixture from teaspoon onto a well-greased skillet. Cook to a golden brown on both sides. Makes about 12 medium-sized pancakes.
Famous American Recipes

FRIED CATFISH

Ernest Matthew Mickler, author of White Trash Cooking, *says of this dish: "If you serve it with anything else but hush puppies, grits, cole slaw, and home fries, it'll get up and walk off the plate."*

6 small catfish, cleaned, or 12 fillets
2 cups buttermilk
2 cups white cornmeal
Salt to taste
Freshly ground black pepper to taste
Oil for frying

Soak the catfish in buttermilk 30 minutes to overnight.
Mix cornmeal, salt, and pepper in a paper bag. Drain the catfish and drop into the bag, one at a time, and shake until coated. Heat 1½ inches oil to 360° F. Measure the thickness of the catfish and for each inch of thickness fry 5 minutes on each side until golden brown. Drain on a paper towel. Serve hot. Serves 6.
New Southern Cooking

SIDE DISHES

WILTED LETTUCE SALAD

Traditionally, this was a good dish to fix in the spring and early summer before the garden started producing. Fresh food was a welcome sight on the table after a winter of canned and dried fruits and vegetables.

6 slices bacon, preferably lean, cut into ¼-inch dice
⅓ cup white or cider vinegar
2 bunches leaf lettuce, washed, dried, and shredded, or 4 cups shredded lettuce
¼ cup minced scallions
¼ to ½ teaspoon salt
¼ teaspoon freshly ground pepper
2 teaspoons sugar
2 hard-cooked eggs, chopped

In a large frying pan, cook the bacon until crisp. If bacon is fat, pour off all but 4 to 6 tablespoons of fat. Add the vinegar to bacon and fat. Heat through over very low heat. Remove from heat and add the lettuce, scallions, salt, pepper and sugar. Toss 1 to 2 minutes to wilt the lettuce. Add the chopped eggs and toss again. Makes 4 servings
American Home Cooking

POTATO SALAD WITH BOILED DRESSING

James Beard, whose recipe follows, says of it: "One of the earliest and most popular of American potato salads, this used to be standard picnic fare, especially throughout New England and the Middle West."

6 large, firm, waxy potatoes, unpeeled

BOILED DRESSING:
4 eggs
5 tablespoons boiling vinegar
1 tablespoon butter
½ pint heavy cream
2 tablespoons finely chopped onion
1 teaspoon dry mustard
1 teaspoon salt
Dash of cayenne
½ teaspoon white pepper
2 tablespoons finely chopped parsley

Boil the potatoes in their skins in

140

salted water to cover until tender. While they are cooking, beat together the eggs and vinegar in the top of a double boiler. Cook the mixture until it thickens slightly, and stir in the butter. Then add the cream, onion, and seasonings. Drain the potatoes. Peel and slice into a bowl while still hot. Pour the dressing over them. Mix thoroughly, sprinkle with the parsley, and chill for several hours. Makes 4 to 6 servings.
The New James Beard

FRIED GREEN TOMATOES

A recipe just right for those tomatoes still green when the first frost threatens. Or as Camille Glenn puts it, "When the crickets and the katydids are singing their hearts out under the porch or in the garden, and the ham is cooking on the stove to be eaten with the last of the fresh corn and fried green tomatoes . . . one knows that another summer has gone, but autumn has blessed our table and life is good."

Wash green tomatoes and pat dry. Thickly slice. Dip into stone-ground cornmeal, flour, or fine bread crumbs seasoned with salt and pepper. Shake off the excess coating. Sauté tomatoes until lightly browned in a butter-oil combination or in bacon fat. (You can also cook ripe tomatoes this way, as long as they are firm.)
The Victory Garden Cookbook

HOPPING JOHN

In the South legend has it that unless Hopping John is served on New Year's Day bad luck will follow. Our favorite story about this dish is the
following from Carson McCullers's novel The Member of the Wedding: *"Now hopping-john was F. Jasmine's very favorite food. She had always warned them to wave a plate of rice and peas before her nose when she was in her coffin, to make certain there was no mistake; for if a breath of life was left in her, she would sit up and eat, but if she smelled the hopping-john, and did not stir, then they could just nail down the coffin and be certain she was truly dead."*

2 cups dried black-eyed peas or cowpeas, soaked overnight and drained
1 piece fatback (salt pork), slashed in several places
1 hot red pepper
1 medium onion, chopped
Salt
Freshly ground black pepper
1 cup uncooked rice
4 tablespoons drippings, preferably bacon

Place the peas in a large pot, cover with water, and add 3 cups more water. Add the fatback, red pepper, onion, salt, and pepper, and bring to the boil. Cover, reduce the heat, and simmer until the peas are tender. Add more water as needed. Remove the peas, and reserve enough liquid in the pot (about 3 cups) to cook the rice. Add the rice and drippings to the pot. Bring

back to the boil, cover, reduce the heat, and simmer until the rice is cooked, about 30 minutes. Return the peas to the pot, stir together, and cook for a few minutes more. Turn into a large dish and serve. Serves 6 to 8.
New Southern Cooking

LEATHER BRITCHES

Drying green beans was one way to preserve them through the winter. As Celestine Sibley says in her book A Place Called Sweet Apple: "Although canned and frozen green beans are now plentiful . . . they do not replace leather britches. If you have eaten leather britches on a snowy winter day in the mountains, nothing really replaces them."

Pick the green beans when young and string them on heavy thread, like long beads, one after the other. Hang the lines in a sunny place to dry thoroughly. It may take as long as a month or even two. When dried, store in baskets for winter use. To use, wash the beans well and soak 2 cups dried beans in 2 quarts of water for an hour or so. Add ¼ pound diced salt pork, salt and pepper. Bring to a boil and reduce heat. Stir, then simmer very gently for at least 3 hours or until beans are tender, adding boiling water if needed to keep them from burning.
Manna: Foods of the Frontier

GREEN BEANS WITH SALT PORK

Nika Hazelton (the following recipe is from her book American Home Cooking) advises: "Use either pole beans or bush beans; pole beans are Southern favorites."

141

½ pound salt pork with a lean streak
1½ cups water
1½ pounds green beans, trimmed
Salt to taste

Wash excess salt off salt pork. Place it in a saucepan large enough to hold the beans, and add the water. Simmer covered for 30 minutes. Add the beans and bring to boiling point. Lower heat and simmer covered for about 40 minutes. Beans will be a pale green. Turn beans with a spatula two or three times to insure even cooking. When done, there should be very little pan liquid. Makes 4 to 6 servings.
American Home Cooking

CRISP FRIED OKRA

People who think they don't like okra have probably just never had it fixed this way. It's best picked right before cooking and served immediately afterwards—hot and crispy brown.

1 pound fresh young okra
Flour
1 egg, beaten with 1 tablespoon salad oil or water
1 cup yellow or white cornmeal or fine dry bread crumbs
4 tablespoons lard, bacon fat, or salad oil
Salt
Freshly ground pepper

Trim off the tips and stems of the okra pods. Cut the pods diagonally into ¼-inch slices. Dip the slices first in flour, coating them on all sides, then in the beaten egg, and finally in the cornmeal or bread crumbs. The okra should be evenly coated; shake off excess meal or crumbs. Put the okra slices on paper towels. Heat the fat in a large heavy frying pan. Add the okra slices. Over medium heat, sauté the okra for about 2 minutes or until golden brown. Turn and sauté 1 to 2 minutes longer, or until evenly browned on all sides. Drain on paper towels and place on a heated serving dish. Sprinkle with salt and pepper and serve hot. Makes 4 servings.
American Home Cooking

GREENS AND POT LIKKER

Marjorie Kinnan Rawlings wrote about this dish in her 1942 classic, Cross Creek: *"Greens probably save more backwoods lives than the doctors, for they are the one vegetable, aside from cowpeas, for which country folk have a passion. . . . Turnip greens, mustard greens and above all, collard greens, cooked with white bacon, with corn bread on the side, make an occasion."*

1 pound salt pork
2 quarts water
3 pounds turnip greens, mustard greens or collards
Salt and pepper
Dash of Tabasco

Boil the salt pork in water about 1 hour. Add the washed and picked greens and boil 1 hour. Remove the greens, cut rather coarsely, and season well with salt and pepper and a dash of Tabasco. Place on a

platter with slices of the pork and some of the pot likker. This calls for corn pone, corn bread, or corn dodgers.
James Beard's American Cookery

HOMINY GRITS

Grits are hominy that has been dried and finely ground. Bob Jeffries says in his book, Soul Food Cookbook: *"Grits made its daily appearance on our table back home as regularly as potatoes appeared in other parts of the country. Smooth, creamy, and thick, cooked with milk, butter, and just the right amount of salt . . . [they] are really delicious served piping hot with country fried ham or thick slices of broiled bacon."*

2 cups grits
1 quart water
1 teaspoon salt

If you are using quick-cooking [or packaged] grits, follow directions on the package.

Wash the grits well. Drain. Cover with 1 quart water and soak several hours. Add salt. Bring to a boil over direct heat in the top of a double boiler, then place over the bottom part of the boiler and cook over simmering water 1 to 1½ hours. Stir occasionally. Serve with butter or cream.

FRIED HOMINY GRITS:
Pour boiled grits into a loaf pan or a square or oblong dish and allow to cool. Cut into slices about ½ inch thick. Dip in beaten egg and bread crumbs, and sauté in butter until nicely browned on each side. Or flour lightly and sauté in butter or oil till nicely browned and crisp at the edges. Delicious with pheasant, wild duck, quail, or any game.

142

HOMINY GRITS CASSEROLE:
Prepare a double recipe of boiled hominy grits. Combine with 6 tablespoons butter, 3 well-beaten eggs, additional salt if needed, and ¾ teaspoon freshly ground pepper. Pour into a buttered 2-quart baking dish and top with 1 cup grated Cheddar or Gruyère cheese, which should be stirred into the grits. Dot with butter. Bake at 400° F. just long enough to brown the top—about 15 minutes.
James Beard's American Cookery

FRIED CORNMEAL MUSH

Cornmeal mush was also called "hasty pudding." In a poem by that name, Joel Barlow wrote, ". . . how I blush/To hear the Pennsylvanians call thee Mush." Chilled, sliced and fried, it is delicious served with maple syrup or honey.

2 cups boiling water
½ teaspoon salt
½ cup cornmeal

If you are using quick-cooking [or packaged] cornmeal, follow directions on the package.

Bring the water and salt to a boil either in the top of a double boiler or in a heavy saucepan. Stirring constantly, pour the meal gradually into the water. When all is added, let it come to a boil and boil 5 minutes. Continue to stir. Then place it over simmering water to cook 1 hour, or if cooking in a saucepan, cook over medium flame 45 to 50 minutes, stirring often.

Pour the cooked mush into a mold or bread pan and let it chill thoroughly. Remove, cut into slices, and sauté in butter or fat until crisp and brown. Serve as a breakfast dish with syrup or honey

and butter, or serve with game or with dishes such as chili, or highly seasoned stews and ragouts.
James Beard's American Cookery

HUSH PUPPIES

To be served with freshly caught and fried fish. In Cross Creek *Marjorie Kinnan Rawlings tells the origin of their name: "It came, old-timers say, from hunting trips of long ago. . . . Although the hunting dogs tethered to nearby trees had been fed their evening meal, they smelled the good smells of man's victuals, and tugged at their leashes, and whined for a tidbit extra. Then cook or helper or huntsman would toss the leftover little corn patties to the dogs, calling, 'Hush, puppies!' And the dogs bolted the toothsome morsels and hushed, in their great content."*

1½ cups cornmeal
½ cup all-purpose flour
2 teaspoons baking powder
½ teaspoon salt
1 egg, well beaten
¾ cup milk
1 small onion, grated
Fat for deep-fat frying

Sift together cornmeal, flour, baking powder, and salt. Mix egg, milk, and onion in a bowl. Combine with dry ingredients and drop from a spoon into hot fat.

When Hush Puppies are crisp and golden (about 1 minute), lift from fat with slotted spoon and drain on paper towels. Serve hot. Makes about 20.
The American Heritage Cookbook

RED BEET EGGS

Of Pennsylvania Dutch origin, this was one of the "seven sweets and seven sours" served at a family dinner. The recipe following comes from Mrs. Mary Rohrer of Lancaster County, Pennsylvania. The 2 to 3 days marinating time allows the beet juice to seep all the way through the hard-cooked egg whites, giving the dish its name.

1 can (1 pound) small whole beets (do not drain)
1 cup cider vinegar
⅓ cup sugar
¾ teaspoon salt
8 hard-cooked eggs, shelled
¼ cup water (about)

Empty beets and their liquid into a small saucepan; add vinegar, sugar and salt and heat just until sugar dissolves; cool to room temperature.

Place eggs in a medium-sized bowl (or in a half-gallon preserving jar, which is the way Mrs. Rohrer does it), pour in beet mixture and add just enough water so that liquid covers eggs. Cover and marinate in the refrigerator 2 to 3 days, stirring now and then, or inverting the jar of eggs and beets gently a few times, so that all eggs redden evenly. Makes 6 servings.
The Grass Roots Cookbook

143

pie pan; do not trim edge. Roll remaining pastry into a 12-inch circle and cut steam slits in center; cover with cloth while you prepare filling. Toss rhubarb and strawberries with enough sugar to sweeten, then mix in flour and salt. Pile in pie shell and dot with butter. Brush pastry rim with cold water, fit top crust, trim, seal, and crimp edges. For a special occasion, top with a lattice crust. For a glistening crust, brush with milk and sprinkle with sugar. Bake 40 to 50 minutes (with foil on rack underneath to catch drips) until browned and bubbling. Cool 5 to 10 minutes before cutting. Good with cream, whipped cream, or vanilla ice cream. Makes 8 servings.
The Doubleday Cookbook

MOTHER'S STACK CAKE

Nathalie Dupree, from whose cookbook this recipe comes, relates an Alabama friend's story about the history of stack cake in her family: "This is my favorite winter-fall-type cake. Mother made it during the holidays like she made biscuit dough and always used apples that we dried from our green apple tree. It works with fresh apples or chunky applesauce but dried apples are better. . . . Traditionally, guests would each bring a layer to a wedding or church supper, and then they would put it all together to make a stack cake."

Note: *The cake pans are turned upside down and the dough baked on the outside bottom of the pans.*

6 cups all-purpose soft-wheat flour
1 cup solid vegetable shortening
1 cup sugar
2 teaspoons baking soda
2 teaspoons ginger
½ cup molasses
½ cup buttermilk

FILLING:
1 pound dried apples
2 to 3 cups sugar
3 to 4 teaspoons allspice

Preheat the oven to 350° F. With a pastry cutter or two forks, mix the flour, shortening, sugar, baking soda, and ginger together until the mixture looks like biscuit mix. Add the molasses and buttermilk and stir with a fork just until the dough holds together. Divide into five or six equal parts. Press the dough out to ¾-inch thickness on the outside bottom of five or six greased and floured 8-inch cake pans. Bake the layers about 10 minutes, until firm. Cool slightly, remove from bottom of the pans and let cool on racks.

To make the filling: Cook the dried apples with water as directed on the package. Or place the dried apples in water to cover and cook until the apples are soft and the water nearly evaporated. Add sugar and allspice to taste. Layer the cake and applesauce until you have a 5- or 6-layer cake with the apple mixture between layers and on top. The cake is best if it sits 24 hours before cutting. Serves 8 to 10.
New Southern Cooking

SHOOFLY PIE

This historic pie is Pennsylvania Dutch in origin. The fact that flies are attracted to the molasses in it accounts for the colorful name.

Pastry for a 1-crust pie (page 145)

FILLING:
⅔ cup boiling water
½ teaspoon baking soda
½ cup molasses

CRUMB TOPPING:
1½ cups sifted flour
¼ teaspoon salt
¾ cup firmly packed light brown sugar
⅓ cup butter, margarine, or shortening

Preheat oven to 350° F. Prepare pastry as directed and fit into a 9-inch pie pan, making a high fluted edge; do not bake. Mix filling. Also mix flour, salt, and sugar and cut in butter with a pastry blender until the texture of coarse meal. Sprinkle about ⅓ cup topping into pie shell, pour in filling, and sprinkle evenly with remaining topping. Bake on center oven rack 35 to 40 minutes until well browned. Cool on a wire rack and serve slightly warm or cold. Good with whipped cream or vanilla ice cream. Makes 6 to 8 servings.
The Doubleday Cookbook

POUND CAKE

James Beard, whose recipe follows, says: "Every homemaker in the late nineteenth and early twentieth century kept a loaf or two of this cake in the pantry to serve to unexpected callers. . . . The name is derived from the quantity of the ingredients—a pound each of butter, sugar, eggs, and flour."

147

2 cups butter
2 cups sugar
8 to 10 large eggs, separated
2 tablespoons rum, brandy, or
 orange juice
1 teaspoon vanilla
4½ cups sifted cake flour
¾ teaspoon salt

Cream the butter until very fluffy, easiest done with an electric mixer. Cream in the sugar, or reserve ½ cup for the egg whites. The butter and sugar mixture should be like sweetened whipped cream in texture.

If using a mixer, drop the egg yolks in one at a time with mixer on medium-to-high speed. If mixing by hand, beat the yolks with a rotary beater or whisk until very light and lemon-colored. Add to the butter and sugar mixture and beat vigorously. The mixture should be even lighter after the egg yolks are added.

Stir or beat in the flavorings. It is customary to use several flavorings—that is, a combination of orange juice and vanilla or rum, or brandy with a little vanilla, or 1 tablespoon each of rum and brandy. (Some cooks insist that pound cake should also have 1 teaspoon of nutmeg or mace added, which was invariably true of New England pound cakes.)

Sift the flour with salt, then sift several times more, holding the sifter high to incorporate as much air as possible. Stir into the creamed mixture until well blended. If using an electric mixer, do this at lowest speed. In any event, be sure to keep the batter wiped down from the sides and bottom of the bowl with a rubber or plastic spatula.

Beat the egg whites until foamy, and if you like add 1 teaspoon lemon juice or cream of tartar at this point to stabilize the egg whites. If you have reserved ½ cup of sugar, add it gradually during beating of whites. Beat until stiff but not dry—the mixture should hold soft peaks. Fold into the cake batter with a rubber spatula. Turn immediately into two buttered and lightly floured loaf pans 9 x 5 x 3 inches. Or use smaller loaf pans, filling a little more than half full. (This cake works better in loaf than in sheet cake pans.)

Bake in a moderately slow 325° F. oven for about an hour, depending upon size of the pans used—it may take 1¼ hours. Test by pressing the center of the cake lightly with the finger. When the cake springs back, and it has pulled away from the sides of the pan, it is done. Transfer to a rack and cool about 15 minutes before loosening from the pan and turning out on the rack to cool. Pound cake is generally considered best after a day or two of "resting." Store in a tightly covered container or place in plastic bags and seal. If kept for several weeks, it is better if stored in the refrigerator. It freezes well. Pound cake is not frosted. Makes 2 loaves.
James Beard's American Cookery

SUMMERTIME PEACH ICE CREAM

Roy Webster in Under a Buttermilk Moon *writes: "Did you ever have a big blushing dead ripe peach drop from the limb into your hand just as you reached to pick it . . . ? Did you ever bite into a peach like that and have the juice run down and drip off your chin or run down your arms and drip off your elbows? Folks, if that didn't happen to you when you were a kid, let me tell you right now, you have missed one of the most enjoyable experiences in life."*

Fresh peaches also meant peach ice cream—another summertime treat.

1 cup light cream, or ½ cup milk
 and ½ cup heavy or whipping
 cream
1½ cups milk
1½ cups sugar
4 large egg yolks
8 very ripe large peaches
2 teaspoons fresh lemon juice, or
 more to taste
¼ teaspoon salt
2 cups heavy or whipping cream,
 chilled

Combine the light cream and the milk in a saucepan, and scald. Do not allow it to boil. Set aside.

Add ¾ cup of the sugar to the egg yolks, and mix thoroughly with a whisk or an electric mixer. Add the scalded cream and milk to the egg yolk mixture, stir well, and transfer to the top of a double boiler. Cook over simmering water until the cus-

148

tard lightly coats a wooden spoon, 5 minutes.

Remove from the heat at once, pour into a cool bowl, cover with plastic wrap, and refrigerate until the custard is cold, 35 minutes.

While the custard is cooling, peel and mash the peaches, leaving some lumps. You should have 4 cups. Add the lemon juice, remaining sugar, and salt. Mix. Refrigerate, covered, 1 hour.

When you are ready to make the ice cream, add the cream to the custard mixture and mix thoroughly.

Freeze in an ice-cream freezer following manufacturer's directions until the custard has turned to a soft ice cream. Stop turning, remove the cover of the container, and add the peaches. Mix them in with a long-handled spoon, and continue to freeze. Makes about 1 gallon.

Note: The custard mixture and the peaches must be cold when freezing the ice cream; otherwise, the heavy cream will turn into buttery lumps. *The Heritage of Southern Cooking*

SWEET POTATO PONE

According to Marjorie Kinnan Rawlings, the recipe for this dish varied depending on what one could get. She tells about old Martha, whose basic pone recipe called for grated potatoes, flour, bacon grease, soda, cane syrup and water. But . . . "When Martha has eggs, she adds an egg or two. When she has milk, she uses milk instead of water. When 'the chillen' are coming to visit, she uses butter instead of bacon grease. On these occasions she may have cream to churn, and she chants:

'Come, butter, come.
Grandma waitin' for the chillen to come.' "

The following is a somewhat fancier recipe, but just as authentic and very good. Try it and see if your "chillen" don't agree.

2½ cups raw grated sweet potatoes
1 cup molasses
2 eggs
2 cups rich milk
1 tablespoon melted butter
1 teaspoon ground ginger or grated orange rind
1 tablespoon brown sugar
½ teaspoon powdered cinnamon

Add the molasses, well-beaten eggs, milk, melted butter and ginger or orange rind, in order, to the grated potatoes. Turn into a well-greased baking pan and bake about 45 minutes in a moderate [350° F.] oven, sprinkling the brown sugar and cinnamon over the top at the end of the first 25 minutes.
Cross Creek Cookery

Part III

Country Stories

A Time of Learning

by Jessamyn West

Emmett Maguire, hitching Old Clay to the buckboard, was suddenly convinced of folly. He became too sorrowful to slide the thin tail through the crupper, too pensive to buckle a hame strap. He stood in the sallow early morning light gazing about the farmyard. Fool, he asked himself, where'll you find anything like this?

Just then, as he renounced it, the whole landscape so altered that he felt that for the first time in his nineteen years he was seeing it truly. All the familiar paraphernalia of the farm seemed suddenly to detach themselves from their background, move nearer him, become luminous and significant.

Amos, the blue-nosed mule, stood out against the sulphur-colored sky like sculpture. Emmett could not take his eyes from him. Now he was leaving—he had, in fact, moved heaven and earth to get away— and what did he really know of Amos? He had consigned himself to dabbling and traveling when he might have stayed home and learned, got to the bottom of mules. Against the morning sky, streaked now like a ripening Baldwin, Amos's head hung more heavy and knowledgeable than the rock of ages. Would there be any wisdom in the next county equal to what Amos had?

In the moment of leave-taking Emmett doubted it. Leaving, what could he expect? Girls and fritterings. No doubt sleep with the swine at the last, too, he supposed. But he felt as bound to move on as the prodigal himself, and for a better reason.

A sign and house painter soon paints himself out in his own neighborhood. All who incline toward paint and have money to pay for it

152

come finally either to the end of the houses and sheds and outhouses needing a new coat or to the end of their money. All who care to have their fences decorated with signs for Hi-John Compelling Powder have them so decorated. Then the painter moves on or puts down his brush.

"Having trouble?" Emmett's father came from behind the buckboard, where with Emmett's mother he had been stowing away a round leather box of clean collars.

"No trouble," said Emmett, pulling the long switch tail on through. "I was thinking."

He was thinking, if they shed a tear, I'll have to unhitch, unpack, stay forever. But he was mistaken. Had his father laid a hand on the bridle, or his mother clung to him, he would have been off, as determined and set in his leave-taking as he had been in his preparation to go. But the leave-taking was seemly, no tears shed or protestations made. As he drove away, the known objects continued to move toward him, become big with the brightness and urgency of the willfully rejected.

His parents saw him depart, untransformed: their dear son, artist and thinker, Emmett. Though those were words they had never been permitted to say to him.

Once, in the barn, his father had come upon a picture of Emmett's painting. He had stared at it a long time. It was a big, empty picture with great reaches of unoccupied cardboard. Except for the front of a house, an expanse of white siding dazzling in sunlight, there was almost nothing in the picture at all: shallow wooden steps ascended to a partially open door; beyond the door on the dark floorboards and deep in shadow lay something crumpled, a piece of goods, a ribbon perhaps, and beyond that a naked, retreating heel.

Emmett's father would have enriched the picture with many more objects: set pots of flowers on the steps, put a window next the door and a face at the window. Still empty and unembellished as the picture was, it had a certain power. He had found himself wondering about it: about that heel, more yellow than pink, about its haste, its alarm. Then he had noticed that there was a shadow across the steps, that near the house someone, stock-still, stood and watched. Listened, too, perhaps.

But when he had said to Emmett, who came in and found him staring, "Son, you're an artist," Emmett had taken the corn knife he had in his hand and cut the picture to shreds.

"Don't call me that," he told his father. "Never say that. I can't learn. I'm a house and sign painter."

He was a house painter, or a barn or shed painter when he could find houses and barns and sheds to paint; but in Bucklin County he was treading upon the heels of a competitor. Emmett regarded with scorn the wash of murky green that marked the man's progress. A color not fit to set to the side of a hen house, he thought, not good enough for any privy I'd paint. He thanked God for his contract and painted signs.

He had known for some time that he was being watched. That didn't trouble him. It was almost as if the eyes that followed the movements of his hand gave it added force. It was talk that troubled.

"What's 'Crossing and Un-Crossing Powder?' "

"I don't know," Emmett said, painting on.

"Would you make a sign for what you don't know?"

"Yes," said Emmett, "I would."

"I wouldn't."

Emmett said nothing.

"What's 'David the Fearless Floor Wash?' "

Emmett set his brush in the can of linseed oil, turned away from the granite rock on which he was lettering freehand.

"What's a kid who stands asking questions while you're trying to work?" he asked.

The boy was big but round, round as an apple, and his round black eyes were swallowing the lettering like quagmire.

"A nuisance," Emmett told him shortly.

"What's the sign for?" the boy asked, as if he hadn't heard.

"Make people buy the stuff."

"How can they buy it if they don't know what it is?"

"You couldn't buy if you knew. You haven't got any money."

The boy's pants were tight, his pockets taut, his hands fat; still he managed to squeeze a quarter up to the air.

"All right," said Emmett. "Read that and be quiet." He tossed him the Occult Supplies Catalogue, turned back to his painting.

"Bat's Blood Oil," the boy said and Emmett could hear him moistly swallowing.

"Shut up," said Emmett, "or I'll take it away from you."

The boy shut up. Except for the swallowing he didn't make another sound until the sign was finished. The minute Emmett stepped away from the boulder to judge his completed work, he began again. "Which would you buy," he asked, "Graveyard Dust or Oriental Lover's Powder?"

"Graveyard Dust," said Emmett.

"Not me," said the boy. He pushed his quarter to the surface again. "I'll take three packages Oriental Lover's Powder."

"I don't sell the stuff," Emmett told him. "I just paint the signs. You write them," he pointed to the catalogue, "to get the powders."

"Have you got a pencil so's I could write it down?" the boy asked.

Emmett tore a sheet from the little notebook he carried, handed it and a pencil to the boy.

"What do you figure to do with it?" he asked, watching the boy, who wrote with his tongue as well as his fingers.

The boy looked up, but a sudden film came over his eyes. "None of your business," he said.

"That's right," said Emmett. "It isn't."

He took back the pencil and began to collect his gear.

"That your horse and rig by the bridge?"

"Yes," said Emmett.

"I'll help you carry your paints."

Emmett handed him a bucket. "Watch your step," he advised. "That's valuable."

The boy planted his bare feet as carefully as if walking through nettles. He looked over the amount of material in the back of the buckboard. "Takes an awful lot of paint to paint signs," he said.

"I paint houses, too," Emmett told him.

"Barns?" asked the boy.

"Sure," Emmett said.

"We got a barn to be painted."

"Who's we?"

"Us. My father. He wanted the other man to do it but Ivy said his paint looked like scum on a frog pond."

"Who's Ivy?" Emmett asked, thinking she'd picked the right word for it.

"My sister. But Ma said, 'There's things worse than scum, Miss Ivy.' "

"Don't your mother want the barn painted?"

"Oh, sure."

"I'll apply for the job," Emmett said. "You want to ride on home with me?"

They went by the river road. Red dust clung to the lush green growth that arched above their heads and Old Clay methodically lifted more of it to their faces. Even in the gloom of red dust and green shadows the boy bent over the catalogue, reading or rereading, Emmett didn't know which, the wondrous items. Emmett himself was

156

rehearsing a sales talk; reassuring himself, before he tried to convince others, that he was the man for the job.

When they turned away from the river, made for the open, rolling farmlands, Emmett asked the boy his name.

"Oral," he said, not looking up from his reading.

"Oral," Emmett repeated. "How do you spell that?"

Oral spelled it. "I'm named for a bird," he said, keeping his place in the catalogue with one finger. "A yellow, singing bird that sang where my mother used to live."

Emmett looked at the cannonball boy, his black eyes and white hair. "You're not very yellow, Oral," he said. "Can you sing?"

The boy didn't smile and he closed his catalogue. "No," he said, "nor lay eggs, neither."

"Excuse me, Oral," Emmett said.

There was no more talk for a time. Finally Oral said, "You're not very big for a man."

"Big enough," said Emmett.

"You ain't bad-looking, though."

Emmett nodded his thanks.

"You got a girl?" Oral asked.

"No girl," Emmett said. "I'm off girls."

"Not me," said Oral. "I got two."

"You don't look very old to be having girls," Emmett told him.

"Old enough," said Oral and went back to his reading.

He roused to point out his home before they got there. It and its outbuildings were planted on a gentle rise of land, visible, as they approached, from every hilltop: a substantial brick house and a big weather-beaten, two-story barn. Three-story, it proved to be when they arrived, the hillside on the back having been scooped away to make room for stalls for the animals.

Oral's father, who was Oral expanded and coated with hoarfrost, heartily welcomed Emmett.

"I'm C. B. Lish," he said after Emmett had stated his own name and business, "and I'm pleased to make your acquaintance. The barn needs painting the worst way."

Emmett then delivered the rehearsed speech, speaking, as he thought right, of the quality of his paints: linseed base, lead content, color, time a coat would last; of his own work, skillful, experienced, painstaking. But C. B. Lish was reading.

"Candle Powder," he said wonderingly. "Now the way I always heard that was candle *power*."

"This is something different," Emmett explained, wishing the catalogue had never fallen into Lish hands. "This is a powder."

"Now, how," said C. B. Lish, "do you reckon they go about getting a Candle Powder? Grind 'em up?"

"I don't know," Emmett said. "I just paint the signs."

"Bible Bouquet Oil," he said reading on and sniffing as he read. "There's a concoction ought to be mighty sweet. You sell this, boy?"

"No, sir," Emmett said, "I don't. I'm a painter. I'd like to get the job painting your barn."

C. B. Lish was turning the pages. "Jinxers. Four inches tall."

"I don't sell that stuff," Emmett reminded him. "I paint."

C. B. Lish nodded, but didn't look up. "That's what you told me before. You walk on up to the house and talk to Emma and Ivy. They're the ones to decide."

Emmett never forgot the room he stepped into. After the summer dust and heat it was as if he had plunged into water, shadowed and cool. He closed his eyes once or twice as he would have done under water, to feel the coolness on his eyelids. The bricks, he supposed, were what made the room cool, the pulled blinds kept it dim.

The room was a kitchen because it had a stove in it: unlit, cool-looking, even, black and shiny like a stoat fresh from a shady wallow. But besides the kitchen furniture—the safe, the cabinet, the set table—there was much else in the room. There was a sofa, a small bird in a big wooden cage, a secretary whose space was about evenly divided between books and dishes, a diamond-shaped mirror with pegs for hats and coats at each corner. Beneath one of the pulled blinds, Emmett guessed, a prism was hanging, for onto the bleached floorboards fell shafts of multicolored lights.

And there was a girl in the room. Emmett saw her last of all. She stood in the darkest corner of the room, leaning against the sink, grating nutmeg on a pudding of some kind. Emmett could smell the vanilla, sweet and sharp, above the sweet muskiness of the nutmeg.

The girl looked up at Emmett, then grated away, not saying a word. Emmett prepared to speak, but could not for a minute. He knew what a beautiful girl should look like; he had often thought about it; he knew exactly what it took. So far as he could see, nothing was missing.

The girl had on a white dress. She curved in and she curved out. Her waist went in to a span as narrow and supple as a grapevine; else-where she had the fullness of the clusters. Her hair was like Oral's, but her eyes when she had looked up at Emmett were like the best milk-agates he had ever owned. O God, Emmett silently prayed, I thank thee for not letting me stay home and study mules.

O God, Emmett silently prayed, I thank thee for not letting me stay home and study mules.

158

She was a calm-looking girl, but seeing Emmett, she dropped the nutmeg, and the sound it made rolling along the bare floorboards brought him back to speech.

"Your nutmeg, Miss," said Emmett, getting it before it stopped rolling.

"Thank you," said the girl.

"I'm Emmett Maguire, house painter," Emmett told her.

"I'm pleased to meet you," said the girl. "I'm Miss Ivy Lish."

That night in the south upstairs chamber, a hot little room where a full-leafed chinaberry tree shut all the air from the single window, Emmett lay in a kind of trance. Sometimes he slept but more often he was awake, and every time he awakened he rejoiced as though he were Lazarus newly come to life. Sleeping, he dreamed of Ivy, but awake he thought of her. And, since he reckoned thinking to be one step nearer reality than dreaming, he hated to lose time in anything as secondhand as sleep.

He would awaken, wonder for a minute where he was, hear the leaves of the chinaberry tree moving outside his window with a watery ripple, say, "Ivy, Ivy." Inside himself he would feel a happiness so great it made him a little sick: a feeling like that he had tobogganing each winter on Sugar Slide, when at the final curve he always thought, I'll die this is so wonderful—joy and pain being at that point so delicately balanced.

Once he got out of his bed and laid the palms of both hands first against the west wall of his room, then against the east, telling himself as he did so, one inch of wood may be all that separates us. But all he heard as he stood, hands pressed to either wall, was a serene snoring: too delicate for Oral, probably C. B. Lish himself.

He had been in love before but always unlucky, and never able to do much but suffer. Once with a girl who was engaged, who had bent down and kissed him twice on the eyelids, but would have no more to do with him; once with a girl whose father had promised to shoot any man or boy who came on the place, and Emmett, after hearing the first load of buckshot whistle past his legs, had never again been able to feel the same about her; the last time had been with a girl in Mercer, but before he had a horse of his own, and in the weeks when he had not been able to see her, she had met and married a coffee salesman.

But now he was lucky: in love and beneath the same roof with the girl he loved. And going to be beneath the same roof with her for two more weeks at the least. For the barn painting, if he did a good job, would take that long; and he intended doing not only a good job, but a job so wonderful people for miles around would marvel at it. He intended to paint the Lish barn as if it were a miniature, with every brush stroke being set on ivory.

The last time he awakened the summer night had ended. The air in the room had cooled and outside in the chinaberry tree the awakening birds were whetting their bills and stretching their throats.

I could paint her, Emmett thought. I see just how to do it, where she should stand, how turn her head. I would paint her in her white dress, full length, a shadow at the base of her throat. In his hand he already felt the brush and the strokes it would make so that Ivy would stand curving in, curving out, alive upon cardboard. Alive with a reality beyond life because to her store of realness he would add all of his own.

There was nothing in the next week he did not do well. He was so filled with power and sureness he walked about his scaffolding as if gravity were a force from which he was exempt. He laid the brush against the barn each day in strokes so solid that the barn rose up clear and bright again, rebuilt, it almost seemed, as well as repainted.

At night, untired after the day's work, he washed first in turpentine and then in water, and talked with the family.

Privately, he said to C. B. Lish, "I'll paint the toolshed free if I can borrow your buggy, Sunday."

"What you want of the buggy?" Mr. Lish asked.

"I want to take Ivy to church."

Mr. Lish whistled. "So that's the way the wind blows."

"Yes, sir," said Emmett, "it is."

"Ivy's no churchgoer," Mr. Lish told him.

Emmett was taken aback. He had supposed all nice girls were churchgoers. He had no idea where else he could take a girl on Sunday, or what other entertainment she could want. Though he would never have denied that for himself coming and going would be the best part of it. Still this was Bucklin County, not home, and he hated a man who was set in his ways.

"Wherever she wants to go, I'll take her."

"The novelty of it," her father admitted, "might appeal to her."

Ivy said yes when he asked her, as if novelty had nothing to do with it.

Upon himself, upon Old Clay and the buggy, Emmett had done an amount of polishing just short of abrasion. A stroke or two more and varnish and hide, human and horse alike, would have given away. Tender and glittering, they drove churchward.

There was nothing Emmett could think of to say which did not seem too personal for words. His mind was filled with Ivy: her sweet, flowery smell, which it was probably wrong even to notice, let alone mention; the blue vein in her forehead; the way a fold of her full skirt lay across his shinbone, where its lightness weighed upon him like a burning glass.

They drove through heat waves rippling like lake water. Already the leaves hung downward, giving the sun only their sharp edges to taste. Old Clay was discolored by sweat and on the fence rails the birds rested with lifted wings.

"Ivy," said Emmett, "will you let me paint your picture?"

"Can you paint people, too?" Ivy asked. "Besides barns, I mean?"

"Yes," said Emmett, with sudden knowledge, "I can," and he used the word he had forbidden his father. "I'm an artist."

"Perhaps you would make me look funny," said Ivy.

"Funny," repeated Emmett. "What do you mean, funny?"

"Queer," Ivy told him. "Not pretty. Maybe you don't know how to paint well enough. Maybe you would make my eyes look funny. Eyes are very hard to paint."

"I know how to paint eyes," Emmett said. "I know how to paint all of a person. I would make you look the way you are, Ivy."

"How am I, Emmett?" asked Ivy.

"Beautiful," said Emmett, trembling with frankness.

From there on, the drive to church went by in a flash, the church time, too, though Ivy was unable to attend the services with Emmett. In the churchyard Arod Johnson had awaited her. His mother was sick, pining to see Ivy, and with Emmett's permission he would drive Ivy to his place, have her back by the time church was over. He was considerably later than that, and Emmett was sorry for Ivy cooped up with a sick old woman while he sat in the shaded churchyard. Still, he had been so deep in thought about his painting of her that he had not had time for much pity.

"Let's go home the long way," Ivy said when she got back.

They went home the long way through the hot afternoon.

"Tell me about my picture," Ivy said.

"I will paint you," Emmett said, "in the parlor bay window. I will push the lace curtains back so that on each side of the picture will be just their ripple. You will stand in your white dress before the clear glass and behind you will be the mock orange."

"How will I look?" asked Ivy.

"You will look," Emmett said slowly, seeing her like a white column budding for flowers—"fine."

"We came home the long way," Ivy told Oral, who was in the barnyard when they drove in. "We came home the long way and had to go slow beause of the heat." She gave Emmett both her hands when he helped her from the buggy and walked at once to the house.

Oral helped with the unhitching.

"I reckon you seen Old Arod," he said.

"Arod Johnson?" asked Emmett.

"You know any other Arods?"

"No," said Emmett, "I don't. His mother was sick."

"She seems to be a mighty weak old lady," Oral told him, he himself leading Clay to the barn.

In the second week Emmett began work on the barn each morning at sunup. In that way he made time for his painting of Ivy. He had never supposed hand and brush could work so well together. It was as if the lines of Ivy's body flowed downward of themselves, through his arm and hand, and onto the cardboard; it was as if her colors stained his fingers and he had only to touch his brush for them to be left where and as they should be.

"What do you think of while you paint?" Ivy asked.

He thought of very little. Then he was lost in the work; in the brush strokes, in the leaf-shaped shadows on the white dress, on the way Ivy's roundness and solidity were transferred by means of his skill so that in thin paint and upon a flat surface, still she was round and solid.

Afterward, when he was not painting, he thought: in later days the picture will hang in a special place in the house and I will say to visitors, that is my beautiful wife, Ivy Lish Maguire; and to the children I'll say, that is the first picture I ever painted of your mother. And I will never part with it, no matter what I should be offered for it.

"I would like my eyelashes made longer," said Ivy.

"No," said Emmett, "that would be wrong."

"Wrong?" said Ivy. "They are longer."

"But not looking at you," Emmett told her, "this way against the light."

162

If someone had told him, you have never said the word love, he would have been surprised. Everything he did said the word, every look, every tone, every gesture. He himself heard no other sound.

"Is it finished?" asked Ivy.

"One more day," said Emmett. "Do you like it?"

"The eyelashes should be longer," said Ivy, but Emmett could tell by the way she stood looking at the picture, turning her head, smiling, that she liked it.

That night he worked until late on the barn and went early to bed. He lay in his upstairs bedroom listening to the chirr of summer insects, and thought, tomorrow night the picture will be finished and I will put, in one corner of the picture, my name, in the other, hers.

He was still awake when Oral came in, noisy in his unaccustomed shoes, and sat on the edge of his bed. Oral moved his feet back and forth across the floorboards, the bed squeaked as his weight shifted, a bird sang a note or two as if, awakening suddenly, it had mistaken the moonlight for dawn.

"Well, Oral?" asked Emmett.

"I got me a date with one of my girls," said Oral as if answering the question.

"Which one?" Emmett asked sleepily, not caring, thinking, he's got no one else to talk to about his girls.

"The best one," Oral said.

Emmett yawned silently, shut his eyes. The moonlight here in the corner, he thought, isn't strong enough for him to tell whether my eyes are open or shut.

"Two's too many," Oral said, "if you've got one good girl."

"One good girl's enough," Emmett agreed, smiling at Oral's wisdom. "How's the other one taking it?" he asked.

"She's down in the mouth," Oral admitted, "but she'll get over it."

"Sure," Emmett echoed out of his drowsiness, "they all get over it."

"Emmett," Oral asked, "who's that picture belong to, you or Ivy?"

"Ivy," Emmett said, wanting to say her name, though he had thought of the picture as theirs together.

"That's all right, then," Oral said, getting off the bed.

"It's Ivy's and mine together," Emmett amended.

"She's given away your half too, then," Oral told him. "Both halves together to Arod Johnson."

Emmett sat up in bed. Oral was standing where the moonlight from the window fell across his broad and sorrowful face.

"I could've told you," he said, "but there wasn't ever a time when you'd hear to it.

"It's gone," he assured him, as Emmett got out of bed. "Wrapped in butcher paper and given away."

Emmett sat down again.

"My girl's waiting for me," Oral said. At the door he turned back. "Ivy's a born two-timer. You ain't the first."

For a long time after Oral left, Emmett sat on the edge of his bed. He felt numbed, beyond feeling anything, but when he stood up his hands and face were wet, and he saw that without knowing it he had been crying. The thing to do, he decided, is to get out, pack and leave. Get gone before I have to look on any of their faces again.

Outside, his carpetbag in his hand, he stood for a time in the barnyard. He could see that it was still early, a moonlit summer night, cooling off now so that the river mists were flowing up into the draws. He could hear the soft, slow movements of the animals in their stalls and once in a while, as the air freshened, a slight fluttering of leaves.

Old Clay came quietly to the fence, hung his head across the top rail, and, with eyes glassy in the moonlight, looked at Emmett.

"Let's get out of here," Emmett said.

But when he saw the ladder and scaffolding still against the barn, and the unpainted section around the haymow door, he determined, stubbornly, to finish the job. "I'll not go and leave a stroke undone," he told Old Clay, as if his horse had argued with him about it.

Once he was on the scaffolding, brush in hand, another idea came to him: she took my picture and gave it away. I'll leave another here that can't be given away, and I'll paint her this time as she really is, so no eye can miss it.

He went down the ladder and brought up his other paints, and while he was doing this he was filled with hate and scorn, thinking, I'll put her on the barn so that everyone can see what a slut looks like. But he could not do it.

He did not know which way it was: whether he was unable to paint and hate at the same time, or whether actually he would never be able to hate Ivy, no matter what she might do. Whichever way it was— whether the brush strokes took away his hate, or he was without real hate to begin with—he was painting a picture not much different from his first. And better, too, he knew; though whether on that surface, with the paints he had, it would show as much, he couldn't tell. There would be no rippling lace curtains in this picture because it would be Ivy herself, unobscured by any of his imaginings. He remembered what he had thought: a tower of white. And budding; and

remembering, spat with disgust over the edge of the scaffolding.

From below someone whispered, "Look out for me," and there in the moonlight, gazing upward, was Oral.

"What you doing out this time of night?" Emmett asked.

"Getting home," Oral whispered, so that Emmett, answering, whispered too—though the house was far enough away to keep anyone from hearing. "You better get on to bed. You'll catch a strapping, staying out all night this way."

"Strapping," Oral scoffed. "I'm not sleeping in the house anyway," he said. "I'm sleeping in the haymow." He stood, stocky legs far apart, head thrown back so that his white hair shone in the moonlight like dandelion fuzz.

"What you painting her again for?" he whispered scornfully. "Whyn't you paint something nice for a change? Whyn't you paint something pretty up there? A big sunflower or a rooster?"

"Be quiet, can't you?" Emmett said. "This makes me feel better."

Oral went inside the barn and Emmett could hear him mounting the ladder into the haymow, then rustling about as he hollowed himself a place to sleep.

Long after Emmett had supposed him to be sleeping, he heard Oral's voice very near at hand as if he were speaking with his mouth close to a knothole or crack.

"Emmett?"

"What you want now, Oral?"

"Whyn't you get some of them powders, Emmett?"

"Powders?" asked Emmett.

"The ones from the catalogue. They work good, Emmett." Oral's voice was filled with kindness.

"I didn't know they'd come."

"Oh, sure, they came. They're strong and good. I wish you'd try some, Emmett."

"No," Emmett told him, "they wouldn't work for me. No powder'll do me any good. I've just got to learn."

"Don't waste any more time on her," urged Oral. "Paint something nice. Paint a picture of a field of punkins."

"When I finish this," said Emmett, "I will."

The moon was still bright when he finished, but the stars had begun to dim and the sky's darkness was fading. He hitched and loaded his stuff into the buckboard, but before he drove away he stood looking up at his work.

"I can paint," he said looking at his picture of Ivy, forgetting Ivy herself.

166

He had driven down the slope from the house and up the first little rise when he heard a clear but controlled halooing behind him. Turning about, he saw that Oral had opened the door of the haymow so that his picture of Ivy was cut in two: a head, then where the upper part of her body should have been, the empty space of the open door, and below that the swelling white skirts.

"Emmett," Oral halooed quietly.

Emmett waved to show that he heard.

"You forgot your catalogue, Emmett."

"Keep it," Emmett called back. "You keep it, Oral. I can get another."

Their gentle voices carried on the quiet morning air. The last stars had faded and the river smell was fresh and sharp.

"Good-bye, Emmett," Oral called as Emmett, waving, drove on.

For as long as Emmett could be seen, Oral stood in the open doorway, not waving, himself, but following the buckboard with his eyes until finally it topped a distant rise and dropped from sight.

THE BAREFOOT BOY

Blessings on thee, little man,
Barefoot boy, with cheek of tan!
With thy turned-up pantaloons,
And thy merry whistled tunes;
With thy red lip, redder still
Kissed by strawberries on the hill;
With the sunshine on thy face,
Through thy torn brim's jaunty grace;
From my heart I give thee joy,—
I was once a barefoot boy!

— *John Greenleaf Whittier*

The Story of the Old Ram

by Mark Twain

Every now and then, in these days, the boys used to tell me I ought to get one Jim Blaine to tell me the stirring story of his grandfather's old ram—but they always added that I must not mention the matter unless Jim was drunk at the time—just comfortably and sociably drunk. They kept this up until my curiosity was on the rack to hear the story. I got to haunting Blaine; but it was of no use, the boys always found fault with his condition; he was often moderately but never satisfactorily drunk. I never watched a man's condition with such absorbing interest, such anxious solicitude; I never so pined to see a man uncompromisingly drunk before. At last, one evening I hurried to his cabin, for I learned that this time his situation was such that even the most fastidious could find no fault with it—he was tranquilly, serenely, symmetrically drunk—not a hiccup to mar his voice, not a cloud upon his brain thick enough to obscure his memory. As I entered, he was sitting upon an empty powder keg, with a clay pipe in one hand and the other raised to command silence. His face was round, red, and very serious; his throat was bare and his hair tumbled; in general appearance and costume he was a stalwart miner of the period. On the pine table stood a candle, and its dim light revealed "the boys" sitting here and there on bunks, candle boxes, powder kegs, etc. They said:

"Sh—! Don't speak—he's going to commence."

I found a seat at once, and Blaine said:

"I don't reckon them times will ever come again. There never was a more bullier old ram than what he was. Grandfather fetched him from Illinois—got him of a man by the name of Yates—Bill Yates—maybe you might have heard of him; his father was a deacon—Baptist—and he was a rustler, too; a man had to get up ruther early to get the start of old Thankful Yates; it was him that put the Greens up to j'ining teams with my grandfather when he moved west. Seth Green was prob'ly the pick of the flock; he married a Wilkerson—Sarah Wilkerson—

good cretur, she was—one of the likeliest heifers that was ever raised in old Stoddard, everybody said that knowed her. She could heft a bar'l of flour as easy as I can flirt a flapjack. And spin? Don't mention it! Independent? Humph! When Sile Hawkins come a-browsing around her, she let him know that for all his tin he couldn't trot in harness alongside of *her*. You see, Sile Hawkins was—no, it warn't Sile Hawkins, after all—it was a galoot by the name of Filkins—I disremember his first name; but he *was* a stump—come into pra'r-meeting drunk, one night, hooraying for Nixon, becuz he thought it was a primary; and old Deacon Ferguson up and scooted him through the window and he lit on old Miss Jefferson's head, poor old filly. She was a good soul—had a glass eye and used to lend it to old Miss Wagner, that hadn't any, to receive company in; it warn't big enough, and when Miss Wagner warn't noticing, it would get twisted around in the socket, and look up, maybe, or out to one side, and every which way, while t'other one was looking as straight ahead as a spyglass. Grown people didn't mind it, but it 'most always made the children cry, it was so sort of scary. She tried packing it in raw cotton, but it wouldn't work, somehow—the cotton would get loose and stick out and look so kind of awful that the children couldn't stand it no way. She was always dropping it out, and turning up her old deadlight on the company empty, and making them oncomfortable, becuz *she* never could tell when it hopped out, being blind on that side, you see. So somebody would have to hunch her and say, 'Your game eye has fetched loose, Miss Wagner, dear'—and then all of them would have to sit and wait till she jammed it in again—wrong side before, as a general thing, and green as a bird's egg, being a bashful cretur and easy sot back before company. But being wrong side before warn't much difference, anyway, becuz her own eye was sky-blue and the glass one was yaller on the front side, so whichever way she turned it it didn't match nohow. Old Miss Wagner was considerable on the borrow, she was. When she had a quilting, or Dorcas S'iety at her house she gen'ally borrowed Miss Higgins's wooden leg to stump around on; it was considerable shorter than her other pin, but much *she* minded that. She said she couldn't abide crutches when she had company, becuz they were so slow; said when she had company and things had to be done, she wanted to get up and hump herself. She was as bald as a jug, and so she used to borrow Miss Jacops's wig—Miss Jacops was the coffin-peddler's wife—a ratty old buzzard, he was, that used to go roosting around where people was sick, waiting for 'em; and there that old rip would sit all day, in the shade, on a coffin that he judged would fit the can'idate; and if it was a slow customer

She was a good soul—had a glass eye and used to lend it to old Miss Wagner, that hadn't any.

170

and kind of uncertain, he'd fetch his rations and a blanket along and sleep in the coffin nights. He was anchored out that way, in frosty weather, for about three weeks, once, before old Robbins's place, waiting for him; and after that, for as much as two years, Jacops was not on speaking terms with the old man, on account of his disapp'inting him. He got one of his feet froze, and lost money, too, becuz old Robbins took a favorable turn and got well. The next time Robbins got sick, Jacops tried to make up with him, and varnished up the same old coffin and fetched it along; but old Robbins was too many for him; he had him in, and 'peared to be powerful weak; he bought the coffin for ten dollars and Jacops was to pay it back and twenty-five more besides if Robbins didn't like the coffin after he'd tried it. And then Robbins died, and at the funeral he bursted off the lid and riz up in his shroud and told the parson to let up on the performances, becuz he could *not* stand such a coffin as that. You see he had been in a trance once before, when he was young, and he took the chances on another, cal'lating that if he made the trip it was money in his pocket, and if he missed fire he couldn't lose a cent. And, by George, he sued Jacops for the rhino and got judgment; and he set up the coffin in his back parlor and said he 'lowed to take his time, now. It was always an aggravation to Jacops, the way that miserable old thing acted. He moved back to Indiany pretty soon—went to Wellsville—Wellsville was the place the Hogadorns was from. Mighty fine family. Old Maryland stock. Old Squire Hogadorn could carry around more mixed licker, and cuss better than 'most any man I ever see. His second wife was the Widder Billings—she that was Becky Martin; her dam was Deacon Dunlap's first wife. Her oldest child, Maria, married a missionary and died in grace—et up by the savages. They et *him*, too, poor feller—biled him. It warn't the custom, so they say, but they explained to friends of his'n that went down there to bring away his things, that they'd tried missionaries every other way and never could get any good out of 'em—and so it annoyed all his relations to find out that that man's life was fooled away just out of a dern'd experiment, so to speak. But mind you, there ain't anything ever reely lost; everything that people can't understand and don't see the reason of does good if you only hold on and give it a fair shake; Prov'dence don't fire no blank ca'tridges, boys. That there missionary's substance, unbeknowns to himself, actu'ly converted every last one of them heathens that took a chance at the barbecue. Nothing ever fetched them but that. Don't tell *me* it was an accident that he was biled. There ain't no such a thing as an accident. When my Uncle Lem was leaning up agin a scaffolding once, sick, or drunk, or suthin, an Irishman with a hod full of bricks fell on him out of the third story and broke the old man's back in two places. People said it was an accident. Much accident there was about that. He didn't know what he was there for, but he was there for a good object. If he hadn't been there the Irishman would have been killed. Nobody can ever make me believe anything different from that. Uncle Lem's dog was there. Why didn't the Irishman fall on the dog? Becuz the dog would 'a' seen him a-coming and stood from under. That's the reason the dog warn't app'inted. A dog can't be depended on to carry out a special prov'dence. Mark my words, it was a put-up thing. Accidents don't happen, boys. Uncle Lem's dog—I wish you could 'a' seen that dog. He was a reg'lar shepherd—or ruther he was part bull and part shepherd—splendid animal; belonged to Parson Hagar before Uncle Lem got him. Parson Hagar belonged to the Western Reserve Hagars; prime family; his mother was a Watson; one of his sisters married a Wheeler; they settled in Morgan County, and he got nipped by the machinery in a carpet factory and went through in less than a quarter of a minute; his widder bought the piece of carpet that had his remains wove in, and people come a hundred mile to 'tend the funeral. There was fourteen yards in the piece. She wouldn't let them roll him up, but planted him just so—full length. The church was middling small where they preached the funeral, and they had to let one end of the coffin stick out of the window. They didn't bury him—they planted one end, and let him stand up, same as a monument. And they nailed a sign on it and put—put on—put on it—sacred to—the m-e-m-o-r-y— of fourteen y-a-r-d-s—of three-ply—car-pet—containing all that was—m-o-r-t-a-l—of—of—W-i-l-l-i-a-m—W-h-e—"

Jim Blaine had been growing gradually drowsy and drowsier—his head nodded, once, twice, three times—dropped peacefully upon his breast, and he fell tranquilly asleep. The tears were running down the boys' cheeks—they were suffocating with suppressed laughter— and had been from the start, though I had never noticed it. I perceived that I was "sold." I learned then that Jim Blaine's peculiarity was that whenever he reached a certain stage of intoxication, no human power could keep him from setting out, with impressive unction, to tell about a wonderful adventure which he had once had with his grand-father's old ram—and the mention of the ram in the first sentence was as far as any man had ever heard him get, concerning it. He always maundered off, interminably, from one thing to another, till his whiskey got the best of him, and he fell asleep. What the thing was that happened to him and his grandfather's old ram is a dark mystery to this day, for nobody has ever yet found out.

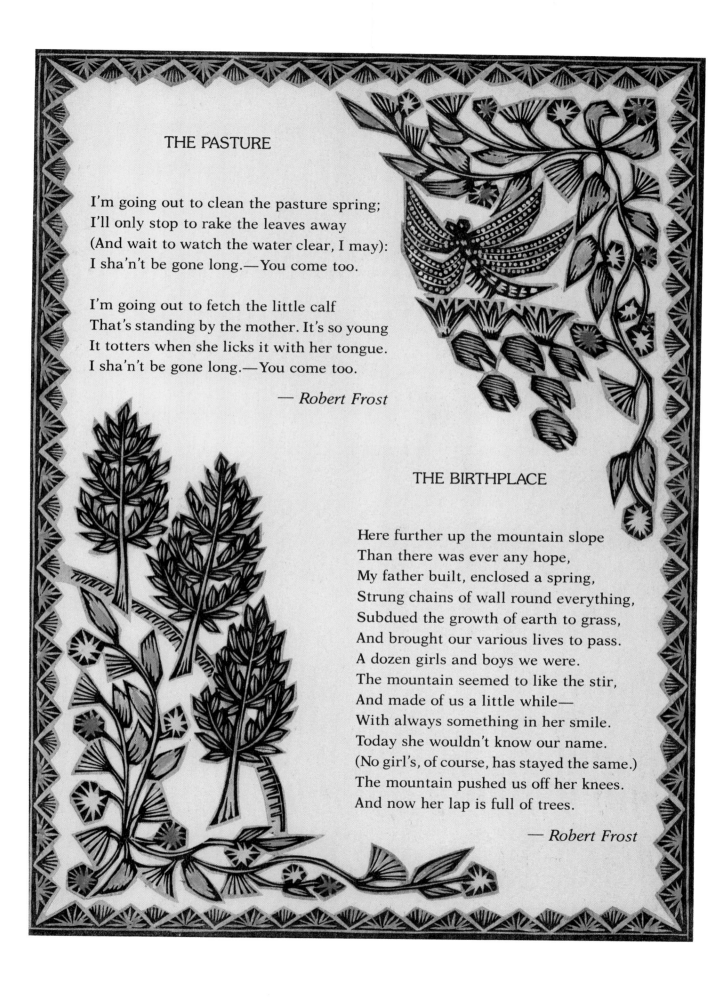

THE PASTURE

I'm going out to clean the pasture spring;
I'll only stop to rake the leaves away
(And wait to watch the water clear, I may):
I sha'n't be gone long.—You come too.

I'm going out to fetch the little calf
That's standing by the mother. It's so young
It totters when she licks it with her tongue.
I sha'n't be gone long.—You come too.

— Robert Frost

THE BIRTHPLACE

Here further up the mountain slope
Than there was ever any hope,
My father built, enclosed a spring,
Strung chains of wall round everything,
Subdued the growth of earth to grass,
And brought our various lives to pass.
A dozen girls and boys we were.
The mountain seemed to like the stir,
And made of us a little while—
With always something in her smile.
Today she wouldn't know our name.
(No girl's, of course, has stayed the same.)
The mountain pushed us off her knees.
And now her lap is full of trees.

— Robert Frost

Lily Daw and the Three Ladies

by Eudora Welty

Mrs. Watts and Mrs. Carson were both in the post office in Victory when the letter came from the Ellisville Institute for the Feeble-Minded of Mississippi. Aimee Slocum, with her hand still full of mail, ran out in front and handed it straight to Mrs. Watts, and they all three read it together. Mrs. Watts held it taut between her pink hands, and Mrs. Carson underscored each line slowly with her thimbled finger. Everybody else in the post office wondered what was up now.

"What will Lily say," beamed Mrs. Carson at last, "when we tell her we're sending her to Ellisville!"

"She'll be tickled to death," said Mrs. Watts, and added in a guttural voice to a deaf lady, "Lily Daw's getting in at Ellisville!"

"Don't you all dare go off and tell Lily without me!" called Aimee Slocum, trotting back to finish putting up the mail.

"Do you suppose they'll look after her down there?" Mrs. Carson began to carry on a conversation with a group of Baptist ladies waiting in the post office. She was the Baptist preacher's wife.

"I've always heard it was lovely down there, but crowded," said one.

"Lily lets people walk over her so," said another.

"Last night at the tent show—" said another, and then popped her hand over her mouth.

"Don't mind me, I know there are such things in the world," said Mrs. Carson, looking down and fingering the tape measure which hung over her bosom.

"Oh, Mrs. Carson. Well, anyway, last night at the tent show, why, the man was just before making Lily buy a ticket to get in."

"A ticket!"

"Till my husband went up and explained she wasn't bright, and so did everybody else."

The ladies all clucked their tongues.

"Oh, it was a very nice show," said the lady who had gone. "And Lily acted so nice. She was a perfect lady—just set in her seat and stared."

"Oh, she can be a lady—she can be," said Mrs. Carson, shaking her

175

head and turning her eyes up. "That's just what breaks your heart."

"Yes'm, she kept her eyes on—what's that thing makes all the commotion?—the xylophone," said the lady. "Didn't turn her head to the right or to the left the whole time. Set in front of me."

"The point is, what did she do after the show?" asked Mrs. Watts practically. "Lily has gotten so she is very mature for her age."

"Oh, Etta!" protested Mrs. Carson, looking at her wildly for a moment.

"And that's how come we are sending her to Ellisville," finished Mrs. Watts.

"I'm ready, you all," said Aimee Slocum, running out with white powder all over her face. "Mail's up. I don't know how good it's up."

"Well, of course, I do hope it's for the best," said several of the other ladies. They did not go at once to take their mail out of their boxes; they felt a little left out.

The three women stood at the foot of the water tank.

"To find Lily is a different thing," said Aimee Slocum.

"Where in the wide world do you suppose she'd be?" It was Mrs. Watts who was carrying the letter.

"I don't see a sign of her either on this side of the street or on the other side," Mrs. Carson declared as they walked along.

Ed Newton was stringing Redbird school tablets on the wire across the store.

"If you're after Lily, she come in here while ago and tole me she was fixin' to git married," he said.

"Ed Newton!" cried the ladies all together, clutching one another. Mrs. Watts began to fan herself at once with the letter from Ellisville. She wore widow's black, and the least thing made her hot.

"Why she is not. She's going to Ellisville, Ed," said Mrs. Carson gently. "Mrs. Watts and I and Aimee Slocum are paying her way out of our own pockets. Besides, the boys of Victory are on their honor. Lily's not going to get married, that's just an idea she's got in her head."

"More power to you, ladies," said Ed Newton, spanking himself with a tablet.

When they came to the bridge over the railroad tracks, there was Estelle Mabers, sitting on a rail. She was slowly drinking an orange Ne-Hi.

"Have you seen Lily?" they asked her.

"I'm supposed to be out here watching for her now," said the Mabers girl, as though she weren't there yet. "But for Jewel—Jewel says Lily come in the store while ago and picked out a two-ninety-eight hat and wore it off. Jewel wants to swap her something else for it."

176

"Oh, Estelle, Lily says she's going to get married!" cried Aimee Slocum.

"Well, I declare," said Estelle; she never understood anything.

Loralee Adkins came riding by in her Willys-Knight, tooting the horn to find out what they were talking about.

Aimee threw up her hands and ran out into the street. "Loralee, Loralee, you got to ride us up to Lily Daw's. She's up yonder fixing to get married!"

"Hop in, my land!"

"Well, that just goes to show you right now," said Mrs. Watts, groaning as she was helped into the backseat. "What we've got to do is persuade Lily it will be nicer to go to Ellisville."

"Just to think!"

While they rode around the corner Mrs. Carson was going on in her sad voice, sad as the soft noises in the hen house at twilight. "We buried Lily's poor defenseless mother. We gave Lily all her food and kindling and every stitch she had on. Sent her to Sunday school to learn the Lord's teachings, had her baptized a Baptist. And when her old father commenced beating her and tried to cut her head off with the butcher knife, why, we went and took her away from him and gave her a place to stay."

The paintless frame house with all the weather vanes was three stories high in places and had yellow-and-violet stained-glass windows in front and gingerbread around the porch. It leaned steeply to one side, toward the railroad, and the front steps were gone. The car full of ladies drew up under the cedar tree.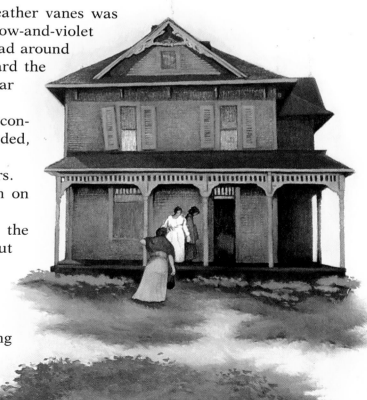

"Now Lily's almost grown up," Mrs. Carson continued. "In fact, she's grown," she concluded, getting out.

"Talking about getting married," said Mrs. Watts disgustedly. "Thanks, Loralee, you run on home."

They climbed over the dusty zinnias onto the porch and walked through the open door without knocking.

"There certainly is always a funny smell in this house. I say it every time I come," said Aimee Slocum.

Lily was there, in the dark of the hall, kneeling on the floor by a small open trunk.

When she saw them she put a zinnia in her mouth, and held still.

"Hello, Lily," said Mrs. Carson reproachfully.

"Hello," said Lily. In a minute she gave a suck on the zinnia stem that sounded exactly like a jaybird. There she sat, wearing a petticoat for a dress, one of the things Mrs. Carson kept after her about. Her milky-yellow hair streamed freely down from under a new hat. You could see the wavy scar on her throat if you knew it was there.

Mrs. Carson and Mrs. Watts, the two fattest, sat in the double rocker. Aimee Slocum sat on the wire chair donated from the drugstore that burned.

"Well, what are you doing, Lily?" asked Mrs. Watts, who led the rocking.

Lily smiled.

The trunk was old and lined with yellow-and-brown paper, with an asterisk pattern showing in darker circles and rings. Mutely the ladies indicated to each other that they did not know where in the world it had come from. It was empty except for two bars of soap and a green washcloth, which Lily was now trying to arrange in the bottom.

"Go on and tell us what you're doing, Lily," said Aimee Slocum.

"Packing, silly," said Lily.

"Where are you going?"

"Going to get married, and I bet you wish you was me now," said Lily. But shyness overcame her suddenly, and she popped the zinnia back into her mouth.

"Talk to me, dear," said Mrs. Carson. "Tell old Mrs. Carson why you want to get married."

"No," said Lily, after a moment's hesitation.

"Well, we've thought of something that will be so much nicer," said Mrs. Carson. "Why don't you go to Ellisville!"

"Won't that be lovely?" said Mrs. Watts. "Goodness, yes."

"It's a lovely place," said Aimee Slocum uncertainly.

"You've got bumps on your face," said Lily.

"Aimee, dear, you stay out of this, if you don't mind," said Mrs. Carson anxiously. "I don't know what it is comes over Lily when you come around her."

Lily stared at Aimee Slocum meditatively.

"There! Wouldn't you like to go to Ellisville now?" asked Mrs. Carson.

"No'm," said Lily.

"Why not?" All the ladies leaned down toward her in impressive astonishment.

" 'Cause I'm goin' to get married," said Lily.

"Well, and who are you going to marry, dear?" asked Mrs. Watts.

She knew how to pin people down and make them deny what they'd already said.

Lily bit her lip and began to smile. She reached into the trunk and held up both cakes of soap and wagged them.

"Tell us," challenged Mrs. Watts. "Who you're going to marry, now."

"A man last night."

There was a gasp from each lady. The possible reality of a lover descended suddenly like a summer hail over their heads. Mrs. Watts stood up and balanced herself.

"One of those show fellows! A musician!" she cried.

Lily looked up in admiration.

"Did he—did he do anything to you?" In the long run, it was still only Mrs. Watts who could take charge.

"Oh, yes'm," said Lily. She patted the cakes of soap fastidiously with the tips of her small fingers and tucked them in with the washcloth.

"What?" demanded Aimee Slocum, rising up and tottering before her scream. "What?" she called out in the hall.

"Don't ask her what," said Mrs. Carson, coming up behind. "Tell me, Lily—just yes or no—are you the same as you were?"

"He had a red coat," said Lily graciously. "He took little sticks and went *ping-pong! ding-dong!*"

"Oh, I think I'm going to faint," said Aimee Slocum, but they said, "No, you're not."

"The xylophone!" cried Mrs. Watts. "The xylophone player! Why, the coward, he ought to be run out of town on a rail!"

"Out of town? He is out of town, by now," cried Aimee. "Can't you read?—the sign in the café—Victory on the ninth, Como on the tenth? He's in Como. Como!"

"All right! We'll bring him back!" cried Mrs. Watts. "He can't get away from me!"

"Hush," said Mrs. Carson. "I don't think it's any use following that line of reasoning at all. It's better in the long run for him to be gone out of our lives for good and all. That kind of a man. He was after Lily's body alone and he wouldn't ever in this world make the poor little thing happy, even if we went out and forced him to marry her like he ought—at the point of a gun."

"Still—" began Aimee, her eyes widening.

"Shut up," said Mrs. Watts. "Mrs. Carson, you're right, I expect."

"This is my hope chest—see?" said Lily politely in the pause that followed. "You haven't even looked at it. I've already got soap and a washrag. And I have my hat—on. What are you all going to give me?"

"Lily," said Mrs. Watts, starting over, "we'll give you lots of gor-

179

geous things if you'll only go to Ellisville instead of getting married."

"What will you give me?" asked Lily.

"I'll give you a pair of hemstitched pillowcases," said Mrs. Carson.

"I'll give you a big caramel cake," said Mrs. Watts.

"I'll give you a souvenir from Jackson—a little toy bank," said Aimee Slocum. "Now will you go?"

"No," said Lily.

"I'll give you a pretty little Bible with your name on it in real gold," said Mrs. Carson.

"What if I was to give you a pink crêpe de Chine brassière with adjustable shoulder straps?" asked Mrs. Watts grimly.

"Oh, Etta."

"Well, she needs it," said Mrs. Watts. "What would they think if she ran all over Ellisville in a petticoat looking like a Fiji?"

"I wish *I* could go to Ellisville," said Aimee Slocum luringly.

"What will they have for me down there?" asked Lily softly.

"Oh! lots of things. You'll have baskets to weave, I expect. . . ." Mrs. Carson looked vaguely at the others.

"Oh, yes indeed, they will let you make all sorts of baskets," said Mrs. Watts; then her voice too trailed off.

"No'm, I'd rather get married," said Lily.

"Lily Daw! Now that's just plain stubbornness!" cried Mrs. Watts. "You almost said you'd go and then you took it back!"

"We've all asked God, Lily," said Mrs. Carson finally, "and God seemed to tell us—Mr. Carson, too—that the place where you ought to be, so as to be happy, was Ellisville."

Lily looked reverent, but still stubborn.

"We've really just got to get her there—now!" screamed Aimee Slocum all at once. "Suppose—! She can't stay here!"

"Oh, no, no, no," said Mrs. Carson hurriedly. "We mustn't think that."

They sat sunken in despair.

"Could I take my hope chest—to go to Ellisville?" asked Lily shyly, looking at them sidewise.

"Why, yes," said Mrs. Carson blankly.

Silently they rose once more to their feet.

"Oh, if I could just take my hope chest!"

"All the time it was just her hope chest," Aimee whispered.

Mrs. Watts struck her palms together. "It's settled!"

"Praise the fathers," murmured Mrs. Carson.

Lily looked up at them, and her eyes gleamed. She cocked her head and spoke out in a proud imitation of someone—someone utterly unknown.

"O.K.—Toots!"

The ladies had been nodding and smiling and backing away toward the door.

"I think I'd better stay," said Mrs. Carson, stopping in her tracks. "Where—where could she have learned that terrible expression?"

"Pack up," said Mrs. Watts. "Lily Daw is leaving for Ellisville on Number One."

In the station the train was puffing. Nearly everyone in Victory was hanging around waiting for it to leave. The Victory Civic Band had assembled without any orders and was scattered through the crowd. Ed Newton gave false signals to start on his bass horn. A crateful of baby chickens got loose on the platform. Everybody wanted to see Lily all dressed up, but Mrs. Carson and Mrs. Watts had sneaked her into the train from the other side of the tracks.

The two ladies were going to travel as far as Jackson to help Lily change trains and be sure she went in the right direction.

Lily sat between them on the plush seat with her hair combed and pinned up into a knot under a small blue hat which was Jewel's exchange for the pretty one. She wore a traveling dress made out of part of Mrs. Watts's last summer's mourning. Pink straps glowed through. She had a purse and a Bible and a warm cake in a box, all in her lap.

Aimee Slocum had been getting the outgoing mail stamped and bundled. She stood in the aisle of the coach now, tears shaking from her eyes. "Good-bye, Lily," she said. She was the one who felt things.

"Good-bye, silly," said Lily.

"Oh, dear, I hope they get our telegram to meet her in Ellisville!" Aimee cried sorrowfully, as she thought how far away it was. "And it was so hard to get it all in ten words, too."

"Get off, Aimee, before the train starts and you break your neck," said Mrs. Watts, all settled and waving her dressy fan gaily. "I declare, it's so hot, as soon as we get a few miles out of town I'm going to slip my corset down."

"Oh, Lily, don't cry down there. Just be good, and do what they tell you—it's all because they love you." Aimee drew her mouth down. She was backing away, down the aisle.

Lily laughed. She pointed across Mrs. Carson's bosom out the window toward a man. He had stepped off the train and just stood there, by himself. He was a stranger and wore a cap.

"Look," she said, laughing softly through her fingers.

"Don't—look," said Mrs. Carson very distinctly, as if, out of all she had ever spoken, she would impress these two solemn words upon Lily's soft little brain. She added, "Don't look at anything till you get to Ellisville."

In the station the train was puffing. Nearly everyone in Victory was hanging around waiting for it to leave.

181

Outside, Aimee Slocum was crying so hard she almost ran into the stranger. He wore a cap and was short and seemed to have on perfume, if such a thing could be.

"Could you tell me, madam," he said, "where a little lady lives in this burg name of Miss Lily Daw?" He lifted his cap—and he had red hair.

"What do you want to know for?" Aimee asked before she knew it.

"Talk louder," said the stranger. He almost whispered, himself.

"She's gone away—she's gone to Ellisville!"

"Gone?"

"Gone to Ellisville!"

"Well, I like that!" The man stuck out his bottom lip and puffed till his hair jumped.

"What business did you have with Lily?" cried Aimee suddenly.

"We was only going to get married, that's all," said the man.

Aimee Slocum started to scream in front of all those people. She almost pointed to the long black box she saw lying on the ground at the man's feet. Then she jumped back in fright.

"The xylophone! The xylophone!" she cried, looking back and forth from the man to the hissing train. Which was more terrible? The bell began to ring hollowly, and the man was talking.

"Did you say Ellisville? That in the state of Mississippi?" Like lightning he had pulled out a red notebook entitled, "Permanent Facts & Data." He wrote down something. "I don't hear well."

Aimee nodded her head up and down, and circled around him.

Under "Ellis-Ville Miss" he was drawing a line; now he was flicking it with two little marks. "Maybe she didn't say she would. Maybe she said she wouldn't." He suddenly laughed very loudly, after the way he had whispered. Aimee jumped back. "Women!—Well, if we play anywheres near Ellisville, Miss., in the future I may look her up and I may not," he said.

The bass horn sounded the true signal for the band to begin. White steam rushed out of the engine. Usually the train stopped for only a minute in Victory, but the engineer knew Lily from waving at her, and he knew this was her big day.

"Wait!" Aimee Slocum did scream. "Wait, mister! I can get her for you. Wait, Mister Engineer! Don't go!"

Then there she was back on the train, screaming in Mrs. Carson's and Mrs. Watts's faces.

"The xylophone player! The xylophone player to marry her! Yonder he is!"

"Nonsense," murmured Mrs. Watts, peering over the others to look where Aimee pointed. "If he's there I don't see him. Where is he? You're looking at One-Eye Beasley."

"The little man with the cap—no, with the red hair! Hurry!"

"Is that really him?" Mrs. Carson asked Mrs. Watts in wonder. "Mercy! He's small, isn't he!"

"Never saw him before in my life!" cried Mrs. Watts. But suddenly she shut up her fan.

"Come on! This is a train we're on!" cried Aimee Slocum. Her nerves were all unstrung.

"All right, don't have a conniption fit, girl," said Mrs. Watts. "Come on," she said thickly to Mrs. Carson.

"Where are we going now?" asked Lily as they struggled down the aisle.

"We're taking you to get married," said Mrs. Watts. "Mrs. Carson, you'd better phone up your husband right there in the station."

"But I don't want to git married," said Lily, beginning to whimper. "I'm going to Ellisville."

"Hush, and we'll all have some ice-cream cones later," whispered Mrs. Carson.

Just as they climbed down the steps at the back end of the train, the band went into "Independence March."

The xylophone player was still there, patting his foot. He came up and said, "Hello, Toots. What's up—tricks?" and kissed Lily with a smack, after which she hung her head.

"So you're the young man we've heard so much about," said Mrs. Watts. Her smile was brilliant. "Here's your little Lily."

"What say?" asked the xylophone player.

"My husband happens to be the Baptist preacher of Victory," said Mrs. Carson in a loud, clear voice. "Isn't that lucky? I can get him here in five minutes: I know exactly where he is."

They were in a circle around the xylophone player, all going into the white waiting room.

"Oh, I feel just like crying, at a time like this," said Aimee Slocum. She looked back and saw the train moving slowly away, going under the bridge at Main Street. Then it disappeared around the curve.

"Oh, the hope chest!" Aimee cried in a stricken voice.

"And whom have we the pleasure of addressing?" Mrs. Watts was shouting, while Mrs. Carson was ringing up the telephone.

The band went on playing. Some of the people thought Lily was on the train, and some swore she wasn't. Everybody cheered, though, and a straw hat was thrown into the telephone wires.

Reverend Black Douglas

by Alex Haley

The congregation of Henning's New Hope Colored Methodist Episcopal Church could not have been more surprised when the bishop of the West Tennessee District arrived in his car one Sunday morning in 1923. The bishop explained that he had come to fill in for New Hope's longtime and well-liked pastor, whom he had asked to go and substitute for an ailing, aged pastor of a large and prestigious church in Memphis, fifty miles south.

The presence of a bishop in the small church was no everyday honor, and although the sermon he preached that Sunday morning was of only fairly ordinary caliber, still some of the older members took pains to be certain that he heard some good, old-fashioned, heavy foot-patting, along with a nice sprinkling of "Yaymans" to show he was both welcomed and appreciated.

Following the sermon and the morning collection, the bishop returned to the pulpit and dropped a real shock upon the congregation. In all probability, their regular pastor would be needed for quite an extended period in Memphis. In his stead, the New Hope Church would receive "a truly unusual young preacher."

The bishop asked that a fair, unprejudiced hearing be given to this young man, who had recently reached the age of twenty-nine. His name was Douglas, the bishop said, and he had grown up as a farm boy near Millington, Tennessee. One day out plowing in a field of young cotton, he'd heard a heavenly voice commanding him to go forth and preach. His proud, hardworking farmer parents had helped him to enter the Fuller Theological School in Memphis. In his graduating year, he had easily won a competition of free-style ten-minute sermons, a competition whose judges had included the bishop. For nearly seven years since then, the young man had been a guest preacher at a variety of small country churches.

The bishop said that the time was ripe for the natural-born pulpit talents of the young Reverend Douglas to be displayed for just the right congregation, in just the right church—which the bishop felt sure was none other than New Hope CME Church in Henning. And, he affirmed, if the New Hope congregation didn't like the young man, then of course he would immediately be replaced.

185

That Sunday saw the beginning of a week of heavy discussions within the homes of New Hope church members. The two principal issues were, first, the prospective preacher was unknown, unseen and unheard; second, and worse, his twenty-nine years of age made him no more than wet behind the ears by comparison with the average age of preachers who were regarded with pride and respect by their congregations.

The youth factor finally triggered the public tongues and tempers of the older Methodist sisters who belonged to the Golden Deeds Society. They began visiting key families, fuming that no bishop or anybody else should be allowed to foist off some unknown "boy preacher" upon the congregation. Friday afternoon the Golden Deeds Society sisters assembled themselves and went marching directly to Uncle Jim Green, who was chairman of the board of the church. In no uncertain terms, the sisters told Uncle Jim Green to telephone the bishop and tell him that a majority of the New Hope congregation wished to cancel, in advance, any hearing of a preacher who was obviously too immature for a serious church.

But Uncle Jim Green looked the Golden Deeds sisters square in the eyes as he told them that the New Hope Church had given its formal promise to the bishop, and therefore it was a matter of church honor that, on the Sunday approaching, the young reverend must be given a fair tryout. At the same time, Uncle Jim Green knew all too well the many pressures which irate Golden Deeds sisters could exert, so he quickly offered a compromise. Once the young man had preached one sermon, if the Golden Deeds sisters voted unanimously against him, the bishop would be telephoned.

On Sunday morning families who belonged to the New Hope Church set out as much as an hour earlier than usual, hoping to arrive in enough time to be certain of a pew seat for the eleven o'clock worship service. As the families arrived at the church ground, literally each and every young marriageable woman gave a gasp upon her first glimpse of Reverend Douglas—which their observing mothers and grandmothers understood. He was a good-looking, velvety-black six-feet-four of muscle, bone and sinew. Greeting easily the people who were approaching the church, he looked straight into the eyes of even the children and solemnly shook their hands. Against the smooth blackness of his face, his teeth seemed made of pearls, while his big, solid shoulders, arms, hands and feet spoke to all that he knew how to handle a mule, a plow, a sledgehammer or an ax. The church's hardworking old and young men members found themselves privately approving him on sight.

Only the sisters of the Golden Deeds Society expressed indignation. "Look at them young gals grinnin' at him like fools!" snapped Sister Hattie Locust. "That's the pushy way they all actin' nowdays!"

Sister Cornelius Johnson exclaimed, "Jes' heared one them tellin' her mama that's the way a man s'posed to look!"

"Well, he sho' don't look it to me!" declared eighty-two-year-old Sister Dindy, reminding them of the Golden Deeds' public pledge to vote him out. "Jes' everybody keep in mind that lookin' sho' ain't preachin'!"

An excited congregation found seats as the church pianist played "Rock of Ages." Then the young Reverend Douglas walked forward and placed his Holy Bible atop the preaching stand. He didn't make any of the expected "I-hope-you'll-like-me" appeals of average preachers who were being tried out. He just opened the Bible to his marked place and, looking down at the congregation, led them in singing "Amazing Grace" in a fine, strong baritone.

The hymn ended, and, not preaching yet but just speaking in that rich voice, he let the people know that whatever else he had learned in theology school, he certainly had never forgotten how it was to have grown up helping his folks in scrabbling out a living on a farm.

"Brothers and sisters," he began, "I don't have to say to anybody here that we're in a time of trouble. For seven or eight weeks now, there's been nothin' but little sprinklin' rains, an' out there in your fields, maybe the boll weevils thicker'n your cotton. An' it look like, from all we can hear, that for whatever little cotton will finally get picked, The Man won't be payin' hardly nothin'."

He leaned his head a little bit backward as he continued: "Ahhhh, yessss! Lots of people, the white as well as the black, startin' to say it seem like might not be too much longer before time will be no more!"

Before long, young sisters who never had exclaimed out loud in church were shouting "Hallelujah!" and "Yes, preach! Preach!" The old Golden Deeds sisters glared at them as the sermon went on.

"But I'm privileged to be standing up here to tell all of you on this good-news morning, brothers and sisters: there's a *just* God sitting up there in heaven! There's a God up there who *cares* about us this Sunday morning! There's a God who *knows* where you and I are chosen to be this Sunday morning . . . here, in His church!"

Amidst a chorusing of shouts from the young church sisters—along with no few older members' "Yaymans!"—Reverend Douglas held his thick, black Holy Bible up high. "Ohhhhh, yessss, my brothers and sisters! The greatest book ever in the living world! And it says, in First Kings, seventeenth chapter, the sixth verse—"

"Preach it, preach it, brother!"

"Look at them young gals grinnin' at him like fools!" snapped Sister Hattie Locust.

"It says that God made a hoecake out of the atmosphere! And God sent it down by the raven, to feed that poor Elijah!"

"Oh, yes, He did."

"Because Elijah had faith!"

"Oh, yes, Lord, *faith!*"

"Sisters and brothers, there's no such thing as a *little* faith! There's no such thing as a *lot* of faith! You've just got to have *faith!* So my text this good-news Sunday morning is *faith!* Without faith, you've got nothing! But *with* faith, then you've got upon you the grace and the glory of God!"

His text finally stated, the young Reverend Douglas mopped at his face with a big white handkerchief. He preached so strong that, later on, even old Sister Pinder—who was a Holy Roller—sitting clear across the road on her front porch, declared that she never missed a word. He gave a fascinating description of Moses fending for the Hebrew children against all of Pharaoh's cruelties and evils. With most of the young women jumping up, flinging their arms, shouting, and many older members also exclaiming, the preacher practically made the congregation hear, see and feel the fierce storm winds parting the Red Sea for Moses to lead those Hebrew children across the riverbed, not even getting their feet-soles wet.

As the sermon ended, the choir began singing softly, and the church's treasurer stood up and announced the offering.

Afterward the young Reverend Douglas led the singing of "I come to the garden alone/While the dew is still on the roses. . . ."

When the hymn concluded, he described how the imps of hell were steadily shoveling more fatty-pine knots into the fiery furnace, and he urged every sinner present to think hard on his or her need to be saved before it was too late. But he wasn't going to make any formal call for sinners to come and fall upon bended knees before the mourners' bench, as he felt that only a church's regular minister should make that call. He said the bishop had made him fully aware that he was visiting Henning entirely on a tryout basis before the New Hope congregation, whom he thanked for having heard him.

There was no further talk about the bishop being telephoned. Before long, Henning's black Methodists were not only praising but even outright bragging about their young preacher. And after only a little while, an odd thing happened.

Up in Haywood County was another preacher, a much older, "dust-stomper" type, whose last name also was Douglas. Henning's Methodists had nothing against him, but they reacted strongly when people confused their new young Douglas with the Haywood County Douglas.

Finally someone, taking into consideration that the Haywood County preacher was quite light-complexioned, came up with a descriptive nickname which Henning's New Hope Methodists all but seized upon. "Oh, no!" they'd exclaim. "Ours is the *black* Douglas!"

As the Sundays came and went, a steadily increasing number of people attended the New Hope services to hear and see the exciting young "Black Douglas" in action, until every morning of worship saw even the aisles filled with visitors seated in folding chairs borrowed from the schoolhouse. By the end of the third month, the church board advised the bishop that Reverend Black Douglas was desired on a permanent basis.

What put Reverend Black Douglas on the road to becoming really famous, even far beyond Henning, was New Hope Church's annual fall revival eight years later, in 1931. There he accomplished two incredible feats, involving the main measures of any revival's success: first, how big a total collection was raised; and second, how many sinners were drawn to the mourners' bench for their souls to be saved.

Preaching his hardest and his finest twice daily for three days running, he had achieved an unbelievable total of over $500 in collections, right in the heart of the Depression, and the revival had actually netted seven pewsful of sinners! It was the greatest harvest of souls—Methodist or Baptist, black or white—ever heard of in the county.

Afterward Reverend Douglas always insisted that it could never have been done without Brother Rich Harrell, the church's chief usher and champion shouter. Finishing the revival's final sermon, which had practically set the packed congregation afire, the preacher gestured to the choir to sing. His call for sinners was due now. Instinctively, he glanced to confirm that Brother Harrell was sitting in his usual left-side pew. Then the minister walked down from the pulpit area to the church floor.

Halting before the empty three pews that he'd kept reserved for what he hoped would be that many sinners, Reverend Black Douglas raised his hands. With a voice ragged from the consecutive days of hard preaching, he began the appeal: "Whosoever will embrace the Holy Ghost, won't you just please come forward to the mourners' bench?... Won't you accept Him today, in your heart?"

189

As always happened at big revivals, several folk instantly sprang up and went rushing forward, most of them weeping, their bodies shaking. But most of the older heads among the congregation quite loudly groaned their skepticism of these "rushers," suspecting them of deliberately staged performances.

When the rushing seemed done, Brother Rich Harrell rose slowly from his pew. He scanned the thickly packed crowd, then began picking his way through the people seated in the aisles.

The choir was singing softly, and all could hear Reverend Douglas intoning, "Oh, sinners, the church *pleads* to you, like a weeping angel, won't you come, won't you please come? Home to Jesus!"

And wherever the roving Brother Harrell spotted anyone whom he knew—or even guessed—harbored an unsaved soul, right there was where he stopped stock-still. *"Mercy!"* he'd exclaim and plead tearfully, "please have mercy upon him [or her]! Oh Lord, mercy!"

Brother Harrell could make anyone who was unsaved feel sinful, guilty and downright dirty. No one knew how many new church members he had simply shamed up to the mourners' bench.

That day in 1931 the front three pews filled up so quickly—with steadily more sinners coming forward—that the frantic ushers had to beg members to give up their seats to accommodate them.

It just about amounted to handwriting on the wall when one after another of western Tennessee's black Methodist churches, particularly in the larger cities, began inviting Reverend Black Douglas to be their guest preacher. So it didn't come as really any great surprise when finally, during 1932, New Hope lost Reverend Black Douglas.

Again the bishop came, and this time he asked the congregation to understand that only once in a while did God prepare such a special servant as the one with whom New Hope had been blessed through his seasoning years. It was only fair that he be reassigned to be shared among the maximum of west Tennessee's black Methodists.

Most of the New Hope congregation had wet eyes; so did Reverend Black Douglas when, after the next Sunday's sermon, the time came for him to bid New Hope farewell. But he added, "The bishop has granted my request to return here to my New Hope family every other first Sunday of the month."

The congregation cheered right out, even if they were in a church.

For many years afterward, as he had promised, Reverend Douglas did return to New Hope Church. The country farming families who were church members would start out from their homes immediately after breakfast. With any luck, they'd find seats before every pew got packed and every folding chair taken. After that the standing room would begin to fill up.

The passing years seemed to mature and season the minister in many ways. More stomach became apparent under his suitcoats—a natural result of invitations to special homecooked dinners. And now, when the choir's singing began the services, he would sit in the big pulpit chair with his head tilted back, his hands in a prayerful position under his chin, his eyes closed in deep, silent meditation.

The singing ended, he would move to the pulpit and open the huge Bible. Everyone could tell that he no longer even needed to glance down at the page to read his text, that whatever chapter and verse he wanted, he'd just quote from his memory.

The sermon preached by Reverend Black Douglas that the members of New Hope Methodist Church remembered best of all was given on a warm, bright summer Sunday in 1938, when he was forty-four.

He began speaking quietly: "Last Sunday I was driving toward my boyhood home in Millington, and I was passing all your fine crops so rich and green out there on either side of Highway 51. And, you know, I got to talking to myself. . . .

"Said to myself, I said, 'Douglas, all these years you been going around calling yourself preaching God's word to people. What are you trying to put across? What's the Bible really trying to say to mankind? Fact of the matter, what's everything religious trying to say?'

"And all the week since, I've been studying on this thing, brothers and sisters. And I believe I've finally got it down to just two words: God's love! That's what it is. God's love!

"We're always *talking* about love, we're always *talking* about having religion. But for over nineteen hundred years, God's love has been right here on this earth with us, right here amidst us—and there never has been as much hate and evil in the world as there is today!"

His voice sounded pleading. "If we would only love each other, as all of religion teaches us to do, we wouldn't need no laws, no guns, no fences, no locks, no nothing but each other."

Reverend Douglas seemed close to tears as he raised his big, black, gold-edged Bible up high, then set it back down. "My brothers and sisters, Paul, that greatest of the Apostles, said that you can understand all the mysteries, you can have all the knowledge, you can move mountains—but if you do not have love, you are *nothing!*

"Paul, yes, told us about love—but in all of time, the greatest *act* of love was that of our Heavenly Father, God Almighty!"

Suddenly flinging his arms wide, he shouted, "God so loved the world that to redeem sinful man, He sent Christ Jesus, His only begotten son, to be *crucified!* Up on the Golgotha Hill that morning, Jesus hung on that thick wooden cross, *dying!* Thorns on His head! Iron spikes through His hands! The sun hid its face! Lightning flashed! The very *earth* was trembling. All of *nature* was in agony! *Because sinful, evil man was killing God's child!"*

Most of the congregation were weeping and crying out: "Mercy, Holy Father!" . . . "Forgive us!"

The preacher sobbed. "Our Saviour, Jesus Christ, had died so that every man, forevermore, can find in his own soul—the way . . . to the Truth . . . and to the Light!"

Reverend Douglas walked down from the pulpit to the shiny-brown oak railing, before which people would kneel to take communion.

"Brothers and sisters, what was it Jesus said to His disciples at the Last Supper, when He knew His hour had come?

"Our Saviour said, 'This is my commandment, that ye love one another, as I have loved you.' What does this say to us this morning?"

He walked back to the pulpit and stood looking gravely down at the congregation. "It says we must do more than respect each other. It says we must do more than just *abide* with each other.

"My brothers and sisters"—Reverend Black Douglas was almost whispering—"we have got to learn to *love* each other.

"Let us pray. . . .

"Our Father, this morning may the seed of Thy love have fallen upon fertile ground in our hearts. Father, may Thy love seed in us be warmed by the sunshine of Thy grace—to grow, in faith, toward a rich harvest.

" 'I am the vine, ye are the branches.' Thus spake our Lord and Saviour, the Risen Christ. Amen."

Reverend Douglas sat down in the preacher's chair. His shoulders were shaking, and he dug at his eyes with his big white handkerchief. For the only time that anyone was later able to recall, during an entire sermon nobody had shouted or even exclaimed one single "Yayman!"

The collection was taken up; the choir sang the closing hymn: "I love to tell the story . . . To tell the old, old story/Of Jesus and His love. . . ."

Then the congregation quietly filed outside. Reverend Black Douglas shook the hands of the people, and patted the heads of their babies, also asking how were the sick and aged not present.

Finally the crowd began drifting apart.

"That Douglas preached this morning!" someone exclaimed.

"He did!" agreed others.

And soon all of the congregation were traveling along their various roads and paths, crossing God's brown, dusty earth, wending their way between His growing green grass, heading toward their homes.

Clearing in the Sky

by Jesse Stuart

"This is the way, Jess," said my father, pointing with his cane across the deep valley below us. "I want to show you something you've not seen for many years!"

"Isn't it too hot for you to do much walking?" I wiped the streams of sweat from my face to keep them from stinging my eyes.

I didn't want to go with him. I had just finished walking a half mile uphill from my home to his. I had carried a basket of dishes to Mom. There were two slips in the road and I couldn't drive my car. And I knew how hot it was. It was 97 in the shade. I knew from that January until April my father had gone to eight different doctors. One of the doctors had told him not to walk the length of a city block. He told my father to get a taxi to take him home. But my father walked home five miles across the mountain and told Mom what the doctor had said. Forty years ago a doctor had told him the same thing. And he had lived to raise a family of five children. He had done as much hard work in those years as any man.

I could not protest to him now. He had made up his mind. When he made up his mind to do a thing, he would do it if he had to crawl. He didn't care if it was 97 in the shade or 16 below zero. I wiped more sweat from my face as I followed him down the little path between the pasture and the meadow.

Suddenly he stopped at the edge of the meadow, took his pocket-knife from his pocket, and cut a wisp of alfalfa. He held it up between him and the sun.

"Look at this, Jess!" he bragged. "Did you ever see better alfalfa grow out of the earth?"

"It's the best-looking hay I've seen anyplace," I said. "I've not seen better-looking alfalfa even in the Little Sandy River bottoms!"

"When I bought this little farm everybody around here said I'd end up with my family at the county poor farm if I tried to make a living here," he bragged again. "It took me thirty years to improve these old worn-out acres to make them do this!"

As I stood looking at his meadow of alfalfa, down in the saddle

193

between two hills, I remembered how, down through the years, he had hauled leaves from the woods and spread them over this field in the autumn and then plowed them under and let them rot. All that would grow on this ground when he bought it were scrubby pines and saw briers. The pines didn't grow waist-high. There wasn't enough strength in the ground to push them any higher. And the saw briers didn't grow knee-high. In addition to this, the land was filled with gullies. But he cut the scrubby pines and turned their tops uphill to stop the erosion. And he mowed the saw briers with a scythe and forked them into the gullies on top the pines. Then he plowed the land. He sowed a cover crop and turned it under. Then he sowed a second, a third, and a fourth cover crop. In a few years he had the land producing good crops of corn, wheat, potatoes, and tobacco.

"But this is not what I want to show you, Jess," he said as he threw the wisp of alfalfa to the ground. "Come on. Follow me!"

I followed him through the pasture gate. Then down a little narrow cattle path into the deep hollow.

"Where are we going?" I asked when he started to walk a log across the creek toward a steep, timbered bluff.

"Not up or down the hollow," he laughed. "But there." He pointed toward a wooded mountaintop. "That's the way we are goin'!"

"But there's not even a path leading up there," I said.

"There's a path up there now," he said. "I've made one."

I followed him across the foot log he had made by chopping down a white oak, felling it over the deep-channeled stream. It was a foot log a flash flood couldn't carry away because its top branches rested on the far side of the channel behind a big tree. He hadn't chopped the white oak all the way off at the trunk. He had left a little of the tree to hold it at the stump. His doctor had told him not to use an ax. But he had cut this white oak to make a foot log across the stream so he could reach the rugged mountain slope.

Now I followed my father up the winding footpath under the tall hickory trees, a place where I used to come with him when I was a little boy to hunt for squirrels. We would shoot squirrels from the tall scaly-bark hickories and black walnuts with our long rifles. But that had been nearly thirty years ago. And through the years, from time to time, I had walked over this rugged mountain slope and there was never a path on it until my father had made this one. It was a pretty little footpath under the high canopy of hickory, walnut, and oak leaves. We couldn't see the sky above our heads. Our eyes could not find an opening among the leaves.

In front of me walked the little man who once walked so fast I had to run to follow him. But it wasn't that way now. Time had slowed him. The passing of the years and much hard labor had bent his shoulders. His right shoulder, the one he used to carry his loads, sagged three inches below the left one. His breath didn't come as easy as it used to come. For he stopped twice, and leaned on his cane to rest, before we reached the top of the first bluff. Then we came to a flat where the ground wasn't so steep.

"I like these woods, Jess," my father said. "Remember when we used to come here to hunt for squirrels? Remember when we sat beneath these hickories and the squirrels threw green hickory shells down at us? The morning wind just at the break of day in August was so good to breathe. I can't forget those days. And in October when the rabbits were ripe and the frosts had come and the hickory leaves had turned yellow and when the October winds blew they rustled the big leaves from the trees and they fell like yellow raindrops to the ground! Remember," he said, looking at me with his pale blue eyes, "how our hounds, Rags and Scout, would make the rabbits circle! Those were good days, Jess! That's why I remember this mountain."

"Is that what you wanted to show me?" I asked.

"Oh, no, no," he said as he began to climb the second bluff that lifted abruptly from the flat toward the sky. The pines on top of the mountain above us looked as if the fingers of their long boughs were fondling the substance of a white cloud. Whatever my father wanted me to see was on top of the highest point on my farm. And with the exception of the last three years, I had been over this point many times. I had never seen anything extraordinary upon this high point of rugged land. I had seen the beauty of many wild flowers, a few rock cliffs, and many species of hard- and softwood trees.

"Why do you take the path straight up the point?" I asked. "Look at these other paths! What are they doing here?"

Within the distance of a few yards, several paths left the main path and circled around the slope, gradually climbing the mountain.

"All paths go to the same place," he answered.

"Then why take the steep one?" I asked.

"I'll explain later," he spoke with half breaths.

He rested a minute to catch his second wind while I managed to stand on the path by holding to a little sapling, because it was too steep for my feet to hold unless I braced myself.

Then my father started to move slowly up the path again, supporting himself with his cane. I followed at his heels. Just a few steps in front of him a fox squirrel crossed the path and ran up a hickory tree.

"See that, Jess!" he shouted.

"Yes, I did," I answered.

"That brings back something to me," he said. "Brings back the old days to see a fox squirrel. But this won't bring back as much as something I'm goin' to show you."

My curiosity was aroused. I thought he had found a new kind of wild grass, or an unfamiliar herb, or a new kind of tree. For I remembered the time he found a coffee tree in our woods. It is, as far as I know, the only one of its kind growing in our county.

Only twice did my father stop to wipe the sweat from his eyes as he climbed the second steep bluff toward the fingers of the pines. We reached the limbless trunks of these tall straight pines whose branches reached toward the blue depth of sky, for the white cloud was now gone. I saw a clearing, a small clearing of not more than three-fourths of an acre in the heart of this wilderness right on the mountaintop.

"Now, you're comin' to something, son," he said as he pushed down the top wire so he could cross the fence. "This is something I want you to see!"

"Who did this?" I asked. "Who cleared this land and fenced it? Fenced it against what?"

"Stray cattle if they ever get out of the pasture," he answered me curtly. "I cleared this land. And I fenced it!"

"But why did you ever climb to this mountaintop and do this?" I asked him. "Look at the fertile land we have in the valley!"

"Fertile," he laughed as he reached down and picked up a double handful of leaf-rot loam. "This is the land, son! This is it. I've tried all kinds of land!"

Then he smelled of the dirt. He whiffed and whiffed the smell of this wild dirt into his nostrils.

"Just like fresh air," he said as he let the dirt run between his fingers. "It's pleasant to touch, too," he added.

"But, Dad—" I said.

"I know what you think," he interrupted. "Your mother thinks the same thing. She wonders why I ever climbed to this mountaintop to raise my potatoes, yams, and tomatoes! But, Jess," he almost whispered, "anything grown in new ground like this has a better flavor. Wait until my tomatoes are ripe! You'll never taste sweeter tomatoes in your life!"

"They'll soon be ripe, too," I said as I looked at the dozen or more rows of tomatoes on the lower side of the patch.

Then above the tomatoes were a half-dozen rows of yams. Above the yams were, perhaps, three dozen rows of potatoes.

I saw a clearing, a small clearing of not more than three-fourths of an acre in the heart of this wilderness right on the mountaintop.

197

"I don't see a weed in this patch." I laughed. "Won't they grow here?"

"I won't let 'em," he said. "Now this is what I've been wanting you to see!"

"This is the cleanest patch I've ever seen," I bragged. "But I still don't see why you climbed to the top of this mountain to clear this patch. And you did all this against your doctor's orders!"

"Which one?" he asked, laughing.

Then he sat down on a big oak stump and I sat down on a small black-gum stump near him. This was the only place on the mountain where the sun could shine to the ground. And on the lower side of the clearing there was a rim of shadow over the rows of dark stalwart plants loaded with green tomatoes.

"What is the reason for your planting this patch up here?" I asked.

"Twenty times in my life," he said, "a doctor has told me to go home and be with my family as long as I could. Told me not to work. Not to do anything but to live and enjoy the few days I had left me. If the doctors have been right," he said, winking at me, "I have cheated death many times! Now, I've reached the years the Good Book allows to man in his lifetime upon this earth! Threescore years and ten!"

He got up from the stump and wiped the raindrops of sweat from his red-wrinkled face with his big blue bandanna.

"And something else, Jess," he said, motioning for me to follow him to the upper edge of the clearing, "you won't understand until you reach threescore and ten! After these years your time is borrowed. And when you live on that kind of time, then something goes back. Something I cannot explain. You go back to the places you knew and loved. See this steep hill slope." He pointed down from the upper rim of the clearing toward the deep valley below. "Your mother and I, when she was nineteen and I was twenty-two, cleared this mountain slope together. We raised corn, beans, and pumpkins here," he continued, his voice rising with excitement—he talked with his hands, too. "Those were the days. This wasn't land one had to build up. It was already here as God had made it and all we had to do was clear the trees and burn the brush. I plowed this mountain with cattle the first time it was ever plowed. And we raised more than a barrel of corn to the shock. That's why I came back up here. I went back to our youth. And this was the only land left like that was.

"And, Jess," he bragged, "regardless of my threescore years and ten, I plowed it. Plowed it with a mule! I have, with just a little help, done all the work. It's like the land your mother and I used to farm here when I brought my gun to the field and took home a mess of fox squirrels every evening!"

I looked at the vast mountain slope below where my mother and father had farmed. And I could remember, years later, when they farmed this land. It was on this steep slope that my father once made me a little wooden plow. That was when I was six years old and they brought me to the field to thin corn. I lost my little plow in a furrow and I cried and cried until he made me another plow. But I never loved the second plow as I did the first one.

Now, to look at the mountain slope, grown up with tall trees, many of them big enough to have sawed into lumber at the mill, it was hard to believe that my father and mother had cleared this mountain slope and had farmed it for many years. For many of the trees were sixty feet tall and the wild vines had matted their tops together.

"And, Jess," he almost whispered, "the doctors told me to sit still and to take life easy. I couldn't do it. I had to work. I had to go back. I had to smell this rich loam again. This land is not like the land I had to build to grow alfalfa. This is real land. It's the land that God left. I had to come back and dig in it. I had to smell it, sift it through my fingers again. And I wanted to taste yams, tomatoes, and potatoes grown in this land."

From this mountaintop I looked far in every direction over the rugged hills my father and mother had cleared and farmed in corn, tobacco, and cane. The one slope they hadn't cleared was the one from which my father had cleared his last, small patch.

I followed him from his clearing in the sky, down a new path, toward the deep valley below.

"But why do you have so many paths coming from the flat up the steep second bluff?" I asked, since he had promised that he would explain this to me later.

"Oh, yes," he said. "Early last spring, I couldn't climb straight up the steep path. That was when the doctor didn't give me a week to live. I made a longer, easier path so I wouldn't have to do so much climbing. Then, as I got better," he explained, "I made another path that was a little steeper. And as I continued to get better, I made steeper paths. That was one way of knowing I was getting better all the time!"

I followed him down the path, that wound this way and that, three times the length of the path we had climbed.

Two Soldiers

by William Faulkner

Me and Pete would go down to Old Man Killegrew's and listen to his radio. We would wait until after supper, after dark, and we would stand outside Old Man Killegrew's parlor window, and we could hear it because Old Man Killegrew's wife was deaf, and so he run the radio as loud as it would run, and so me and Pete could hear it plain as Old Man Killegrew's wife could, I reckon, even standing outside with the window closed.

And that night I said, "What? Japanese? What's a pearl harbor?" and Pete said, "Hush."

And so we stood there, it was cold, listening to the fellow in the radio talking, only I couldn't make no heads nor tails neither out of it. Then the fellow said that would be all for a while, and me and Pete walked back up the road to home, and Pete told me what it was. Because he was nigh twenty and he had done finished the Consolidated last June and he knowed a heap: about them Japanese dropping bombs on Pearl Harbor and that Pearl Harbor was across the water.

"Across what water?" I said. "Across that Government reservoy up at Oxford?"

"Naw," Pete said. "across the big water. The Pacific Ocean."

We went home. Maw and pap was already asleep, and me and Pete laid in the bed, and I still couldn't understand where it was, and Pete told me again—the Pacific Ocean.

"What's the matter with you?" Pete said. "You're going on nine years old. You been in school now ever since September. Ain't you learned nothing yet?"

"I reckon we ain't got as fer as the Pacific Ocean yet," I said.

We was still sowing the vetch then that ought to been all finished by the fifteenth of November, because pap was still behind, just like he had been ever since me and Pete had knowed him. And we had firewood to git in, too, but every night me and Pete would go down to Old Man Killegrew's and stand outside his parlor window in the cold and listen to his radio; then we would come back home and lay in the bed and Pete would tell me what it was. That is, he would tell me for a while. Then he wouldn't tell me. It was like he didn't want to talk about it no more. He would tell me to shut up because he wanted to go to sleep, but he never wanted to go to sleep.

He would lay there, a heap stiller than if he was asleep, and it would be something, I could feel it coming out of him, like he was mad at me even, only I knowed he wasn't thinking about me, or like he was worried about something, and it wasn't that neither, because he never had nothing to worry about. He never got behind like pap, let alone stayed behind. Pap give him ten acres when he graduated from the Consolidated, and me and Pete both reckoned pap was durn glad to get shut of at least ten acres, less to have to worry with himself; and Pete had them ten acres all sowed to vetch and busted out and bedded for the winter, and so it wasn't that. But it was something. And still we would go down to Old Man Killegrew's every night and listen to his radio, and they was at it in the Philippines now, but General Mac-Arthur was holding um. Then we would come back home and lay in the bed, and Pete wouldn't tell me nothing or talk at all. He would just lay there still as a ambush and when I would touch him, his side or his leg would feel hard and still as iron, until after a while I would go to sleep.

Then one night—it was the first time he had said nothing to me except to jump on me about not chopping enough wood at the wood tree where we was cutting—he said, "I got to go."

"Go where?" I said.

"To that war," Pete said.

"Before we even finish gettin' in the firewood?"

"Firewood, hell," Pete said.

"All right," I said. "When we going to start?"

But he wasn't even listening. He laid there, hard and still as iron in the dark. "I got to go," he said. "I jest ain't going to put up with no folks treating the Unity States that way."

"Yes," I said. "Firewood or no firewood, I reckon we got to go."

This time he heard me. He laid still again, but it was a different kind of still.

"You?" he said. "To a war?"

"You'll whup the big uns and I'll whup the little uns," I said.

Then he told me I couldn't go. At first I thought he just never wanted me tagging after him, like he wouldn't leave me go with him when he went sparking them girls of Tull's. Then he told me the Army wouldn't leave me go because I was too little, and then I knowed he really meant it and that I couldn't go nohow noways. And somehow I hadn't believed until then that he was going himself, but now I knowed he was and that he wasn't going to leave me go with him a-tall.

"I'll chop the wood and tote the water for you-all then!" I said. "You got to have wood and water!"

Anyway, he was listening to me now. He wasn't like iron now.

He turned onto his side and put his hand on my chest because it was me that was laying straight and hard on my back now.

"No," he said. "You got to stay here and help pap."

"Help him what?" I said. "He ain't never caught up nohow. He can't get no further behind. He can sholy take care of this little shirttail of a farm while me and you are whupping them Japanese. I got to go too. If you got to go, then so have I."

"No," Pete said. "Hush now. Hush." And he meant it, and I knowed he did. Only I made sho from his own mouth. I quit.

"So I just can't go then," I said.

"No," Pete said. "You just can't go. You're too little, in the first place, and in the second place—"

"All right," I said. "Then shut up and leave me go to sleep."

So he hushed then and laid back. And I laid there like I was already asleep, and pretty soon he was asleep and I knowed it was the wanting to go to the war that had worried him and kept him awake, and now that he had decided to go, he wasn't worried any more.

The next morning he told maw and pap. Maw was all right. She cried.

"No," she said, crying, "I don't want him to go. I would rather go myself in his place, if I could. I don't want to save the country. Them Japanese could take it and keep it, so long as they left me and my family and my children alone. But I remember my brother Marsh in that other war. He had to go to that one when he wasn't but nineteen, and our mother couldn't understand it then any more than I can now. But she told Marsh if he had to go, he had to go. And so, if Pete's got to go to this one, he's got to go to it. Jest don't ask me to understand why."

But pap was the one. He was the feller. "To the war?" he said.

"Why, I just don't see a bit of use in that. You ain't old enough for the draft, and the country ain't being invaded. Our President in Washington, D.C., is watching the conditions and he will notify us. Besides, in that other war your ma just mentioned, I was drafted and sent clean to Texas and was held there nigh eight months until they finally quit fighting. It seems to me that that, along with your Uncle Marsh who received a actual wound on the battlefields of France, is enough for me and mine to have to do to protect the country, at least in my lifetime. Besides, what'll I do for help on the farm with you gone? It seems to me I'll get mighty far behind."

"You been behind as long as I can remember," Pete said. "Anyway, I'm going. I got to."

"Of course he's got to go," I said. "Them Japanese—"

"You hush your mouth!" maw said, crying. "Nobody's talking to you! Go and get me a armful of wood! That's what you can do!"

So I got the wood. And all the next day, while me and Pete and pap was getting in as much wood as we could in that time because Pete said how pap's idea of plenty of wood was one more stick laying against the wall that maw ain't put on the fire yet, maw was getting Pete ready to go. She washed and mended his clothes and cooked him a shoe box of vittles. And that night me and Pete laid in the bed and listened to her packing his grip and crying, until after a while Pete got up in his nightshirt and went back there, and I could hear them talking, until at last maw said, "You got to go, and so I want you to go. But I don't understand it, and I won't never, and so don't expect me to." And Pete come back and got into the bed again and laid again still and hard as iron on his back, and then he said, and he wasn't talking to me, he wasn't talking to nobody, "I got to go. I just got to."

"Sho you got to," I said. "Them Japanese—" He turned over hard, he kind of surged over onto his side, looking at me in the dark.

"Anyway, you're all right," he said. "I expected to have more trouble with you than with all the rest of them put together."

"I reckon I can't help it neither," I said. "But maybe it will run a few years longer and I can get there. Maybe someday I will jest walk in on you."

"I hope not," Pete said. "Folks don't go to wars for fun. A man don't leave his maw crying just for fun."

"Then why are you going?" I said.

"I got to," he said. "I just got to. Now you go on to sleep. I got to ketch that early bus in the morning."

"All right," I said. "I hear tell Memphis is a big place. How will you find where the Army's at?"

"I'll ask somebody where to go to join it," Pete said. "Go on to sleep now."

"Is that what you'll ask for? Where to join the Army?" I said.

"Yes," Pete said. He turned onto his back again. "Shut up and go to sleep."

We went to sleep. The next morning we et breakfast by lamplight because the bus would pass at six o'clock. Maw wasn't crying now. She jest looked grim and busy, putting breakfast on the table while we et it. Then she finished packing Pete's grip, except he never wanted to take no grip to the war, but maw said decent folks never went nowhere, not even to a war, without a change of clothes and something to tote them in. She put in the shoe box of fried chicken and biscuits and she put the Bible in, too, and then it was time to go. We didn't know until then that maw wasn't going to the bus. She jest brought Pete's cap and overcoat, and still she didn't cry no more, she jest stood with her hands on Pete's shoulders and she didn't move, but somehow, and just holding Pete's shoulders, she looked as hard and fierce as when Pete had turned toward me in the bed last night and tole me that anyway I was all right.

"They could take the country and keep the country, so long as they never bothered me and mine," she said. Then she said, "Don't never forget who you are. You ain't rich and the rest of the world outside of Frenchman's Bend never heard of you. But your blood is good as any blood anywhere, and don't you never forget it."

Then she kissed him, and then we was out of the house, with pap toting Pete's grip whether Pete wanted him to or not. There wasn't no dawn even yet, not even after we had stood on the highway by the mailbox, a while. Then we seen the lights of the bus coming and I was watching the bus until it come up and Pete flagged it, and then, sho enough, there was daylight—it had started while I wasn't watching. And now me and Pete expected pap to say something else foolish, like he done before, about how Uncle Marsh getting wounded in France and that trip to Texas pap taken in 1918 ought to be enough to save the Unity States in 1942, but he never. He done all right too. He jest said, "Good-bye, son. Always remember what your ma told you and write her whenever you find the time." Then he shaken Pete's hand, and Pete looked at me a minute and put his hand on my head and rubbed my head durn nigh hard enough to wring my neck off and jumped into the bus, and the feller wound the door shut and the bus began to hum; then it was moving, humming and grinding and whining louder and louder; it was going fast, with two little red lights behind it that never seemed to get no littler, but just seemed to be running together until

Maw said decent folks never went nowhere, not even to a war, without a change of clothes and something to tote them in.

pretty soon they would touch and jest be one light. But they never did, and then the bus was gone, and even like it was, I could have pretty nigh busted out crying, nigh to nine years old and all.

Me and pap went back to the house. All that day we worked at the wood tree, and so I never had no good chance until about middle of the afternoon. Then I taken my slingshot and I would have liked to took all my bird eggs, too, because Pete had give me his collection and he holp me with mine, and he would like to git the box out and look at them as good as I would, even if he was nigh twenty years old. But the box was too big to tote a long ways and have to worry with, so I just taken the shikepoke egg, because it was the best un, and wropped it up good into a matchbox and hid it and the slingshot under the corner of the barn. Then we et supper and went to bed, and I thought then how if I would 'a' had to stayed in that room and that bed like that even for one more night, I jest couldn't 'a' stood it. Then I could hear pap snoring, but I never heard no sound from maw, whether she was asleep or not, and I don't reckon she was. So I taken my shoes and drapped them out the window, and then I clumb out like I used to watch Pete do when he was still jest seventeen and pap held that he was too young yet to be tomcatting around at night, and wouldn't leave him out, and I put on my shoes and went to the barn and got the slingshot and the shikepoke egg and went to the highway.

It wasn't cold, it was jest durn confounded dark, and that highway stretched on in front of me like, without nobody using it, it had stretched out half again as fer just like a man does when he lays down, so that for a time it looked like full sun was going to ketch me before I had finished them twenty-two miles to Jefferson. But it didn't. Daybreak was jest starting when I walked up the hill into town. I could smell breakfast cooking in the cabins and I wished I had thought to brought me a cold biscuit, but that was too late now. And Pete had told me Memphis was a piece beyond Jefferson, but I never knowed it was no eighty miles. So I stood there on that empty square, with daylight coming and coming and the street lights still burning and that Law looking down at me, and me still eighty miles from Memphis, and it had took me all night to walk jest twenty-two miles, and so, by the time I got to Memphis at that rate, Pete would 'a' done already started for Pearl Harbor.

"Where do you come from?" the Law said.

And I told him again. "I got to get to Memphis. My brother's there."

"You mean you ain't got any folks around here?" the Law said. "Nobody but that brother? What are you doing way off down here and your brother in Memphis?"

And I told him again, "I got to get to Memphis. I ain't got no time to waste talking about it and I ain't got time to walk it. I got to git there today."

"Come on here," the Law said.

We went down another street. And there was the bus, just like when Pete got into it yestiddy morning, except there wasn't no lights on it now and it was empty. There was a regular bus dee-po like a railroad dee-po, with a ticket counter and a feller behind it, and the Law said, "Set down over there," and I set down on the bench, and the Law said, "I want to use your telephone," and he talked in the telephone a minute and put it down and said to the feller behind the ticket counter, "Keep your eye on him. I'll be back as soon as Mrs. Habersham can arrange to get herself up and dressed." He went out. I got up and went to the ticket counter.

"I want to go to Memphis," I said.

"You bet," the feller said. "You set down on the bench now. Mr. Foote will be back in a minute."

"I don't know no Mr. Foote," I said. "I want to ride that bus to Memphis."

"You got some money?" he said. "It'll cost you seventy-two cents."

I taken out the matchbox and unwropped the shikepoke egg. "I'll swap you this for a ticket to Memphis," I said.

"What's that?" he said.

"It's a shikepoke egg," I said. "You never seen one before. It's worth a dollar. I'll take seventy-two cents fer it."

"No," he said, "the fellers that own that bus insist on a cash basis. If I started swapping tickets for bird eggs and livestock and such, they would fire me. You go and set down on the bench now, like Mr. Foote—"

I started for the door, but he caught me, he put one hand on the ticket counter and jumped over it and caught up with me and reached his hand out to ketch my shirt. I whupped out my pocketknife and snapped it open.

"You put a hand on me and I'll cut it off," I said.

I tried to dodge him and run at the door, but he could move quicker than any grown man I ever see, quick as Pete almost. He cut me off and stood with his back against the door and one foot raised a little, and there wasn't no other way to get out. "Get back on that bench and stay there," he said.

And there wasn't no other way out. And he stood there with his back against the door. So I went back to the bench. And then it seemed like to me that dee-po was full of folks. There was that Law again, and

there was two ladies in fur coats and their faces already painted. But they still looked like they had got up in a hurry and they still never liked it, a old one and a young one, looking down at me.

"He hasn't got a overcoat!" the old one said. "How in the world did he ever get down here by himself?"

"I ask you," the Law said. "I couldn't get nothing out of him except his brother is in Memphis and he wants to get back up there."

"That's right," I said. "I got to git to Memphis today."

"Of course you must," the old one said. "Are you sure you can find your brother when you get to Memphis?"

"I reckon I can," I said. "I ain't got but one and I have knowed him all my life. I reckon I will know him again when I see him."

The old one looked at me. "Somehow he doesn't look like he lives in Memphis," she said.

"He probably don't," the Law said. "You can't tell though. He might live anywhere, overhalls or not. This day and time they get scattered overnight from he— hope to breakfast; boys and girls, too, almost before they can walk good. He might have been in Missouri or Texas either yestiddy, for all we know. But he don't seem to have any doubt his brother is in Memphis. All I know to do is send him up there and leave him look."

"Yes," the old one said.

The young one set down on the bench by me and opened a hand satchel and taken out a artermatic writing pen and some papers.

"Now, honey," the old one said, "we're going to see that you find your brother, but we must have a case history for our files first. We want to know your name and your brother's name and where you were born and when your parents died."

"I don't need no case history neither," I said. "All I want is to get to Memphis. I got to get there today."

"You see?" the Law said. He said it almost like he enjoyed it. "That's what I told you."

"You're lucky, at that, Mrs. Habersham," the bus feller said. "I don't think he's got a gun on him, but he can open that knife da— I mean, fast enough to suit any man."

But the old one just stood there looking at me.

"Well," she said. "Well. I really don't know what to do."

"I do," the bus feller said. "I'm going to give him a ticket out of my own pocket, as a measure of protecting the company against riot and bloodshed. And when Mr. Foote tells the city board about it, it will be a civic matter and they will not only reimburse me, they will give me a medal too. Hey, Mr. Foote?"

But never nobody paid him no mind. The old one still stood looking down at me. She said "Well," again. Then she taken a dollar from her purse and give it to the bus feller. "I suppose he will travel on a child's ticket, won't he?"

"Wellum," the bus feller said, "I just don't know what the regulations would be. Likely I will be fired for not crating him and marking the crate Poison. But I'll risk it."

Then they were gone. Then the Law come back with a sandwich and give it to me.

"You're sure you can find that brother?" he said.

"I ain't yet convinced why not," I said. "If I don't see Pete first, he'll see me. He knows me too."

Then the Law went out for good, too, and I et the sandwich. Then more folks come in and bought tickets, and then the bus feller said it was time to go, and I got into the bus just like Pete done, and we was gone.

I seen all the towns. I seen all of them. When the bus got to going good, I found out I was jest about wore out for sleep. But there was too much I hadn't never saw before. We run out of Jefferson and run past fields and woods, then we would run into another town and out of that un and past fields and woods again, and then into another town with stores and gins and water tanks, and we run along by the railroad for a spell and I seen the signal arm move, and then I seen the train and then some more towns, and I was jest about plumb wore out for sleep, but I couldn't resk it.

Then Memphis begun. It seemed like, to me, it went on for miles. We would pass a patch of stores and I would think that was sholy it and the bus would even stop. But it wouldn't be Memphis yet and we would go on again past water tanks and smokestacks on top of the mills, and if they was gins and sawmills, I never knowed there was that many and I never seen any that big, and where they got enough cotton and logs to run um I don't know.

Then I see Memphis. I knowed I was right this time. It was standing up into the air. It looked like about a dozen whole towns bigger than Jefferson was set up on one edge in a field, standing up into the air higher than ara hill in all Yoknapatawpha County. Then we was in it, with the bus stopping ever' few feet, it seemed like to me, and cars rushing past on both sides of it and the street crowded with folks from ever'where in town that day, until I didn't see how there could 'a' been nobody left in Mis'sippi a-tall to even sell me a bus ticket, let alone write out no case histories. Then the bus stopped. It was another bus dee-po, a heap bigger than the one in Jefferson. And I said, "All right. Where do folks join the Army?"

210

"What?" the bus feller said.

And I said it again, "Where do folks join the Army?"

"Oh," he said. Then he told me how to get there. I was afraid at first I wouldn't ketch on how to do in a town big as Memphis. But I caught on all right. I never had to ask but twice more. Then I was there, and I was durn glad to git out of all them rushing cars and shoving folks and all that racket for a spell, and I thought, It won't be long now, and I thought how if there was any kind of a crowd there that had done already joined the Army, too, Pete would likely see me before I seen him. And so I walked into the room. And Pete wasn't there.

He wasn't even there. There was a soldier with a big arrerhead on his sleeve, writing, and two fellers standing in front of him, and there was some more folks there, I reckon. It seems to me I remember some more folks there.

I went to the table where the soldier was writing, and I said, "Where's Pete?" and he looked up and I said, "My brother. Pete Grier. Where is he?"

"What?" the soldier said. "Who?"

And I told him again. "He joined the Army yestiddy. He's going to Pearl Harbor. So am I. I want to ketch him. Where you-all got him?" Now they were all looking at me, but I never paid them no mind. "Come on," I said. "Where is he?"

The soldier had quit writing. He had both hands spraddled out on the table. "Oh," he said. "You're going, too, hah?"

"Yes," I said. "They got to have wood and water. I can chop it and tote it. Come on. Where's Pete?"

The soldier stood up. "Who let you in here?" he said. "Go on. Beat it."

"Durn that," I said. "You tell me where Pete—"

I be dog if he couldn't move faster than the bus feller even. He never come over the table, he come around it, he was on me almost before I knowed it, so that I jest had time to jump back and whup out my pocketknife and snap it open and hit one lick, and he hollered and jumped back and grabbed one hand with the other and stood there cussing and hollering.

One of the other fellers grabbed me from behind, and I hit at him with the knife, but I couldn't reach him.

Then both of the fellers had me from behind, and then another soldier come out of a door at the back. He had on a belt with a britching strop over one shoulder.

"What the hell is this?" he said.

"That little son cut me with a knife!" the first soldier hollered. When he said that I tried to get at him again, but both them fellers was holding me, two against one, and the soldier with the backing strop said, "Here, here. Put your knife up, feller. None of us are armed. A man don't knife-fight folks that are barehanded." I could begin to hear him then. He sounded jest like Pete talked to me. "Let him go," he said. They let me go. "Now what's all the trouble about?" And I told him. "I see," he said. "And you come up to see if he was all right before he left."

"No," I said, "I came to—"

But he had already turned to where the first soldier was wropping a handkerchief around his hand.

"Have you got him?" he said. The first soldier went back to the table and looked at some papers.

"Here he is," he said. "He enlisted yestiddy. He's in a detachment leaving this morning for Little Rock." He had a watch stropped on his arm. He looked at it. "The train leaves in about fifty minutes. If I know country boys, they're probably all down there at the station right now."

"Get him up here," the one with the backing strop said. "Phone the station. Tell the porter to get him a cab. And you come with me," he said.

It was another office behind that un, with jest a table and some chairs. We set there while the soldier smoked, and it wasn't long; I knowed Pete's feet soon as I heard them. Then the first soldier opened the door and Pete come in. He never had no soldier clothes on. He looked jest like he did when he got on the bus yestiddy morning, except it seemed to me like it was at least a week, so much had happened, and I had done had to do so much traveling. He come in and there he was, looking at me like he hadn't never left home, except that here we was in Memphis, on the way to Pearl Harbor.

"What in durnation are you doing here?" he said.

And I told him, "You got to have wood and water to cook with. I can chop it and tote it for you-all."

"No," Pete said. "You're going back home."

"No, Pete," I said. "I got to go too. I got to. It hurts my heart, Pete."

"No," Pete said. He looked at the soldier. "I jest don't know what could have happened to him, lootenant," he said. "He never drawed a knife on anybody before in his life." He looked at me. "What did you do it for?"

"I don't know," I said. "I jest had to. I jest had to git here. I jest had to find you."

"Well, don't you never do it again, you hear?" Pete said. "You put that knife in your pocket and you keep it there. If I ever again hear of you drawing it on anybody, I'm coming back from wherever I am at and whup the fire out of you. You hear me?"

"I would pure cut a throat if it would bring you back to stay," I said. "Pete," I said. "Pete."

"No," Pete said. Now his voice wasn't hard and quick no more, it was almost quiet, and I knowed now I wouldn't never change him. "You must go home. You must look after maw, and I am depending on you to look after my ten acres. I want you to go back home. Today. Do you hear?"

"I hear," I said.

"Can he get back home by himself?" the soldier said.

"He come up here by himself," Pete said.

"I can get back, I reckon," I said. "I don't live in but one place. I don't reckon it's moved."

Pete taken a dollar out of his pocket and give it to me. "That'll buy your bus ticket right to our mailbox," he said. "I want you to mind the lootenant. He'll send you to the bus. And you go back home and you take care of maw and look after my ten acres and keep that durn knife in your pocket. You hear me?"

"Yes, Pete," I said.

"All right," Pete said. "Now I got to go." He put his hand on my head again. But this time he never wrung my neck. He just laid his hand on my head a minute. And then I be dog if he didn't lean down and kiss me, and I heard his feet and then the door, and I never looked up and that was all, me setting there, rubbing the place where Pete kissed me and the soldier throwed back in his chair, looking out the window and coughing. He reached into his pocket and handed something to me without looking around. It was a piece of chewing gum.

"Much obliged," I said. "Well, I reckon I might as well start back. I got a right fer piece to go."

"Wait," the soldier said. Then he telephoned again and I said again I better start back, and he said again, "Wait. Remember what Pete told you."

So we waited, and then another lady come in, old, too, in a fur coat, too, but she smelled all right, she never had no artermatic writing pen nor no case history neither. She come in and the soldier got up, and she looked around quick until she saw me, and come and put her hand on my shoulder light and quick and easy as maw herself might 'a' done it.

"Come on," she said. "Let's go home to dinner."

"Nome," I said. "I got to ketch the bus to Jefferson."

"I know. There's plenty of time. We'll go home and eat dinner first."

She had a car. And now we was right down in the middle of all them other cars. We was almost under the busses, and all them crowds of people on the street close enough to where I could have talked to them

213

if I had knowed who they was. After a while she stopped the car. "Here we are," she said, and I looked at it, and if all that was her house, she sho had a big family. But all of it wasn't. We crossed a hall with trees growing in it and went into a little room without nothing in it but a feller dressed up in a uniform a heap shinier than them soldiers had, and he shut the door, and then I hollered, "Look out!" and grabbed, but it was all right; that whole little room jest went right on up and stopped and the door opened and we was in another hall, and the lady unlocked a door and we went in, and there was another soldier, a old feller, with a britching strop, too, and a silver-colored bird on each shoulder.

"Here we are," the lady said. "This is Colonel McKellogg. Now, what would you like for dinner?"

"I reckon I'll jest have some ham and eggs and coffee," I said.

She had done started to pick up the telephone. She stopped. "Coffee?" she said. "When did you start drinking coffee?"

"I don't know," I said. "I reckon it was before I could remember."

"You're about eight, aren't you?" she said.

"Nome," I said. "I'm eight and ten months. Going on eleven months."

She telephoned then. Then we set there and I told them how Pete had jest left that morning for Pearl Harbor and I had aimed to go with him, but I would have to go back home to take care of maw and look after Pete's ten acres, and she said how they had a little boy about my size, too, in a school in the East. Then a feller in a short kind of shirttail coat rolled a kind of wheelbarrer in. It had my ham and eggs and a glass of milk and a piece of pie, too, and I thought I was hungry. But when I taken the first bite I found out I couldn't swallow it, and I got up quick.

"I got to go," I said.

"Wait," she said.

"I got to go," I said.

"Just a minute," she said. "I've already telephoned for the car. It won't be but a minute now. Can't you drink the milk even? Or maybe some of your coffee?"

"Nome," I said. "I ain't hungry. I'll eat when I git home." Then the telephone rung. She never even answered it.

"There," she said. "There's the car." And we went back down in that 'ere little moving room with the dressed-up feller. This time it was a big car with a soldier driving it. I got into the front with him. She give the soldier a dollar. "He might get hungry," she said. "Try to find a decent place for him."

"O.K., Mrs. McKellogg," the soldier said.

Then we was gone again. And now I could see Memphis good, bright in the sunshine, while we was swinging around it. And first thing I knowed, we was back on the same highway the bus run on this morning—the patches of stores and them big gins and sawmills, and Memphis running on for miles, it seemed like to me, before it begun to give out. Then we was running again between the fields and woods, running fast now, and except for that soldier, it was like I hadn't never been to Memphis a-tall. We was going fast now. At this rate, before I knowed it we would be home again, and I thought about me riding up to Frenchman's Bend in this big car with a soldier running it, and all of a sudden I begun to cry. I never knowed I was fixing to, and I couldn't stop it. I set there by that soldier, crying. We was going fast.

The Bedquilt

by Dorothy Canfield Fisher

Of all the Elwell family Aunt Mehetabel was certainly the most unimportant member. It was in the New England days, when an unmarried woman was an old maid at twenty, at forty was everyone's servant, and at sixty had gone through so much discipline that she could need no more in the next world. Aunt Mehetabel was sixty-eight.

She had never for a moment known the pleasure of being important to anyone. Not that she was useless in her brother's family; she was expected, as a matter of course, to take upon herself the most tedious and uninteresting part of the household labors. On Mondays she accepted as her share the washing of the men's shirts, heavy with sweat and stiff with dirt from the fields and from their own hard-working bodies. Tuesdays she never dreamed of being allowed to iron anything pretty or even interesting, like the baby's white dresses or the fancy aprons of her young lady nieces. She stood all day pressing out a tiresome monotonous succession of dishcloths and towels and sheets.

In preserving-time she was allowed to have none of the pleasant responsibility of deciding when the fruit had cooked long enough, nor did she share in the little excitement of pouring the sweet-smelling stuff into the stone jars. She sat in a corner with the children and stoned cherries incessantly, or hulled strawberries until her fingers were dyed red to the bone.

The Elwells were not consciously unkind to their aunt, they were even in a vague way fond of her; but she was so utterly insignificant a figure in their lives that they bestowed no thought whatever on her. Aunt Mehetabel did not resent this treatment; she took it quite as unconsciously as they gave it. It was to be expected when one was an old-maid dependent in a busy family. She gathered what crumbs of comfort she could from their occasional careless kindnesses and tried to hide the hurt which even yet pierced her at her brother's rough joking. In the winter when they all sat before the big hearth, roasted apples, drank mulled cider, and teased the girls about their beaux and the boys about their sweethearts, she shrank into a dusky corner with her knitting, happy if the evening passed without her brother saying, with a crude sarcasm, "Ask your Aunt Mehetabel about the beaux that used to come a-sparkin' her!" or, "Mehetabel, how was't when you was in love with Abel Cummings." As a matter of fact, she had been the same at twenty as at sixty, a quiet, mouselike little creature, too timid and shy for anyone to notice, or to raise her eyes for a moment and wish for a life of her own.

Her sister-in-law, a big hearty housewife, who ruled indoors with as autocratic a sway as did her husband on the farm, was rather kind in an absent, offhand way to the shrunken little old woman, and it was through her that Mehetabel was able to enjoy the one pleasure of her life. Even as a girl she had been clever with her needle in the way of patching bedquilts. More than that she could never learn to do. The garments which she made for herself were the most lamentable affairs, and she was humbly grateful for any help in the bewildering business of putting them together. But in patchwork she enjoyed a tepid importance. She could really do that as well as anyone else. During years of devotion to this one art she had accumulated a

217

considerable store of quilting patterns. Sometimes the neighbors would send over and ask "Miss Mehetabel" for such and such a design. It was with an agreeable flutter at being able to help someone that she went to the dresser, in her bare little room under the eaves, and extracted from her crowded portfolio the pattern desired.

She never knew how her great idea came to her. Sometimes she thought she must have dreamed it, sometimes she even wondered reverently, in the phraseology of the weekly prayer meeting, if it had not been "sent" to her. She never admitted to herself that she could have thought of it without other help; it was too great, too ambitious, too lofty a project for her humble mind to have conceived. Even when she finished drawing the design with her own fingers, she gazed at it incredulously, not daring to believe that it could indeed be her handiwork. At first it seemed to her only like a lovely but quite unreal dream. She did not think of putting it into execution—so elaborate, so complicated, so beautifully difficult a pattern could be only for the angels in heaven to quilt. But so curiously does familiarity accustom us even to very wonderful things, that as she lived with this astonishing creation of her mind, the longing grew stronger and stronger to give it material life with her nimble old fingers.

She gasped at her daring when this idea first swept over her and put it away as one does a sinfully selfish notion, but she kept coming back to it again and again. Finally she said compromisingly to herself that she would make one "square," just one part of her design, to see how it would look. Accustomed to the most complete dependence on her brother and his wife, she dared not do even this without asking Sophia's permission. With a heart full of hope and fear thumping furiously against her old ribs, she approached the mistress of the house on churning day, knowing with the innocent guile of a child that the country woman was apt to be in a good temper while working over the fragrant butter in the cool cellar.

Sophia listened absently to her sister-in-law's halting, hesitating petition. "Why, yes, Mehetabel," she said, leaning far down into the huge churn for the last golden morsels—"why, yes, start another quilt if you want to. I've got a lot of pieces from the spring sewing that will work in real good." Mehetabel tried honestly to make her see that this would be no common quilt, but her limited vocabulary and her emotion stood between her and expression. At last Sophia said, with a kindly impatience, "Oh, there! Don't bother me. I never could keep track of your quiltin' patterns, anyhow. I don't care what pattern you go by."

With this overwhelmingly, although unconsciously, generous permission Mehetabel rushed back up the steep attic stairs to her room, and in a joyful agitation began preparations for the work of her life. It was even better than she hoped. By some heaven-sent inspiration she had invented a pattern beyond which no patchwork quilt could go.

She had but little time from her incessant round of household drudgery for this new and absorbing occupation, and she did not dare sit up late at night lest she burn too much candle. It was weeks before the little square began to take on a finished look, to show the pattern. Then Mehetabel was in a fever of impatience to bring it to completion. She was too conscientious to shirk even the smallest part of her share of the work of the house, but she rushed through it with a speed which left her panting as she climbed to the little room. This seemed like a radiant spot to her as she bent over the innumerable scraps of cloth which already in her imagination ranged themselves in the infinitely diverse pattern of her masterpiece. Finally she could wait no longer, and one evening ventured to bring her work down beside the fire where the family sat, hoping that some good fortune would give her a place near the tallow candles on the mantelpiece. She was on the last corner of the square, and her needle flew in and out with inconceivable rapidity. No one noticed her, a fact which filled her with relief, and by bedtime she had but a few more stitches to add.

As she stood up with the others, the square fluttered out of her trembling old hands and fell on the table. Sophia glanced at it carelessly. "Is that the new quilt you're beginning on?" she asked with a yawn. "It looks like a real pretty pattern. Let's see it." Up to that moment Mehetabel had labored in the purest spirit of disinterested devotion to an ideal, but as Sophia held her work toward the candle to examine it, and exclaimed in amazement and admiration, she felt an astonished joy to know that her creation would stand the test of publicity.

"Land sakes!" ejaculated her sister-in-law, looking at the many-colored square. "Why, Mehetabel Elwell, where'd you git that pattern?"

"I made it up," said Mehetabel quietly, but with unutterable pride.

"No!" exclaimed Sophia incredulously. "*Did* you! Why, I never see such a pattern in my life. Girls, come here and see what your Aunt Mehetabel is doing."

The three tall daughters turned back reluctantly from the stairs. "I don't seem to take much interest in patchwork," said one listlessly.

"No, nor I neither!" answered Sophia; "but a stone image would take an interest in this pattern. Honest, Mehetabel, did you think of it yourself? And how under the sun and stars did you ever git your courage up to start in a-making it? Land! Look at all those tiny squinchy little seams! Why the wrong side ain't a thing *but* seams!"

The girls echoed their mother's exclamations, and Mr. Elwell himself came over to see what they were discussing. "Well, I declare!" he said, looking at his sister with eyes more approving than she could ever remember. "That beats old Mis' Wightman's quilt that got the blue ribbon so many times at the county fair."

Mehetabel's heart swelled within her, and tears of joy moistened her old eyes as she lay that night in her narrow, hard bed, too proud and excited to sleep. The next day her sister-in-law amazed her by taking the huge pan of potatoes out of her lap and setting one of the younger children to peeling them. "Don't you want to go on with that quiltin' pattern?" she said; "I'd kind o' like to see how you're goin' to make the grapevine design come out on the corner."

By the end of the summer the family interest had risen so high that Mehetabel was given a little stand in the sitting room where she could keep her pieces, and work in odd minutes. She almost wept over such kindness, and resolved firmly not to take advantage of it by neglecting her work, which she performed with a fierce thoroughness. But the whole atmosphere of her world was changed. Things had a meaning now. Through the longest task of washing milk pans there rose the rainbow of promise of her variegated work. She took her place by the little table and put the thimble on her knotted, hard finger with the solemnity of a priestess performing a sacred rite.

She was even able to bear with some degree of dignity the extreme honor of having the minister and the minister's wife comment admiringly on her great project. The family felt quite proud of Aunt Mehetabel as Minister Bowman had said it was work as fine as any he had ever seen, "and he didn't know but finer!" The remark was repeated verbatim to the neighbors in the following weeks when they dropped in and examined in a perverse silence some astonishingly difficult *tour de force* which Mehetabel had just finished.

The family especially plumed themselves on the slow progress of the quilt. "Mehetabel has been to work on that corner for six weeks, come Tuesday, and she ain't half done yet," they explained to visitors. They fell out of the way of always expecting her to be the one to run on errands, even for the children. "Don't bother your Aunt Mehetabel," Sophia would call. "Can't you see she's got to a ticklish place on the quilt?"

The old woman sat up straighter and looked the world in the face. She was a part of it at last. She joined in the conversation and her remarks were listened to. The children were even told to mind her when she asked them to do some service for her, although this she did but seldom, the habit of self-effacement being too strong.

One day some strangers from the next town drove up and asked if

they could inspect the wonderful quilt which they had heard of, even down in their end of the valley. After that such visitations were not uncommon, making the Elwells' house a notable object. Mehetabel's quilt came to be one of the town sights, and no one was allowed to leave the town without having paid tribute to its worth. The Elwells saw to it that their aunt was better dressed than she had ever been before, and one of the girls made her a pretty little cap to wear on her thin white hair.

A year went by and a quarter of the quilt was finished; a second year passed and half was done. The third year Mehetabel had pneumonia and lay ill for weeks and weeks, overcome with terror lest she die before her work was completed. A fourth year and one could really see the grandeur of the whole design; and in September of the fifth year, the entire family watching her with eager and admiring eyes, Mehetabel quilted the last stitches in her creation. The girls held it up by the four corners, and they all looked at it in a solemn silence. Then Mr. Elwell smote one horny hand within the other and exclaimed, "By ginger! That's goin' to the county fair!" Mehetabel blushed a deep red at this. It was a thought which had occurred to her in a bold moment, but she had not dared to entertain it. The family acclaimed the idea, and one of the boys was forthwith dispatched to the house of the neighbor who was chairman of the committee for their village. He returned with radiant face. "Of course he'll take it. Like's not it may git a prize, so he says; but he's got to have it right off, because all the things are goin' tomorrow morning."

Even in her swelling pride Mehetabel felt a pang of separation as the bulky package was carried out of the house. As the days went on she felt absolutely lost without her work. For years it had been her one preoccupation, and she could not bear even to look at the little stand, now quite bare of the litter of scraps which had lain on it so long. One of the neighbors, who took the long journey to the fair, reported that the quilt was hung in a place of honor in a glass case in "Agricultural Hall." But that meant little to Mehetabel's utter ignorance of all that lay outside of her brother's home. The family noticed the old woman's depression, and one day Sophia said kindly, "You feel sort o' lost without the quilt, don't you, Mehetabel?"

"They took it away so quick!" she said wistfully; "I hadn't hardly had one real good look at it myself."

Mr. Elwell made no comment, but a day or two later he asked his sister how early she could get up in the morning.

"I dun'no'. Why?" she asked.

"Well, Thomas Ralston has got to drive clear to West Oldton to see a lawyer there, and that is four miles beyond the fair. He says if you can git up so's to leave here at four in the morning he'll drive you over to the fair, leave you there for the day, and bring you back again at night."

Mehetabel looked at him with incredulity. It was as though someone had offered her a ride in a golden chariot up to the gates of heaven. "Why, you can't *mean* it!" she cried, paling with the intensity of her emotion. Her brother laughed a little uneasily. Even to his careless indifference this joy was a revelation of the narrowness of her life in his home. "Oh, 'tain't so much to go to the fair. Yes, I mean it. Go git your things ready, for he wants to start tomorrow morning."

All that night a trembling, excited old woman lay and stared at the rafters. She, who had never been more than six miles from home in her life, was going to drive thirty miles away—it was like going to another world. She who had never seen anything more exciting than a church supper was to see the county fair. To Mehetabel it was like making the tour of the world. She had never dreamed of doing it. She could not at all imagine what it would be like.

Nor did the exhortations of the family, as they bade good-bye to her, throw any light on her confusion. They had all been at least once to the scene of gaiety she was to visit, and as she tried to eat her breakfast they called out conflicting advice to her till her head whirled. Sophia told her to be sure and see the display of preserves. Her brother said not to miss inspecting the stock, her nieces said the fancywork was the only thing worth looking at, and her nephews said she must bring them home an account of the races. The buggy drove up to the door, she was helped in, and her wraps tucked about her. They all stood together and waved good-bye to her as she drove out of the yard. She waved back, but she scarcely saw them. On her return home that evening she was very pale, and so tired and stiff that her brother had to lift her out bodily, but her lips were set in a blissful smile. They crowded around her with thronging questions, until Sophia pushed them all aside, telling them Aunt Mehetabel was too tired to speak until she had had her supper. This was eaten in an enforced silence on the part of the children, and then the old woman was helped into an easy chair before the fire. They gathered about her, eager for news of the great world, and Sophia said, "Now, come, Mehetabel, tell us all about it!"

Mehetabel drew a long breath. "It was just perfect!" she said; "finer even than I thought. They've got it hanging up in the very middle of a sort o' closet made of glass, and one of the lower corners is ripped and turned back so's to show the seams on the wrong side."

She who had never seen anything more exciting than a church supper was to see the county fair. To Mehetabel it was like making the tour of the world.

223

"What?" asked Sophia, a little blankly.

"Why, the quilt!" said Mehetabel in surprise. "There are a whole lot of other ones in that room, but not one that can hold a candle to it, if I do say it who shouldn't. I heard lots of people say the same thing. You ought to have heard what the women said about that corner, Sophia. They said—well, I'd be ashamed to *tell* you what they said. I declare if I wouldn't!"

Mr. Elwell asked, "What did you think of that big ox we've heard so much about?"

"I didn't look at the stock," returned his sister indifferently. "That set of pieces you gave me, Maria, from your red waist, come out just lovely!" she assured one of her nieces. "I heard one woman say you could 'most smell the red silk roses."

"Did any of the horses in our town race?" asked young Thomas.

"I didn't see the races."

"How about the preserves?" asked Sophia.

"I didn't see the preserves," said Mehetabel calmly. "You see, I went right to the room where the quilt was, and then I didn't want to leave it. It had been so long since I'd seen it. I had to look at it first real good myself, and then I looked at the others to see if there was any that could come up to it. And then the people begun comin' in and I got so interested in hearin' what they had to say I couldn't think of goin' anywheres else. I ate my lunch right there too, and I'm as glad as can be I did, too; for what do you think?"—she gazed about her with kindling eyes—"while I stood there with a sandwich in one hand didn't the head of the hull concern come in and open the glass door and pin 'First Prize' right in the middle of the quilt!"

There was a stir of congratulation and proud exclamation. Then Sophia returned again to the attack. "Didn't you go to see anything else?" she queried.

"Why, no," said Mehetabel. "Only the quilt. Why should I?"

She fell into a reverie where she saw again the glorious creation of her hand and brain hanging before all the world with the mark of highest approval on it. She longed to make her listeners see the splendid vision with her. She struggled for words; she reached blindly after unknown superlatives. "I tell you it looked like—" she said, and paused, hesitating. Vague recollections of hymnbook phraseology came into her mind, the only form of literary expression she knew; but they were dismissed as being sacrilegious, and also not sufficiently forcible. Finally, "I tell you it looked real *well!*" she assured them, and sat staring into the fire, on her tired old face the supreme content of an artist who has realized his ideal.

Hot-Collared Mule

by Jesse Stuart

"Keep that mule a-goin'," Pa hollered as I passed by where he was sitting on a log under the shade fanning himself with sourwood leaves. "Run 'im until he's hot as blue blazes!"

I couldn't answer Pa. My tongue was out of my mouth and I was getting my breath hard. If you have never owned a cold-collared mule then you wouldn't understand what a job it is to run one long enough to get him hot so he'll work in the harness. What you do when you run him is put a collar on him and run along behind and slap him across the back with the lines when he begins to slow down.

The bad thing for Pa and me was, we had a mule we couldn't ride or work until we got his collar hot. Pa had tried to ride him. Pa went over his head when he bucked and came down belly-flat on the hard road in front of the mule, knocking all the wind out of him. When I had him galloping, he stopped suddenly with me. I bounced up in the air like a rubber ball. It was done so quickly I couldn't come down to the ground on my feet. I came down a-sittin' in the middle of the road. And I sat there seeing stars. Of all the trading Pa had done, he'd never got a mule like Rock.

"He's a-gettin' warmed up," I grunted to Pa as I passed him on the second lap.

"Fetch 'im around agin and I'll take 'im," Pa said. "Just be keerful and don't do any hollerin'."

If I had wanted to holler at Rock I couldn't, for I was so short of

225

breath. I was running Rock up a logging road to the turn of the hill; there we turned right up a cowpath that wound up the hill and connected with another logging road which ran parallel to the one below and then turned perpendicular down the hill and connected with the first road. The circle of narrow road looked cool, for it was bordered by culled trees whose clouds of green leaves sagged in wilted pods. These leaves were so thick they not only obscured the sun but they kept out the little August breeze that idly swayed the wilted pods of leaves. It was a close smothery warmth down under the trees that heated up a man faster than it did a cold-collared mule.

"All right, Pa," I grunted as I came in on my last lap. "It's your time now."

"Hit'll be the last time one of us has to run this mule," Pa said as he took the lines.

I dropped down on the log where Pa was sitting and picked up the sourwood fan. Sweat ran from my face like little streams pour from the face of a hill after an April shower. I'd run Rock three laps around the circle. Now Pa would run him two. Pa couldn't run as well as I could, for he was older and his legs were stiffer and his breath came harder. While I sat fanning, I watched him go out of sight, running stiff-legged like a cold buck rabbit in the wintertime. The twist of burley leaf was jumping up and down in his hip pocket as he made the turn to climb the hill.

"Hit's a hard way to git a mule to work," Pa grunted as he passed me going into his second lap.

I was fanning fast as I could fan. I had cooled down some, but my clothes were as wet as if I had jumped into the river.

When Pa came around on his second lap, I didn't think he'd make it. But he did. His face was red as a sliced beet, and his clothes were as wet as mine were. But a sweaty foam had gathered under Rock's flanks and his shoulders were wet around his collar.

"He's in shape to work now," Pa said as he dropped to the ground. "I'll wind a minute before we hitch 'im to the drag."

But Pa didn't wind very long. He sat there long enough to catch his second wind. We couldn't wait until Rock's shoulders cooled. We threw the gears over his back, hitched a trace chain to the singletree, and let him draw the log chain to the dead oak that Pa had chopped down for us to haul to the woodyard.

"When Cyrus sees my mule pull a log like this," Pa said as he wrapped the log chain around the log, "he'll swap that good mule o' his 'n and give me ten 'r fifteen dollars to boot! See, this log's heavier than Rock. He'll be a-pullin' more than his weight on the ground," he went on as he fastened the log chain around the drag. "I'm a-goin' to ast 'im twenty-five dollars to boot. Then, maybe, I'll drop to fifteen dollars. Remember, I'm through runnin' a cold-collared mule. My ticker ain't good enough fer it and my legs won't stand."

"It's some job for a young man," I said.

"All right, Rock," Pa said, slapping him with a line. "Git down and pull!"

Rock squatted, braced his feet, and pulled, shaking the big log from where it had indented the hard earth. Then, without Pa's telling him, Rock pulled again, and the big log started sliding along while sparks flew from his steel shoes.

"If he wuzn't cold-collared I wouldn't trade 'im fer any animal I ever laid eyes on," Pa said, holding the lines up from the briers.

I walked behind Pa as he drove Rock toward our woodyard.

Maybe our timing was just right. We pulled into our woodyard under the sour-apple tree just as Cyrus Broadfoot rode his harnessed mule up and stopped.

"That's some log, Mick," he said.

"Well, it's purty good-sized," Pa said. "But Rock's pulled a lot bigger logs than this 'n. I'll pull 'im agin any mule of his pounds. Do you want to pull your mule agin 'im?"

"Not necessarily, Mick," Cyrus said, dismounting his mule.

"I thought if you wanted to hitch yer mule to my mule's singletree, we'd let 'em pull agin each other," Pa said as he unhitched the log chain from the drag. "If yer mule pulls mine backwards," Pa went on, "I'll give you my mule. If my mule pulls your mule backwards, then ye give me yer mule! That's fair enough!"

That was the way Pa always started a trade. He would always put the other fellow on the fence. He'd set a price, give or take. And he'd trade at sight unseen. That's how we'd got old Rock. He'd traded with Herb Coloney. Herb told Pa he had a mule that could pull his weight on the ground. That was enough. Pa traded him a two-year-old Jersey bull and got ten dollars to boot right there. Now he was going after Cyrus.

"I don't keer much about tradin' that way, Mick," Cyrus said, pulling a big knife from his pocket with one hand as he picked up a stick with the other.

"Yer mule's bigger 'n mine," Pa said.

"I know that," Cyrus said, whittling a big shaving. "But he ain't as old."

"How old is yer mule?" Pa asked.

"Rye's a-comin' five in the spring," Cyrus said, his words muffled as the sound of his voice was strained through his big mustache.

227

"Rock ain't but four," Pa bragged. "He ain't shed his colt's teeth yet."

Then Pa picked up a stick, pulled his knife from his pocket, and began to whittle. While Pa whittled big shavings from a poplar stick, Cyrus opened Rock's mouth and looked at his teeth.

"He's still got his colt's teeth all right," Cyrus said. "Don't ye want to look in my Rye's mouth, Mick?"

"I'll take your word fer his age, Cyrus," Pa said, whittling away. "Ye've allus been a good neighbor and a truthful man!"

Pa's words didn't please Cyrus. Maybe Cyrus was thinking about the last time he had traded with Pa. Pa had said these same words and patted Cyrus on the back when he sold three steers for a hundred and forty-three dollars. Cyrus kept them all that winter, put them on grass next spring and summer, and sold them late in the fall for a hundred forty-four dollars. He knew Pa was a good trader, the best among the hills.

"Jist how much boot are you a-goin' to ast me, Mick?" Cyrus asked.

"Tell you what I'll do, Cyrus," Pa said, laying his stick and knife down so he could pull his galluses out and let them fly back like he always did when he was trading. "Since it's you, I'll take twenty-five dollars to boot and trade."

"That's a lot of boot, Mick," he said.

"Won't take a cent less," Pa said.

"I won't give you a penny," Cyrus said, whittling a long shaving.

"I'll tell you what us do," Pa said. "Let's split the difference!"

"Okay," Cyrus said.

Cyrus pulled a ten-dollar bill, two ones, and a fifty-cent piece from a Bull Durham tobacco sack he was carrying in the little watch pocket on the bib of his overalls.

"Jist a minute," Pa said, before he took the money. "That means we're trading harness too!"

"Right," Cyrus said.

Then Pa took the money. I knew Pa had got a barg'in on the harness. Rock's harness was wrapped and tied in many places with groundhog-hide strings.

"You've got a pullin' mule," Pa said as Cyrus picked up the rope lines to drive Rock away. "He's the only mule in these parts that can pull his weight on the ground."

Then Pa looked at me and winked. I knew what Pa meant, for Cyrus didn't know how we had to run old Rock to get up steam. In a cold collar he wouldn't pull the hat off a man's head.

"I'm satisfied, Mick," were Cyrus's last words as he drove Rock up the hollow.

I wasn't sorry to see Rock go.

"Now we've got a mule," Pa said. "We'll hitch 'im to the express wagon and take that load of melons to town."

With all the confidence of a strutting turkey gobbler, Pa drove Rye to our express wagon. He was proud of his trade, and I was too. I never wanted to see another mule that I had to run to get steamed up like I had to run Rock. I never wanted to see another cold-collared mule.

Our express wagon was loaded with watermelons and parked under the shade of a white oak in our backyard. When Mom saw Pa backing the new mule between the shafts she came out at the door.

"I told ye, Sall, I'd have a new mule to take these melons to Greenup," Pa bragged. "I really set Cyrus on fire in that trade! I really give 'im a good burnin'. One he'll never forget!"

"I guess it's all right to do that, Mick," Mom said. "Men do such things. But one of these days you're goin' to get a good swindlin'."

"Not me," Pa said, laying the lines down and pulling at his galluses. "I've made you a good livin', ain't I?"

"Yes," Mom agreed by nodding her head.

"And I've done hit mostly by tradin', ain't I?" Pa went on bragging as I hitched the trace chains to the singletree.

"Yes, by cheating people," Mom said. "I feel bad about Cyrus Broadfoot's six little children. Never have a pair of shoes on their feet all winter!"

Then Mom turned around and went back into the house.

"Funny how softhearted wimmen are," Pa said as he fastened a chain through the loop while I fastened the other. "If wimmen had to make a livin' and men stay in the house, wouldn't that be funny? Could ye imagine yer mom out a-mule-swappin'?"

Pa laughed at his own joke as he climbed up on the express seat and I climbed up beside him. With a light tap from the line, Rye moved the loaded express wagon across the yard and down the road toward Greenup. Pa sat straight as a young poplar with his whip across his shoulder and a chew of burley leaf under his suntanned beardy jaw.

As we drove down the sandy jolt-wagon road, I never heard such bragging as Pa did. He talked about the trades he had made in his lifetime, how he had cheated people from the time he began mule trading. That was when he was sixteen. He would tell about cheating people, then he would laugh. And when he spoke of how he had traded a cold-collared mule to Cyrus, he would bend over, slap his knees with his hands, and laugh until people walking along the road would stop and look at us.

"When old Cyrus starts runnin' Rock . . ." Pa would never be able to finish what he started out to say for laughing. He laughed until I had to take the lines and drive so he would have both hands free to slap his knees.

"Old Cyrus will get hot under the collar," Pa went on. "I can just see old Cyrus a-takin' off behind old Rock. . . ."

The tears rolled from Pa's eyes down his sunburnt face.

"Wonder if he'll know what's the matter with . . ." and Pa got down on the load of melons and rolled around like he was crazy.

At first it was a little funny, but after I thought about what Mom had told him I couldn't laugh any more. And I was ashamed of him the way he rolled over the watermelons, laughing. The people we passed would stop and look at him like he was out of his head. I'd never seen a man in my life enjoy a barg'in like Pa was enjoying his trade with Cyrus.

And Pa had made a barg'in, for Rye pulled the load easily and smoothly along the jolt-wagon road until we reached the turnpike. Now we were on the road to Greenup, where we would soon sell our melons. When we reached the turnpike where there were more people traveling, Pa got back on the seat beside of me, put a cigar between his beardy lips, and took the lines. He would never chew burley when we got near town. He would always light up a cigar, though Pa enjoyed a chew more than he did a smoke. He thought he looked more important with a cigar in his mouth.

Rye had pulled steadily along for three miles or more, and now I noticed there was foaming sweat dripping from his flanks and oozing from beneath his collar and dark shades of sweat on his sleek, curry-combed and brushed brown hair over his ribs. Pa didn't notice the sweat on Rye. He just sat upon the high springboard seat with a whip over his shoulder that he carried for an ornament, a cigar in his mouth to make him look important, and looked down at everybody we passed.

"Pa, you'd better let Rye take it a little easy," I said. "He's gettin' pretty warm!"

"A mule can stand an awful lot of heat," Pa said, driving on.

But when we reached the Lottie Bates Hill, Rye braced his feet and wouldn't move a step.

"Wonder what's wrong with Rye?" Pa asked me.

"I don't know," I said.

"He needs a little ticklin' with the whip." Pa laughed, pulling it from over his shoulder and tapping Rye on the back.

Then Rye started going backwards, shoving the express wagon zigzagging from one side of the road to the other.

"Slap on the brakes," Pa shouted to me.

I put on the brakes as quickly as I could and stopped the wagon. People passing us along the road started laughing. And Pa was really embarrassed. His suntanned face began to change color into a paw-paw-leaf crimson.

"He's a mule that goes backwards," a man said, laughing.

"Somethin's wrong with the harness," Pa said. "Here, take these lines. I'm gettin' down to see what's wrong."

I held the lines while he started to examine the backband and the trace chains. When Pa put his hand on the backband, Rye kicked up with both hind feet and squealed.

"What's the matter with that mule?" Pa said, jumpin' back in a hurry while the strangers walking home with loads on their backs stood at a safe distance and laughed. "He acts like he's crazy. I'm sure it's his harness hurtin' 'im or a blue-tailed fly on his belly."

"See if the bridle bit is cutting his tongue," I said.

When Pa started to open his mouth to look, Rye lunged forward with both front feet in the air and tried to hit Pa, but he sidestepped just in time.

"That mule's dangerous," Pa wailed. "Git this near town when we can see the smoke from the chimneys, then he acts up like this!"

The words weren't out of Pa's mouth when Rye lunged forward and I pulled back on the lines. Then he started going backwards and the express wagon started rolling down a little hill. The endboard came out and the melons rolled like apples from the wagon bed, down the hill into Town Branch.

"There goes our melons," Pa moaned.

Twenty people, who had stopped to enjoy our trouble, all made a run for the melons that were broken and ruined. While all of them but one old beardy-faced man ran for the melons, Rye jumped forward again, veered to one side, and broke the shafts from the express.

"Hold 'im," Pa shouted.

"I'm doing my best," I said, rearing back on the lines until I brought the mule under control.

And now it worried me not so much that the people were eating our melons, but that I was providing entertainment for them while they ate. They could hardly eat our melons for laughing at us. But Pa puffed harder on his cigar and there was a worried look on his face.

"Say, stranger," the old man with the beardy face said as he slowly approached Pa, "I don't want to butt into yer affairs. But I'm an old mule skinner. I ust to drive a mule team when they had the furnaces back in this county. I drove mules fer forty-three years and hauled cordwood," he went on talking, "and I can tell ye what's the matter with that mule. I've seen four 'r five like 'im in my lifetime!"

"Hit must be his harness that's a-hurtin' 'im, Dad," Pa apologized for Rye.

"Nope, that ain't it, stranger," the man said. "He's a hot-collared mule!"

"Never heard of a hot-collared mule," Pa said, throwing up both hands. "I've heard of a cold-collared mule!"

"Well, that's what he is, stranger," the old man said. "Somebody's give ye a good burnin'. He's sold ye a hot-collared mule. And this one is a dangerous animal!"

I looked at Pa and he looked at me.

"And I can prove to ye he's hot-collared," the old man said.

"How can ye do it?" Pa said, turning around to face the old man.

"Take this bucket and go down to the crick and get a bucket of cool water and throw hit over his shoulders," the old man said, as he emptied his groceries so Pa could use it. "Ye'll see that he'll pull when he gits cool shoulders!"

"I'll try anything," Pa said. "I'd like to git my express wagon back home."

Thirty-five or forty people who had now gathered to eat our watermelons looked strangely at Pa when they saw him dip a bucket of water from the creek. They watched Pa carry the water up to the road and throw it on Rye's shoulders, while the mule stood perfectly still as if he enjoyed it.

"It'll take more water," the old man said.

While the people laughed at Pa carrying water to put on a mule's shoulders like he was trying to put out a fire, I thought of what Pa had said about Cyrus's having to run old Rock to get up steam. And the people with watermelon smeared on their faces laughed at Pa more than he had laughed at Cyrus. But after Pa had carried the tenth bucket of water the old man said, "That's enough now, stranger. Ye've put the fire out!"

And when the old man smiled I could see his discolored teeth through his thin dingy-white mustache.

"Now try to drive 'im, young man," the old man said to me.

"Get up, Rye," I said, touching his back lightly with the lines.

The mule moved gently away, pulling the express wagon with the broken shafts which made it zigzag from one side of the road to the other. And when I stopped the mule, Pa came up and said, "It's a new wrinkle on my horn. I never heard of a hot-collared mule but we've got one, Adger. We'll haf to wire up these shafts someway until we can git home. I'll haf to do some more swappin'. Yer mom was right."

Cocks Must Crow

by Marjorie Kinnan Rawlings

I got nothing particular against time. Time's a natural thing. Folks is a kind of accident on the face of the earth, but time was here before us. And when we've done finished messing ourselves up, and when the last man turns over to die, saying, "Now how come us to make such a loblolly of living?"—why, time'll rock right on. But what I do hold against time is this: Time be so all-fired slick. It's slick as a otter slide. And how come me to object to that, don't be on account of you slip down it so fast, but you slip down without noticing what it's a-doing to you.

Time ain't got the decency of a rattlesnake. A rattler most times'll give warning. I almost lost my Will, and me a big fat somebody no man'd look at twicet lessen he was used to me. I almost lost him on account of I had changed and didn't know it, and time never give me the first sign to warn me. Merciful jaybird!

My Will married me—some say I married him—when I was a big feather-bolster kind of a gal, pink-cheeked and laughing and easy-going and heavy-eating. I will say, I always did have a tongue in my head and loved to use it, but I used it fair and open. I'd had men was more to look at than Will come courting me out at Pa's place, but Will had a gold tooth and I always was a fool for a gold tooth. I takened to the little feller first time I seed him. I was a heap bigger'n him even then.

235

Third time Will come out of a Sunday evening, Pa tipped back in his chair on the porch and said, "Better look out, young feller, Quincey don't take you for a play-dolly."

Will looked him square in the eye. "You ever tried to hold a hawk in your bare hand?"

"Why, no," Pa said, "I'd know better."

"Well, a hawk's a heap littler'n you, ain't he? But 'taint his size or your size makes you leave him be. It's his nature. Now the gal ain't growed so big in these flatwoods, could take me for a play-dolly. I ain't got the size to hold Quincey, here, on my lap. But she shore as hell ain't going to hold me on hers."

Pa laughed and slapped hisself. "Will Dover," he said, "if you want her and she don't take you, I'll lick her with my own hands."

"Ain't nobody going to lick Quincey but me," Will said, "and I aim just to reason with her."

"Ain't he something?" Pa said to me. "Quincey, I've always told you, you can't judge no man by the length of his suspenders. You got to judge him by the spirit in him."

And I done so. I takened Will first time he offered. The business he was in was in his favor. He run a livery stable in Oak Bluff, and he come courting in a light trap with a pair of black horses drove tandem. It kind of melted me. I hadn't never see a pair of horses drove tandem.

We hit it off fine right from the start. Will was little and he acted gentle, but couldn't nobody press him no farther than he was o' mind to be pressed. That was one thing I disremembered as the years went by.

When we was fresh-married I said to him, "You're soft-acting, Will Dover, but you got a will as hard as a gopher shell."

"You ain't fooling me none, neither," he said. "You got a tongue as sharp as a new cane knife, but your heart's as big as your behind, and soft as summer butter." He looked at me with his head on one side, and them blue eyes as bright and quick as a mockingbird's. "And that's why I love you, Quincey Dover," he said.

In them days I was full of idees about handling men. They was good idees and mostly this: Man-nature is man-nature, and a woman's a fool to interfere. A man worth his salt can't be helt to heel like a bird dog. Give him his head. Leave him run and he won't run far away from his regular rations. Men is the most regular creatures on earth. All they need is to know they can run if they want to. That satisfies them. And that's what I had to go and forget.

Some things about me didn't never change. My tongue didn't never change and, truth to tell, I'd not want it to. And what Will called my big heart, I don't believe didn't never change. When a old tabby cat has got no place to birth her kittens, or some poor soul in the woods is fool enough to be bringing another young un into the world, and not a piece of cloth to wrap it in, why, I got to light in and fix a bed for that tabby cat or that fool woman.

What did change about me was my size. I had a mighty good start, and seems like ary piece of rations I've ever ate has just wrapped itself around my middle and stayed there. The last time I weighed myself was a ways back on the scales in the express office, and it balanced two hundred and twenty, and I quit weighing.

"Don't let it fret you," Will said. "You was a big gal when I got you, and I'd purely hate to turn you back to your Maker without I had added something to the good thing was give me."

My Will has been a heap of comfort. Can ary one figure how I could be mean to a man like that? Seems to me, I growed so big, I got biggety.

I can't no-ways recollect when the change in me begun. First time I remember cold-out bearing down on Will was about two years ago.

He said to me one evening after supper, "The boys is having a cockfight down to the garage. Reckon I'll ease on down and watch it."

I said, "You'll do no such of a thing. Cockfighting is a low-down nasty business. Men that's got nothing better to do than watch a pair of roosters kill theirselves isn't fitten company."

Will looked at me slantwise and he said, "Don't you reckon I can judge my company, Quincey?"

I said, "Judge all you please, but you'll go to no cockfight."

He filled up his pipe, and he tamped the tobaccy down, and he lit it and he said, "Since when you been telling me where I could go?"

I said, "You heerd me the first time."

Now I felt mighty righteous about it. I'd never seed a cockfight, but I'd heerd tell they was cruel and bloody, and besides, it's agin the law.

Will rocked awhile and he smoked awhile and he said, "Nothing ain't worth quarreling about. I'll just go on down to the station and wait-see do them automobile parts come in on Number Three."

I said, "All right, but don't you go near no cockfight."

He give me a look I hadn't never seed before, and he said, "No, ma'am," in a funny way, and he went on off.

Now I got to put this together the best way I can. I ain't like them story writers can make a tale come out as even as a first-prize patchwork quilt. Life ain't slick like a story, no-ways. I got to remember this, and remember that, and when I'm done it'll make sense. The Widow Tippett moving to Oak Bluff didn't seem to have a thing to do with me at the time. But move to Oak Bluff she did, and get messed up

I ain't like them story writers can make a tale come out as even as a first-prize patchwork quilt. Life ain't slick like a story, no-ways.

237

in my and Will's business, she done so. And that was about a year and a half ago.

First thing I knowed, I heerd a strange widow had bought the old Archer farm. I give her time to get nested down, and one afternoon I went out to welcome her. I takened a basket of my guava preserves and my sour-orange marmalade, and a bundle of cuttings from my porch plants. Minute she come to the door, I seed she had a chip on her shoulder. She was a quiet kind of a woman, right pretty if you like skimmed-milk eyes and sand-colored hair with a permanent wave put to it, and a tippy-tippy way of walking.

"Mis' Tippett?" I said. "I'm Quincey Dover. I come to welcome you."

"Pleased to meet you. I figured that was who 'twas."

I never seed a place kept so careless. The front room looked as if a truck had just backed up to the door and dumped everything out together, and she hadn't never straightened it out and didn't aim to. She hadn't washed her dishes and a big old tomcat was asleep in the dishpan. There was cats and dogs strowed all over the house and yard. A Dominick hen was on the table, pecking at the butter.

"Set down," she said. "I hear tell Oak Bluff just couldn't make out without you."

"When I see my duty, I do it," I said.

"That works good when ever'one sees it the same," she said. "You're the lady don't let her husband go to no cockfight, ain't you?"

"You mighty right," I said.

"Ain't it nice to have a man does just like you tell him?" she said. There was pure sandspurs under that easy voice.

"I find it so," I said. "You're a widow, they tell me. Sod?"

"Water. Water and whiskey."

"I never heerd tell of a water widow."

"He was drunk as ten coots and fell in the water and never did come up. A lake's as good a burying place as any."

"I'm mighty sorry about your loss."

"Don't mention it. I didn't lose much."

I knowed from then on I didn't like the Widow Tippett and didn't mean to have no truck with her. I got up to go and I give her the preserves and the cuttings. She didn't offer me my basket back.

I said, "Pleased to of met you. Call on me if a need come," and I walked down the path. I turned at the gate. "I hope you ain't fixing to farm this land," I said. "It's plumb wore out."

"I thank you," she said. "Just to keep folks from fretting theirselves to death, you can tell Oak Bluff I got steady insurance and aim to raise chickens."

I said to myself, I'll tell Oak Bluff you're the biggetiest woman I know, to look like a curly-headed mouse.

What she thought of me, she told me when the time come.

Now if I'd of takened to her, I'd of give her settings of my eggs. I have game chickens, as they near about feed themselves, ranging. They lays good, and they grows to fryer size the quickest of ary chicken. The breed is the Roundhead, and the roosters is some kind of handsome bronze and red, and now and again a long white feather mixed in with the shiny green tail. 'Tain't everybody wants game chickens, on account of the hens'll steal their nests. Could be, I figured, the Widow Tippett'd not crave to raise Roundheads. I felt a mite mean, just the same, not offering. Then I put it out of my mind.

The next thing Will was asking me for a couple of my frying-size roosters. "Quincey," he said, "can I have a couple of them young roosters to give to a friend?"

"I raised them chickens to put in our own bellies," I said. "Anybody you want to invite to set down and eat fried chicken with us, that's another thing."

"I want to give them away," he said.

"Go catch a mess of fish to give away, if you want to feed the county," I said.

A day-two later he said, "Quincey, can I have a setting of them Roundhead eggs to give away?"

I said, "Now who in tarnation are you so fretted about them having chicken to eat?"

"A customer come to the garage."

"No," I said.

"I do pay for the chicken feed, Quincey."

"No."

"Nothing ain't worth quarreling about," he said.

A week later one morning there wasn't an egg in the nests, and two of them young roosters never come up for their feed. I like to had a fit.

"A varmint likely went with them," Will said.

"Will, you reckon that varmint could of had two legs instead of four?" I looked him in the eye. "Who's this friend you'd steal for?"

"Just a poor soul that don't have much pleasure in life." He laid a dollar on the table. "Things has come to a pretty pass when a man has to buy eggs and chickens off his own wife."

"Well, you rob my nests and roosts one more time, and you'll get the living daylights displeasured outen you."

"Yes, ma'am," and he give me that funny look.

A year rocked on. Twice he give me a quarter for a setting of eggs and fifty cents for two more roosters. Then late this spring, the truth come out. The truth was a red chicken feather in a basket, and ary one thinks a chicken feather in a basket can't boil up hell in a woman, just don't know hell nor women.

I went out to the chicken house on a bright June morning to gather the eggs. My foot catched in something. I backed off so's I could see, and it was a basket. I hadn't left no basket in the chicken house. I looked at it, and I picked it up and turned it over. It was the basket I'd taken preserves in, and cuttings, to the Widow Tippett. She hadn't never come near me nor returned it. I looked at the basket again, and there was a bronzy-red chicken feather stuck to the inside of it. It was a tail feather off a Roundhead rooster.

I seed it plain. That slow-speaking, permanent-headed, buttermilk-faced widow with cats in her dishpan had done tolled my Will into her clutches. He'd stole eggs and chickens from me, his loving and faithful wife, to take and put in her wicked hands. I set right down on the ground of the chicken house, and when I set down on the ground it's serious, for it near about takes a yoke of oxen to get me up again. It seemed to me life had done gone so black I just as lief die and be shut of it.

I thought about all the years me and Will had stuck it out together, him losing money on the livery stable, and cars coming in instead of horses, and finally him building the garage on credit, and learning a new trade, and me making a sack of grits last a fortnight. Then things got good, and we prospered, and seemed to me like man and wife couldn't of got along better together lessen they was a pair of angels.

I set on the ground of the chicken house and I studied. What had I done to deserve such as this? I'd been faithful. 'Course, there'd be them to say a woman as big as me had no choice but being faithful. But I'd been faithful in my mind, and 'taint every woman goes to the movies can say the same. I'd worked, and I'd saved, and Will Dover hadn't never oncet come in late from the garage but I had hot rations on the stove. I reckon a woman can put too much store by hot rations. A warm heart'll freshen a man a heap quicker'n hot rations, but all the hot rations in the world can't warm up a cold female tongue.

I set there. I boiled up inside hotter and higher than the fire in a sinners' hell, and I purely boiled over. That cooled the fire a mite, and I fanned myself with my apron and commenced to study. I laid me a trap for Will. I decided to watch-see when he done ary thing was different from what he generally done. I got a-holt of a wall beam for a lever and finally got myself up off the ground. When Will come in that evening, I was quieted down and set myself to watching, like an alligator watching for a shoat he knows comes to water.

240

That evening Will didn't stir from his rocker, just set and smoked. I thought, Uh-huh, you know I'm watching you. The next evening he put on a clean shirt and I thought, Uh-huh, dressing up for the widow. After supper he eased on out of the house, and I followed along a half hour behind him and, bless Katy, there he was setting on the bench in front of the grocery store, visiting with Doc and Uncle Benny.

I said, "I forgot I was out of shortening," and I got me a pound of lard at the store.

Will said, "I'll go on home with you. I come down to hear the fight on the radio, but it's put off."

I thought, Uh-huh, I just come too soon.

Sunday morning he takened me by surprise. He didn't shave, and he put on the same shirt he'd wore the day before. But he did get out of bed extra early and he acted like he had ants in his pants. But he do that, times, of a Sunday. He's a man is restless when he ain't at his work. I never studied on a thing, until I seed him slip off to the fireplace and pull out the loose brick and take out the money we keep there. I seed him stuff them bills in his pocket and look around as sly as a 'possum.

He come to me and he said, "I'm going on down to town. Don't look for me back to dinner."

My heart lept like a mullet jumping. I thought, Merciful jaybird, now's the time.

I give him about forty minutes' start and I lit out. I walked the two miles to the Widow Tippett's like a road-runner snake on its way home. I was puffing and blowing when I got to her gate, and I thought, In a minute now I'll see Will Dover setting beside her and holding her hand, and he ain't held mine since spring.

I stopped to figure what I'd do; would I just crack their heads together, or would I say, proud and stiff, "So! This be the end."

While I was panting and studying, the Widow Tippett come out with her hat on. "Why, Mis' Dover!" she said. "You look powerful warm."

I said, "I be warm. Tell me the truth, or you'll figure you never knowed what heat was. My Will here?"

"No," she said, "he ain't here."

"He been here?"

She looked me up and down like a woman trying to make up her mind to step on a cockroach. She threwed back her head. "Yes," she said. "He's been here."

I said to myself, "O Lord, give my tongue a long reach," and I takened my tongue and I flicked it, like a man flicking a fishing rod. I takened it like a casting line and I laid it down right where I wanted it.

I said, "You figure I aim to leave a man-snatcher like you stay in Oak Bluff? You figure I aim to leave you go from home to home stealing husbands? You takened my husband and never returned my preserve basket, and that's how come me to catch up with you, on account of a red chicken feather in that basket. And what I aim to do to Will Dover is my business and not yours, but I ain't aiming to let you clean Oak Bluff out of husbands, for could be they's one or two of them worth keeping."

She tipped back her head and begun to laugh.

I takened my tongue and I drawed it back and I laid it down again. "Devils laughs. Devils with buttermilk faces laughs. They laughs right on through damnation and brimstone, and that's what'll be your portion."

She said, "You should of been a lady preacher."

I takened my tongue and I purely throwed it. "I comes to you with a basket of preserves and a bundle of cuttings, and what do you do? You don't even send back a empty basket. What you sends back is a empty husband. You figure I aim to leave the sun go down on you in Oak Bluff one more time? The sun ain't rose, will set on you in Oak Bluff."

She quit laughing. She licked her lips. I could see her drawing back her tongue like I'd done mine. And when she let it loose, seemed to me like I'd not cast mine within ten yards of where I aimed to. For she takened her tongue and she laid it down so accurate I had to stand and admire a expert.

"You was likely a good woman oncet," she said. "You know what you are now? You're nothing but a big old fat hoot-nanny."

I like to of crumpled in the sand. She stepped down off her porch and she walked up to me, and there was nothing between her and me but the gate, and nothing between our souls at all.

She said, "I aim to give you credit for what you was oncet. I come to Oak Bluff, hearing the first day I come that you was a woman wouldn't leave her husband go to no cockfight. I thought, a husband leaves his wife tell him what to do and what not to do, ain't man noways. Then folks told me you was a woman with a tongue sharp enough to slice soft bacon, and a heart like gold. And they told me you was always a great one for leaving a man go his man's way, and seemed like you bearing down on yours was something had slipped up on you."

I said, "Go on."

She said, "Who be I, a stranger, to tell you to give a man his freedom? Who be I to tell you a man that has his freedom is the man don't particular want it? And the man drove with a short rein, do he be a man, is the one just ain't going to be drove?"

I said, "Tell me."

She said, "I'll tell you this. I got a man of my own. We're marrying soon as he sells out the stock in his store and crates up his fighting chickens and moves down here. I don't want your man nor no other woman's man. Now you quit your hassling and pull up your petticoat that's showing in the back, and I'll carry you where you can see just what your husband's been a-doing behind your big fat back."

She stalked out the gate and I followed her.

"Where you carrying me?" I said.

"To the cockfight."

Now if ary one had ever of told me I'd be going to a cockfight, walking along humble behind another woman, feeling scairt and mixed up inside as a Brunswick stew, I'd of figured they was headed for the insane asylum. But that's what I was doing.

I puffed and I blowed but the Widow Tippett kept right on going. The sun beat down and I begun to sweat. She was about ten yards ahead of me. I called out, "If you aim to carry me to the cockfight, you got to wait a minute, else I'll be toted in as dead as one of them poor roosters."

She stopped then and we set down under a live-oak tree to rest.

I said, "I be blessed if I see how I can go to no cockfight. I've stood out against them things all my life. I can't go setting up to one now."

She said, "Can you climb a tree?"

"Can a elephant fly?"

"Then you'll have to let folks see you there." She got up and give me a boost to get me up and she set off again.

The place where she takened me was out in Wilson's Woods. We come up on it from the south, and here was a clearing in the woods, and a cockpit in the sand, with a wooden ring around it. On the north side was some men standing, and the trees was between us and them.

The Widow Tippett said to me, "Now how come me to ask you could you climb a tree, is on account of that big camphor tree has a flat bough leans right out over the cockpit, and could you oncet make that first crotch, you could get you a ringside seat and watch the show, and nobody ever know you was near if you set quiet."

I said, "If you was to push me a mite, could be I'd make the crotch."

She said, "You ain't asking much, be you?" but she put her shoulder under me and pushed with a will, and I got myself up into the camphor tree. It was easy going oncet I was off the ground, and I pulled up a ways and found me a fine seat partways out the bough, and she went on over to where the men was standing.

I hadn't no more than made it, for directly men begun coming in from all over. Most of them had gamecocks tucked under their arms. Some was Roundheads, like mine, and some was White Hackles and Irish Grays, and some was Carolina Blues. They had their combs trimmed and their spurs was cut off to a nub about a half-inch long. Their tail feathers was shaved off till the poor things' butts was naked.

I thought, Merciful jaybird, them fine roosters throwed to the slaughter.

After I'd looked at the cocks, I begun craning my neck careful to look at the men. And after I'd watched their faces it come to me there was two kinds of men there. One kind had the fighting mark on them. They was men with cold hard eyes and I knowed they'd fight theirselves or their chickens merciless. They had a easy kind of way of moving, a gambler's way. I knowed this kind of man would fight until he couldn't get up. And he'd bet his last dollar and his last farm, did the notion take him. He was a kind of man loved to give a licking and could take one, a hard kind of a man, but you had to give him your respect.

Then there was another kind of man there. This kind of man was little, and his eyes was gentle. And I thought to myself, Now what's that kind of man doing at a cockfight?

I inched around on my limb so I got a better peephole through the branches. I seed money change hands. The men that was getting their cocks ready was as nervous as brides sewing on their wedding clothes. I could see one man wrapping little thin strips of leather around the nubs of his rooster's spurs. Then he takened a pair of shiny pointed steel things I knowed must be the gaffs, and he fastened them on, and wrapped them like they was a baby's bandage.

I thought, Why, them things ain't as cruel as the natural spurs. I could see they'd go in quick and clean, and if they didn't reach no vital spot they'd not be much more'n a pin prick.

A gray-looking feller with his hat on the back of his head stepped into the pit. He drawed three lines acrost the sand with his foot. He said, "Let's go."

Two men come ambling into the pit with their chickens. They turned their backs one on t'other. Each man on his side of the pit set his cock down on the sand, keeping holt of its wings, and let it run up and down. The cocks lifted their legs high. Their eyes was bright. They was raring to go.

The referee said, "Bill your cocks."

Seemed like electricity goed through all the men. The two handlers goed up to each other with the cocks cradled in their arms. They

244

poked the cocks' bills together and one cock made him a pass at t'other. Somebody hollered, "Two to one on the Blue!"

The cocks pecked at each other. Their hackles rose.

The referee said, "Pit your cocks."

The handlers set the birds down, each one on his own line.

The referee said, "Pit!"

The cocks flew at each other. They met in the air. When they come down, one just naturally didn't get up again. The handlers picked up the birds and went out. Money passed here and yon.

I thought, Now nobody much got their money's worth outen that.

The next fight were a dandy. Right off, I picked a big Carolina Blue to win. I never did see such a fight. I'd seed men box and I'd seed men wrestle. I'd seed dogfights and catfights. I'd seed a pair of old male 'coons having it. I thought I'd seed fighting. But them game roosters was the fightingest things I ever laid eyes on. They knowed what they was doing. One'd lay quiet for t'other, and he'd flick up his feet, and whip his wings, and pass a lick with them gaffs.

I begun to get uneasy about the Blue I'd picked. Seemed to me he was dodging. He lay still oncet when he had him a fine chancet to hit a lick, and I almost hollered, "Get him now!" Then he kind of shuffled around, and next thing I knowed he laid out the enemy plumb cold. I come near shouting, I was so proud I'd picked the winner. There was three more fights and I picked two of them. I said to myself, "Quincey Dover, take shame. You're purely enjoying yourself."

'Twas too late to feel shame. I couldn't scarcely wait for the next fight to begin. But there was a delay. I could see men look at their watches and I heerd one say, "He knowed he was to fight the Main."

The Widow Tippett called out, "Yonder he comes."

And who come walking in to the cockfight with a big red Round-head rooster tucked under his arm? My Will come in, that's who come.

Now I'd figured, the way the Widow Tippett talked, I could look to see him here. But I sure didn't look to see him walk in with no fighting cock. I cut my eye at that chicken. It was one of my prime young roosters, growed up into the biggest, finest, proudest gamecock I ever did see, and the marks of battle was on him.

Right off I knowed two things. I knowed the Widow Tippett hadn't done a thing but leave Will train his chickens at that sloppy, easy-going place of hers. And I knowed another thing. I knowed my Will was one of them second kind of men come to the cockfight: the little gentle fellers I couldn't make out why they was there. Well, you'd of thought 'twas the Lord of the Jaybirds had come in to the cockfight, 'stead of Will Dover. The men parted a way for him to go into the pit.

I thought I'd seed fighting. But them game roosters was the fightingest things I ever laid eyes on.

245

Will called out, "I got a hundred dollars says this is my day."

I like to shook the camphor tree to pieces. I near about climbed down to say, "Will Dover, don't you go betting that money from the fireplace on no cockfight." But I didn't dast give myself away.

The fight was the big fight of the day. Seemed like Will's rooster was a old winner, and the men figured it were his turn to take a licking. Odds was mostly two to one against him. T'other cock was a Carolina Blue, and directly I seed him my heart sank.

"Bill your cocks," said the referee, and Will and t'other feller billed their cocks. They like to of fought right then and there.

"Pit!"

Nobody didn't have to give his rooster no shove. That pair was mixing it time they hit the ground. Will's Roundhead got hung in the Blue.

"Handle!"

The Blue's owner got him a-loose. Then they was at it again. Now if I hadn't of seed them other fights first, I'd not of appreciated this one. It was a pair of champions, and they both knowed it. They was as neat as a pair of boxers that knowed their footwork. Didn't neither one waste no energy, but when the moment come one seed him a chancet, he was whipping his wings and striking. Now and again they'd both fly up and pass their licks a foot in the air.

"Handle!"

Both chickens was breathing hard. Will picked his up and run his mouth down along his feathers, from the top of his head on down his back, cooling him and soothing him. He blowed on him and he dipped his bill in a pan of water.

"Pit!"

All of a sudden the Blue begun to take the fight. He got in a lick to the head and while the Roundhead lay hurt and dazed, the Blue followed through with another.

"Time!" I takened my first breath in about two minutes.

"Pit!"

This time it looked like it was all over. The Blue come in like a whirlwind and he done a heap of damage. He got hung in the Round-head's back.

"Handle!"

This time when Will turned him a-loose he talked to him. He made queer little sounds, and one of them sounded like a hen a-clucking.

"Pit!"

He set him down, and the light of battle was in the Roundhead's eyes. He fought hard and game, but next thing I knowed the Blue had

246

him out cold, with one wing broke. "He's dead," I said, for he lay on his side just scarcely breathing. I could of cried. The referee begun to count. The Blue give the Roundhead an extra lick as he laid there, and everybody figured that finished him. I begun to sniffle. I just couldn't bear to see that Roundhead take a licking. Well, I reckon he figured the same. He opened his eyes and he drawed a breath and where he lay he reached up and he put them gaffs in that big Blue standing over him, and the Blue dropped like he'd been shot.

A grunt come outen the men like as if it was them had been hit. And you know that Roundhead wavered up to his feet, dragging that broke wing, and he climbed up on that Blue, raised his head, flopped his good wing, and he crowed! He'd won, and he knowed it, and he crowed.

My Will picked him up and stroked him, and wiped the sweat off his own forehead. He kind of lifted up his face and I could see the look on it. And I knowed that without that look a man just ain't a man. And with it, why, he's cock of the walk, no matter how little and runty and put-upon he be. And I knowed why Will and all them other little gentle-looking fellers loved a cockfight. They was men didn't have no other way to be men.

A shame come over me. Times, it's life'll do that to a man. Mostly, it's his woman. And I'd done that to my Will. I'd tried to take his manhood from him, so he didn't have no way to strut but fighting a rooster. Now he'd won, and he was a man again. And I knowed that cocks must crow.

And about that time you know what happened? I reckon I'd been doing a heap of jiggling around in that camphor tree. I heerd a creak and then a crack, and the limb I was setting on busted off as neat as if you'd put a ax to it, and I slid down it, and I catched holt of the limb below, and I slid down that, and I plunked off down outen the camphor tree right smack in the middle of the cockpit.

I reckon everybody thought it was the end of the world. Nobody couldn't do nothing but gape at me.

"Well, get me up off the ground," I said. "You sure as the devil can't fight no chickens with me in the middle of the pit."

Will run to me then, and two-three others, and they hoisted me up. I brushed off my skirt and the Widow Tippett tidied me up.

I looked her in the eye. "I'd be proud to call you my friend," I said.

"All you got to do is call it," she said.

I turned to my Will. His face was in knots. The Lord Hisself couldn't of told what he was thinking.

"Well, Will," I said, "we sure got us some kind of a fighting rooster. Now I'd like a mite softer seat for the next fight."

He drawed a long slow breath. "We ain't staying for the next," he said. "You're like to be hurt. I'm carrying you home."

The men that had lost to him paid him off. He crammed the bills in his pocket and he tucked up the Roundhead under his arm and he led me off to the car. He cranked up and headed out. The Roundhead kind of nested down on the seat between us.

"Will," I said, "I figured you'd been on-faithful to me with the Widow Tippett."

He shook his head.

"I should of knowed better. You ain't that kind of a man. But something in you had drawed off from me."

He nodded.

"I know why you drawed off," I said. "I'd drove you to it."

He never answered.

"Will," I said, "I hope it's in your heart to forgive me. I didn't use to be thataway. Time changed me, Will, and I didn't never notice it."

He kind of blinked his eyes, like he was fixing to cry.

"Will," I said, "you ain't got to go raising no chickens behind my back. I'll raise them for you."

"No, Quincey," he said, slowlike. "No. I reckon I'll quit cockfighting. It's a foolish business, for a man can lose his shirt at it. And you didn't happen to see one of them long, bloody fights, makes a man sick to watch it. No, Quincey, I'm done." He looked at me. "Seems like something inside me is satisfied."

Well, I busted out crying. "Oh, Will," I said. "I wisht I was young again. An awful thing has done happened to me. You know what I be? I be nothing but a big old fat hoot-nanny."

"Why, Quincey," he said. "Don't you dast say such as that. You're my good, sweet Quincey, and I love every hundred pounds of you."

And we busted out laughing.

"Quincey," he said, "you remember when I come courting you and I told you I aimed to fatten you up, for a man couldn't have too much of a good thing?"

I blowed my nose and he put his arm around me.

"Will," I said, "we're on a public highway."

"It's a free road," he said, and he kissed me.

"Will," I said, "home's the place for such as that."

"Ain't I headed for home fast as I can go?" he said, and we laughed like a pair of young uns.

My Will ain't much to look at, but he's mighty good company.

Invisible Boy

by Ray Bradbury

She took the great iron spoon and the mummified frog and gave it a bash and made dust of it, and talked to the dust while she ground it in her stony fists quickly. Her beady gray bird-eyes flickered at the cabin. Each time she looked, a head in the small thin window ducked as if she'd fired off a shotgun.

"Charlie!" cried Old Lady. "You come outa there! I'm fixing a lizard magic to unlock that rusty door! You come out now and I won't make the earth shake or the trees go up in fire or the sun set at high noon!"

The only sound was the warm mountain light on the high turpentine trees, a tufted squirrel chittering around and around on a green-furred log, the ants moving in a fine brown line at Old Lady's bare, blue-veined feet.

"You been starving in there two days, darn you!" she panted, chiming the spoon against a flat rock, causing the plump gray miracle bag to swing at her waist. Sweating sour, she rose and marched at the cabin, bearing the pulverized flesh. "Come out, now!" She flicked a pinch of powder inside the lock. "All right, I'll come get you!" she wheezed.

She spun the knob with one walnut-colored hand, first one way, then the other. "O Lord," she intoned, "fling this door wide!"

When nothing flung, she added yet another philter and held her breath. Her long blue untidy skirt rustled as she peered into her bag of darkness to see if she had any scaly monsters there, any charm finer than the frog she'd killed months ago for such a crisis as this.

She heard Charlie breathing against the door. His folks had pranced off into some Ozark town early this week, leaving him, and he'd run almost six miles to Old Lady for company—she was by way of being an aunt or cousin or some such, and he didn't mind her fashions.

But then, two days ago, Old Lady, having gotten used to the boy around, decided to keep him for convenient company. She pricked her thin shoulder bone, drew out three blood pearls, spat wet over her right elbow, tromped on a crunch-cricket, and at the same instant

251

clawed her left hand at Charlie, crying, "My son you are, you are my son, for all eternity!"

Charlie, bounding like a startled hare, had crashed off into the bush, heading for home.

But Old Lady, skittering quick as a gingham lizard, cornered him in a dead end, and Charlie holed up in this old hermit's cabin and wouldn't come out, no matter how she whammed door, window, or knothole with amber-colored fist or trounced her ritual fires, explaining to him that he was certainly her son *now*, all right.

"Charlie, you *there?*" she asked, cutting holes in the door planks with her bright little slippery eyes.

"I'm all of me here," he replied finally, very tired.

Maybe he would fall out on the ground any moment. She wrestled the knob hopefully. Perhaps a pinch too much frog powder had grated the lock wrong. She always overdid or underdid her miracles, she mused angrily, never doing them just *exact*, Devil take it!

"Charlie, I only wants someone to night-prattle to, someone to warm hands with at the fire. Someone to fetch kindling for me mornings, and fight off the spunks that come creeping of early fogs! I ain't got no fetchings on you for myself, son, just for your company." She smacked her lips. "Tell you what, Charles, you come out and I *teach* you things!"

"What things?" he suspicioned.

"Teach you how to buy cheap, sell high. Catch a snow weasel, cut off its head, carry it warm in your hind pocket. There!"

"Aw," said Charlie.

She made haste. "Teach you to make yourself shotproof. So if anyone bangs at you with a gun, nothing happens."

When Charlie stayed silent, she gave him the secret in a high fluttering whisper. "Dig and stitch mouse-ear roots on Friday during full moon, and wear 'em around your neck in a white silk."

"You're *crazy*," Charlie said.

"Teach you how to stop blood or make animals stand frozen or make blind horses see, all them things I'll teach you! Teach you to cure a swelled-up cow and unbewitch a goat. Show you how to make yourself invisible!"

"Oh," said Charlie.

Old Lady's heart beat like a Salvation tambourine.

The knob turned from the other side.

"You," said Charlie, "are funning me."

"No, I'm not," exclaimed Old Lady. "Oh, Charlie, why, I'll make you like a window, see right through you. Why, child, you'll be surprised!"

"Real invisible?"

"Real invisible!"

"You won't fetch onto me if I walk out?"

"Won't touch a bristle of you, son."

"Well," he drawled reluctantly, "all right."

The door opened. Charlie stood in his bare feet, head down, chin against chest. "Make me invisible," he said.

"First we got to catch us a bat," said Old Lady. "Start lookin'!"

She gave him some jerky beef for his hunger and watched him climb a tree. He went high up and high up and it was nice seeing him there and it was nice having him here and all about after so many years alone with nothing to say good morning to but bird droppings and silvery snail tracks.

Pretty soon a bat with a broken wing fluttered down out of the tree. Old Lady snatched it up, beating warm and shrieking between its porcelain white teeth, and Charlie dropped down after it, hand upon clenched hand, yelling.

That night, with the moon nibbling at the spiced pine cones, Old Lady extracted a long silver needle from under her wide blue dress. Gumming her excitement and secret anticipation, she sighted up the dead bat and held the cold needle steady-steady.

She had long ago realized that her miracles, despite all perspirations and salts and sulphurs, failed. But she had always dreamt that one day the miracles might start functioning, might spring up in crimson flowers and silver stars to prove that God had forgiven her for her pink body and her pink thoughts and her warm body and her warm thoughts as a young miss. But so far God had made no sign and said no word, but nobody knew this except Old Lady.

"Ready?" she asked Charlie, who crouched cross-kneed, wrapping his pretty legs in long goose-pimpled arms, his mouth open, making teeth. "Ready," he whispered, shivering.

"There!" She plunged the needle deep in the bat's right eye. "So!"

"Oh!" screamed Charlie, wadding up his face.

"Now I wrap it in gingham, and here, put it in your pocket, keep it there, bat and all. Go on!"

He pocketed the charm.

"Charlie!" she shrieked fearfully. "Charlie, where *are* you? I can't *see* you, child!"

"Here!" He jumped so the light ran in red streaks up his body. "I'm here, Old Lady!" He stared wildly at his arms, legs, chest, and toes. "I'm here!"

Her eyes looked as if they were watching a thousand fireflies criss-crossing each other in the wild night air.

"Charlie, oh, you went *fast!* Quick as a hummingbird! Oh, Charlie, come *back* to me!"

"But I'm *here!*" he wailed.

"Where?"

"By the fire! And—and I can see myself. I'm not invisible at all!"

Old Lady rocked on her lean flanks. "Course *you* can see *you!* Every invisible person knows himself. Otherwise, how could you eat, walk, or get around places? Charlie, touch me. Touch me so I *know* you."

Uneasily he put out a hand.

She pretended to jerk, startled, at his touch. *"Ah!"*

"You mean to say you can't *find* me?" he asked. "Truly?"

"Not the least half-rump of you!"

She found a tree to stare at, and stared at it with shining eyes, careful not to glance at him. "Why, I sure *did* a trick *that* time!" She sighed with wonder. "Whooeee. Quickest invisible I *ever* made! Charlie. Charlie, how you *feel?*"

"Like creek water—all stirred."

"You'll settle."

Then after a pause she added, "Well, what you going to do now, Charlie, since you're invisible?"

All sorts of things shot through his brain, she could tell. Adventures stood up and danced like hellfire in his eyes, and his mouth, just hanging, told what it meant to be a boy who imagined himself like the mountain winds. In a cold dream he said, "I'll run across wheat fields, climb snow mountains, steal white chickens off 'n farms. I'll kick pink pigs when they ain't looking. I'll pinch pretty girls' legs when they sleep, snap their garters in schoolrooms." Charlie looked at Old Lady, and from the shiny tips of her eyes she saw something wicked shape his face. "And other things I'll do, I'll do, I will," he said.

"Don't try nothing on me," warned Old Lady. *"I'm brittle as spring ice and I don't take handling."*

"Don't try nothing on me," warned Old Lady. "I'm brittle as spring ice and I don't take handling." Then: "What about your folks?"

"My folks?"

"You can't fetch yourself home looking like that. Scare the inside ribbons out of them. Your mother'd faint straight back like timber falling. Think they want you about the house to stumble over and your ma have to call you every three minutes, even though you're in the room next her elbow?"

Charlie had not considered it. He sort of simmered down and whispered out a little "Gosh" and felt of his long bones carefully.

"You'll be mighty lonesome. People looking through you like a

254

water glass, people knocking you aside because they didn't reckon you to be underfoot. And women, Charlie, *women*—"

He swallowed. "What about women?"

"No woman will be giving you a second stare. And no woman wants to be kissed by a boy's mouth they can't even *find!*"

Charlie dug his bare toe in the soil contemplatively. He pouted. "Well, I'll stay invisible, anyway, for a spell. I'll have me some fun. I'll just be pretty careful, is all. I'll stay out from in front of wagons and horses and Pa. Pa shoots at the nariest sound." Charlie blinked. "Why, with me invisible, someday Pa might just up and fill me with buckshot, thinkin' I was a hill squirrel in the dooryard. Oh . . ."

Old Lady nodded at a tree. "That's likely."

"Well," he decided slowly. "I'll stay invisible for tonight, and tomorrow you can fix me back all whole again, Old Lady."

"Now if that ain't just like a critter, always wanting to be what he can't be," remarked Old Lady to a beetle on a log.

"What you mean?" said Charlie.

"Why," she explained, "it was real hard work, fixing you up. It'll take a little *time* for it to wear off. Like a coat of paint wears off, boy."

"You!" he cried. "You did this to me! Now you make me back, you make me seeable!"

"Hush," she said. "It'll wear off, a hand or a foot at a time."

"How'll it look, me around the hills with just one hand showing!"

"Like a five-winged bird hopping on the stones and bramble."

"Or a foot showing!"

"Like a small pink rabbit jumping thicket."

"Or my head floating!"

"Like a hairy balloon at the carnival!"

"How long before I'm *whole?*" he asked.

She deliberated that it might pretty well be an entire year.

He groaned. He began to sob and bite his lips and make fists. "You magicked me, you did this, you did this thing to me. Now I won't be able to run home!"

She winked. "But you *can* stay here, child, stay on with me real comfort-like, and I'll keep you fat and saucy."

He flung it out. "You did this on purpose! You mean old hag, you want to keep me here!"

He ran off through the shrubs on the instant.

"Charlie, come back!"

No answer but the pattern of his feet on the soft dark turf, and his wet choking cry which passed swiftly off and away.

She waited and then kindled herself a fire. "He'll be back," she whispered. And thinking inward on herself, she said, "And now I'll have me my company through spring and into late summer. Then, when I'm tired of him and want a silence, I'll send him home."

Charlie returned noiselessly with the first gray of dawn, gliding over the rimed turf to where Old Lady sprawled like a bleached stick before the scattered ashes.

He sat on some creek pebbles and stared at her.

She didn't dare look at him or beyond. He had made no sound, so how could she know he was anywhere about? She couldn't.

He sat there, tear marks on his cheeks.

Pretending to be just waking—but she had found no sleep from one end of the night to the other—Old Lady stood up, grunting and yawning, and turned in a circle to the dawn.

"Charlie?"

Her eyes passed from pines to soil, to sky, to the far hills. She called out his name, over and over again, and she felt like staring plumb straight at him, but she stopped herself. "Charlie? Oh, Charles!" she called, and heard the echoes say the very same.

He sat, beginning to grin a bit, suddenly, knowing he was close to her, yet she must feel alone. Perhaps he felt the growing of a secret power, perhaps he felt secure from the world, certainly he was *pleased* with his invisibility.

She said aloud, "Now where *can* that boy be? If he only made a noise so I could tell just where he is, maybe I'd fry him a breakfast."

She prepared the morning victuals, irritated at his continuous quiet. She sizzled bacon on a hickory stick. "The smell of it will draw his nose," she muttered.

While her back was turned he swiped all the frying bacon and devoured it tastily.

She whirled, crying out, "Lord!"

She eyed the clearing suspiciously. "Charlie, that *you?*"

Charlie wiped his mouth clean on his wrists.

She trotted about the clearing, making like she was trying to locate him. Finally, with a clever thought, acting blind, she headed straight for him, groping. "Charlie, where *are* you?"

A lightning streak, he evaded her, bobbing, ducking.

It took all her willpower not to give chase; but you can't chase invisible boys, so she sat down, scowling, sputtering, and tried to fry more bacon. But every fresh strip she cut he would steal bubbling off the fire and run away far. Finally, cheeks burning, she cried, "I know where you are! Right *there!* I hear you run!" She pointed to one side of him, not too accurate. He ran again. "Now you're there!" she shouted. "There, and there!" pointing to all the places he was in the next five minutes. "I hear you press a grass blade, knock a flower, snap a twig. I got fine shell ears, delicate as roses. They can hear the stars moving!"

Silently he galloped off among the pines, his voice trailing back, "Can't hear me when I'm set on a rock. I'll just *set!*"

All day he sat on an observatory rock in the clear wind, motionless and sucking his tongue.

Old Lady gathered wood in the deep forest, feeling his eyes weaseling on her spine. She wanted to babble, "Oh, I see you, I see you! I was only fooling about invisible boys! You're right there!" But she swallowed her gall and gummed it tight.

The following morning he did the spiteful things. He began leaping from behind trees. He made toad faces, frog faces, spider faces at her, clenching down his lips with his fingers, popping his raw eyes, pushing up his nostrils so you could peer in and see his brain thinking.

Once she dropped her kindling. She pretended it was a blue jay startled her.

He made a motion as if to strangle her.

She trembled a little.

He made another move as if to bang her shins and spit on her cheek.

These motions she bore without a lid-flicker or a mouth-twitch.

He stuck out his tongue, making strange bad noises. He wiggled his loose ears so she wanted to laugh, and finally she did laugh and explained it away quickly by saying, "Sat on a salamander! Whew, how it poked!"

By high noon the whole madness boiled to a terrible peak.

For it was at that exact hour that Charlie came racing down the valley stark boy-naked!

Old Lady nearly fell flat with shock!

"Charlie!" she almost cried.

Charlie raced naked up one side of a hill and naked down the other—naked as day, naked as the moon, raw as the sun and a newborn chick, his feet shimmering and rushing like the wings of a low-skimming hummingbird.

Old Lady's tongue locked in her mouth. What could she say? Charlie, go dress? For *shame? Stop* that? *Could* she? Oh, Charlie, Charlie, God! Could she say that now? *Well?*

Upon the big rock, she witnessed him dancing up and down, naked as the day of his birth, stomping bare feet, smacking his hands on his knees and sucking in and out his white stomach like blowing and deflating a circus balloon.

She shut her eyes tight and prayed.

After three hours of this she pleaded, "Charlie, Charlie, come here! I got something to *tell* you!"

Like a fallen leaf he came, dressed again, praise the Lord.

"Charlie," she said, looking at the pine trees, "I see your right toe. *There* it is."

"You do?" he said.

"Yes," she said very sadly. "There it is like a horny toad on the grass. And there, up there's your left ear hanging on the air like a pink butterfly."

Charlie danced. "I'm forming in, I'm forming in!"

Old Lady nodded. "Here comes your ankle!"

"Gimme *both* my feet!" ordered Charlie.

"You got 'em."

"How about my hands?"

"I see one crawling on your knee like a daddy longlegs."

"How about the other one?"

"It's crawling too."

"I got a body?"

"Shaping up fine."

"I'll need my head to go home, Old Lady."

To go home, she thought wearily. "No!" she said, stubborn and angry. "No, you ain't got no head. No head at all," she cried. She'd leave that to the very last. "No head, no head," she insisted.

"No head?" he wailed.

"Yes, oh my God, yes, yes, you got your blamed head!" she snapped, giving up. "Now, fetch me back my bat with the needle in his eye!"

He flung it at her. "Haaaa-yoooo!" His yelling went all up the valley, and long after he had run toward home she heard his echoes, racing.

Then she plucked up her kindling with a great dry weariness and started back toward her shack, sighing, talking. And Charlie followed her all the way, *really* invisible now, so she couldn't see him, just hear him, like a pine cone dropping or a deep underground stream trickling, or a squirrel clambering a bough; and over the fire at twilight she and Charlie sat, him so invisible, and her feeding him bacon he wouldn't take, so she ate it herself, and then she fixed some magic and fell asleep with Charlie, made out of sticks and rags and pebbles, but still warm and her very own son, slumbering and nice in her shaking mother arms . . . and they talked about golden things in drowsy voices until dawn made the fire slowly, slowly wither out. . . .

The Corn-Planting

by Sherwood Anderson

The farmers who come to our town to trade are a part of the town life. Saturday is the big day. Often the children come to the high school in town.

It is so with Hatch Hutchenson. Although his farm, some three miles from town, is small, it is known to be one of the best-kept and best-worked places in all our section. Hatch is a little gnarled old figure of a man. His place is on the Scratch Gravel Road and there are plenty of poorly kept places out that way.

Hatch's place stands out. The little frame house is always kept painted, the trees in his orchard are whitened with lime halfway up the trunks, and the barn and sheds are in repair, and his fields are always clean-looking.

Hatch is nearly seventy. He got a rather late start in life. His father, who owned the same farm, was a Civil War man and came home badly wounded, so that, although he lived a long time after the war, he couldn't work much. Hatch was the only son and stayed at home, working the place until his father died. Then, when he was nearing fifty, he married a schoolteacher of forty, and they had a son. The schoolteacher was a small one like Hatch. After they married, they both stuck close to the land. They seemed to fit into their farm life as certain people fit into the clothes they wear. I have noticed something about people who make a go of marriage. They grow more and more alike. They even grow to look alike.

Their one son, Will Hutchenson, was a small but remarkably strong boy. He came to our high school in town and pitched on our town baseball team. He was a fellow always cheerful, bright and alert, and a great favorite with all of us.

For one thing, he began as a young boy to make amusing little drawings. It was a talent. He made drawings of fish and pigs and cows and they looked like people you knew. I never did know before that people could look so much like cows and horses and pigs and fish.

When he had finished in the town high school, Will went to Chicago, where his mother had a cousin living, and he became a student in the Art Institute out there. Another fellow from our town was also in Chicago. He really went two years before Will did. His name is Hal Weyman, and he was a student at the University of Chicago. After he

259

graduated, he came home and got a job as principal of our high school.

Hal and Will Hutchenson hadn't been close friends before, Hal being several years older than Will, but in Chicago they got together, went together to see plays, and, as Hal later told me, they had a good many long talks.

I got it from Hal that, in Chicago, as at home here, when he was a young boy, Will was immediately popular. He was good-looking, so the girls in the art school liked him, and he had a straightforwardness that made him popular with all the young fellows.

Hal told me that Will was out to some party nearly every night, and right away he began to sell some of his amusing little drawings and to make money. The drawings were used in advertisements, and he was well paid.

He even began to send some money home. You see, after Hal came back here, he used to go quite often out to the Hutchenson place to see Will's father and mother. He would walk or drive out there in the afternoon or on summer evenings and sit with them. The talk was always of Will.

Hal said it was touching how much the father and mother depended on their one son, how much they talked about him and dreamed of his future. They had never been people who went about much with the town folks or even with their neighbors. They were of the sort who work all the time, from early morning till late in the evenings, and on moonlight nights, Hal said, and after the little old wife had got the supper, they often went out into the fields and worked again.

You see, by this time old Hatch was nearing seventy and his wife would have been ten years younger. Hal said that whenever he went out to the farm they quit work and came to sit with him. They might be in one of the fields, working together, but when they saw him in the road, they came running. They had got a letter from Will. He wrote every week.

The little old mother would come running following the father. "We got another letter, Mr. Weyman," Hatch would cry, and then his wife, quite breathless, would say the same thing, "Mr. Weyman, we got a letter."

The letter would be brought out at once and read aloud. Hal said the letters were always delicious. Will larded them with little sketches. There were humorous drawings of people he had seen or been with, rivers of automobiles on Michigan Avenue in Chicago, a policeman at a street crossing, young stenographers hurrying into office buildings. Neither of the old people had ever been to the city and they were curious and eager. They wanted the drawings explained, and Hal said

Hal said it was touching how much the father and mother depended on their one son, how much they talked about him and dreamed of his future.

they were like two children wanting to know every little detail Hal could remember about their son's life in the big city. He was always at them to come there on a visit and they would spend hours talking of that.

"Of course," Hatch said, "we couldn't go.

"How could we?" he said. He had been on that one little farm since he was a boy. When he was a young fellow, his father was an invalid and so Hatch had to run things. A farm, if you run it right, is very exacting. You have to fight weeds all the time. There are the farm animals to take care of. "Who would milk our cows?" Hatch said. The idea of anyone but him or his wife touching one of the Hutchenson cows seemed to hurt him. While he was alive, he didn't want anyone else plowing one of his fields, tending his corn, looking after things about the barn. He felt that way about his farm. It was a thing you couldn't explain, Hal said. He seemed to understand the two old people.

It was a spring night, past midnight, when Hal came to my house and told me the news. In our town we have a night telegraph operator at the railroad station and Hal got a wire. It was really addressed to Hatch Hutchenson, but the operator brought it to Hal. Will Hutchenson was dead, had been killed. It turned out later that he was at a party with some other young fellows and there might have been some drinking. Anyway, the car was wrecked, and Will Hutchenson was killed. The operator wanted Hal to go out and take the message to Hatch and his wife, and Hal wanted me to go along.

I offered to take my car, but Hal said no. "Let's walk out," he said. He wanted to put off the moment, I could see that. So we did walk. It was early spring, and I remember every moment of the silent walk we took, the little leaves just coming on the trees, the little streams we crossed, how the moonlight made the water seem alive. We loitered and loitered, not talking, hating to go on.

Then we got out there, and Hal went to the front door of the farmhouse while I stayed in the road. I heard a dog bark, away off somewhere. I heard a child crying in some distant house. I think that Hal, after he got to the front door of the house, must have stood there for ten minutes, hating to knock.

Then he did knock, and the sound his fist made on the door seemed terrible. It seemed like guns going off. Old Hatch came to the door, and I heard Hal tell him. I know what happened. Hal had been trying, all the way out from town, to think up words to tell the old couple in some gentle way, but when it came to the scratch, he couldn't. He blurted everything right out, right into old Hatch's face.

That was all. Old Hatch didn't say a word. The door was opened, he stood there in the moonlight, wearing a funny long white nightgown, Hal told him, and the door went shut again with a bang, and Hal was left standing there.

He stood for a time, and then came back out into the road to me. "Well," he said, and "Well," I said. We stood in the road looking and listening. There wasn't a sound from the house.

And then—it might have been ten minutes or it might have been a half hour—we stood silently, listening and watching, not knowing what to do—we couldn't go away— "I guess they are trying to get so they can believe it," Hal whispered to me. I got his notion all right. The two old people must have thought of their son Will always only in terms of life, never of death.

We stood watching and listening, and then, suddenly, after a long time, Hal touched me on the arm. "Look," he whispered. There were two white-clad figures going from the house to the barn. It turned out, you see, that old Hatch had been plowing that day. He had finished plowing and harrowing a field near the barn.

The two figures went into the barn and presently came out. They went into the field, and Hal and I crept across the farmyard to the barn and got to where we could see what was going on without being seen.

It was an incredible thing. The old man had got a hand corn-planter out of the barn and his wife had got a bag of seed corn, and there, in the moonlight, that night, after they got that news, they were planting corn.

It was a thing to curl your hair—it was so ghostly. They were both in their nightgowns. They would do a row across the field, coming quite close to us as we stood in the shadow of the barn, and then, at the end of each row, they would kneel side by side by the fence and stay silent for a time. The whole thing went on in silence. It was the first time in my life I ever understood something, and I am far from sure now that I can put down what I understood and felt that night—I mean something about the connection between certain people and the earth—a kind of silent cry, down into the earth, of these two old people, putting corn down into the earth. It was as though they were putting death down into the ground that life might grow again— something like that.

They must have been asking something of the earth, too. But what's the use? What they were up to in connection with the life in their field and the lost life in their son is something you can't very well make clear in words. All I know is that Hal and I stood the sight as long as we could, and then we crept away and went back to town, but Hatch Hutchenson and his wife must have got what they were after that night, because Hal told me that when he went out in the morning to see them and to make the arrangements for bringing their dead son home, they were both curiously quiet and Hal thought in command of themselves. Hal said he thought they had got something. "They have their farm and they have still got Will's letters to read," Hal said.

Part IV

Country Songbook

A TIME TO KEEP

by Burl Ives

Burl Ives, age three

To paraphrase what Walt Whitman wrote in *Leaves of Grass*, "There was a child went forth one day and what that child saw he became." To view myself as such a child, I would have to say, "What that child saw, he *heard*, and so became."

A year prior to the portended doomsday of the 1910 appearance of Halley's Comet, there was in southern Illinois a great harmonic oneness of sound and senses. The organ point of roosters crowing, bees, crickets, birds, horses, chickens, cows, geese, crows, robins, meadowlarks, wrens, prairie chickens, faraway voices, rumbling of wagon carts, farm implements, wood splitting, children laughing and singing, dogs barking, a thin stream of milk splattering against a milk bucket, and the splash of milk being churned—giving sweet butter and delicious buttermilk. The smell of fresh cornbread, lily-white hominy, and the powerful smell of kraut fermenting in wooden vats, the canning of fruits and vegetables, the curing and smoking of meat. All of this and much, much more greeted me on June 14, 1909, on a farm in Hunt Township, Jasper County, southeastern part of the great state of Illinois. Sights and sounds that are still to this day seed to my process of becoming. As I recall my first professional appearance at the age of four and my days as a child evangelical singer, I realize that now on the concert stage I'm reaping the harvest of a time long ago when a horse's gait measured the distance you could travel in a day.

I remember as a toddler being the center of attention whilst surrounded by my family—Mother, Dad, three sisters and two brothers. Dad had just bought my sister Audrey, ten years my senior, a pump organ. We had all been singing "We're Marching to Zion" when they became silent, their gazes fixed on me, singing "Come ye who love the Lord and let your joys be known. . . ." Not only did I know the lyrics—all of them—I was singing on pitch. They were astounded! How could a baby know all the words and the melody? Seventy-five years and a lot of music later, I think I might have an answer to that question.

A few miles from where my father "farmed on the shares," there

267

was a little country church where deep-chested farmers and their families assembled for Sunday morning and Tuesday night prayer. My mother always attended, accompanied by her children. I remember her singing hymns with the congregation when I was just a babe in arms. Indeed I believe I was listening to the hearty vibrations of that praise *before* I made my appearance that June morning close to dawn—into a world of summer sounds.

To this day, when I'm out sailing I can remember a small boy running below billowing white sheets on washday—me, the master of my own vessel to starboard of the chicken coop! I remember a world of "come what may and take what it brings" without regret. Today I sometimes long for the huge silences of a sacred sky before the airplane overshadowed the squawk of birds and before the drone of the motorcar invaded the quiet of front porch neighborly gatherings. Those sounds of progress were not yet attained when I grew up among healthy children in a family where there was a song to match almost every occasion, where stories were told to music, where my Grandma Kate taught us the "naughty words" in song rather than have us learn them the "wrong way" in school.

The music I heard and learned as a child was of a fabric woven long before—not of silk, but of flax. The songs that in the oral tradition my forebears brought with them from their homelands have been passed to me and treasured by me through the fine muslin of small-town America. Some of the songs kept style and nuance remarkably well; others, submerged, were lost for a time, to be reborn generations later as American Folklore.

Looking back over my seventy-seven summers, my becoming known as a ballad singer seems as natural to me as a dog taking after a rabbit. I first learned to play the banjo, then the guitar, which seemed better suited to my sound. I remember taking orders for the Larkin Mail Order Company out of Chicago until I had enough money put aside to buy my first banjo. I was about nine or ten years of age at the time.

As a youth, I gravitated to people who shared their songs with me— sometimes very ancient songs. When I was twenty, I traveled to New York with my guitar to see and hear that "great ocean" I had heard so much about. Having been dubbed an indifferent student, I left Eastern Illinois State Teachers College in my third year. Hungering to fill myself with a quality to match an inner yearning, I sang my way through forty-six of the then forty-eight states, honing to the sights and sounds of my country, creating a niche, a style, a web of sound to

The music I heard and learned as a child was of a fabric woven long before— not of silk, but of flax.

Frank and Cordella Ives,
Burl's parents

*Burl Ives (at far left)
in high school, performing
in a group called
"The String Beaners"*

give form to a will to *be* the song which I sang.

I ended up back in New York City in 1933. While there I met a lady who was affiliated with the Columbia University library. I asked her if I might use the library facilities even though I was not a registered student. She arranged for me to do this. To this day I am forever grateful to the Columbia University who welcomed a country boy without funds, for it was there that I became acquainted with the great classics— Tolstoy, Dostoevsky, Thomas Mann, and so many others.

I strove then and still do today to resonate the purity I heard in those hymns early in my life. I knew that songs traveled well, that music was never alien, so I became a wayfarer. I found a new order in my mind, as if the diverse elements composing my spirit, like the winds of my native state, had discarded their random ways. I accepted my destiny. This destiny brought me to New York City, to the Church of St. Mary the Virgin on 46th Street, where I became a specialist in plain chant, then on to The Riverside Church as a tenor singing oratorios and masses.

At the same time, with my guitar I was playing benefits of various kinds with my colleagues in the renaissance of American folk music: Alan Lomax, Josh White, Huddie "Leadbelly" Ledbetter, Earl Robinson, Woody Guthrie, and the Golden Gate Quartet. We all ended up on a CBS radio show produced by Alan Lomax called *Back Where I Come From*—a fitting title indeed because we all had roots in different parts of America and we all possessed "the goods."

However, this was not the first group of folk artists with whom I had performed. At eight years of age in my hometown, I first heard and became active in what is recognized today as bluegrass music. We performed many tunes together on guitar, banjo, mandolin and fiddle. I remember "The Lost Indian," "Sailor's Hornpipe," "The Irish Washerwoman," "Red Wing," "Over the Waves Waltz," and a couple of two-steps, among others.

269

*1975, North Carolina,
reading from the Book of Genesis*

Many people hear songs and they just sort of digest the lyrics and music together without isolating the meaning of the lyric. My songs have become for me, and, I hope, for the audience, a literary experience. I put images to words. An example is "The Red River Valley." I see it as a great drama:

> When you go to your home by the ocean
> May you never forget those sweet hours
> That we spent in the Red River Valley
> And the love we exchanged 'mid the flowers.

It creates a romance that is full like a novel to me. I'll give you an example or two of how this affected me as a young boy.

As a child one hears words. If he doesn't know the meaning of those words, he changes them to something within his own experience. I vividly recall one such example involving a separator—the machine that separates the grain from the straw in the harvest. Back then the power source for this device was a steam engine. There was a large belt that ran from the flywheel of the engine to the separator. Grain came out one way, chaff and straw the other. When the job was done, the engine would pull the separator to the next job. The two vehicles were known as a threshing machine. One day before being pulled over a small bridge near my home, the separator started sliding into the river. It took many shouting men with ropes, block and tackle, and horses pulling to get that separator back on the road.

There was an old hymn we sang in church:

> Rescue the perishing
> Care for the dying
> Jesus is merciful
> Jesus will save.

To my young mind the first line of that hymn was a picture of the rescue of that threshing machine, so I sang "Rescue the perichine [like machine]." I did this for ten years before I realized that the vision I had portrayed in my child's mind, the vision I was singing, was in error.

Another such instance of this wrong impression of sight interfering with sound in my childhood is from my times in Sunday School. We would sing:

> Away far beyond Jordan
> We'll shout in that land
> We'll shout in that land.

In the little one-room church, hanging in front of the pulpit, was a picture representing the weekly Bible study—usually the Old Testament. There was one such picture which showed an ancient festival of the sacrifice of a bull—it may have been to Baal—with Elijah contesting his strength. The congregation was singing the hymn. When they sang the word "Jordan," my young eyes were on the bloody cow and my brain transformed the phrase, which I sang as "Away bloody cow Jordan" instead of "Away far beyond Jordan." At age sixteen I was still unknowingly singing "Away bloody cow Jordan."

To this day I do not remember words. I sing pictures and remembered phrases: pictures representing drama, emotions, and the flow of phrases, creating tales in progress. For instance, through all my years of singing the ancient Scottish air "Barbara Allen" the drama is the same, the casting the same, the setting the same. I cannot start halfway through. My memory visually requires that I begin at the beginning. Many times songs are requested that I haven't sung in years, sometimes as many as forty years, but if I can nail the first two or three words I'm off and running. The entire song comes back to my mind and I remember the drama.

I realize now that all through my life I have been instinctively trying to simplify ideas, songs, music, poetry, in an effort to distill from them their essence. The greatest wrestling match has been with myself: to remove myself from my work and bring to the audience that which I have distilled from my beginnings in the country. For years I thought it was just my imagination, nostalgia perhaps, that made me think that the sun shone brighter back then, the rain seemed sweeter, the sky bluer, the grass greener. But now with what we know of ecology and pollution I realize that the sky *was* bluer, the grass greener, the rain more sparkling. I also know that I was privileged to partake of a world long gone, a world in flower, innocent perhaps but still lovely, still young and, for me, filled with harmony.

Burl and Dorothy Ives

Amazing Grace

Words by John Newton

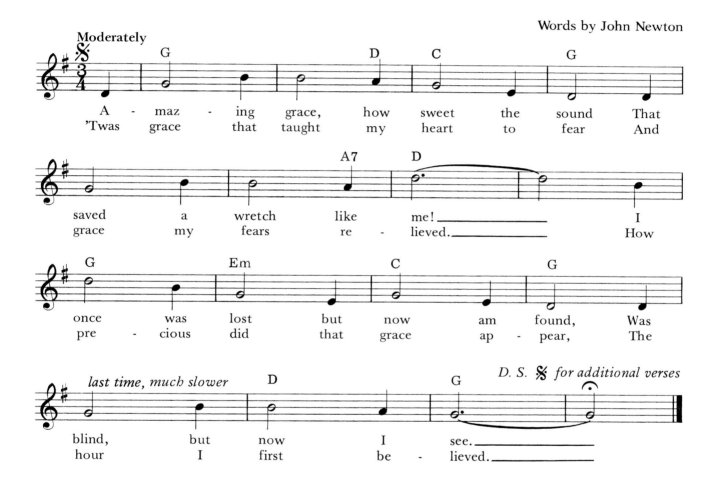

Moderately

G ... D ... C ... G

A - maz - ing grace, how sweet the sound That
'Twas grace that taught my heart to fear And

A7 ... D

saved a wretch like me! I
grace my fears re - lieved. How

G ... Em ... C ... G

once was lost but now am found, Was
pre - cious did that grace ap - pear, The

last time, much slower ... D ... G ... *D. S. 𝄋 for additional verses*

blind, but now I see.
hour I first be - lieved.

Additional Verses

Through many dangers, toils and snares
I have already come;
'Tis grace hath brought me safe thus far,
And grace will lead me home.

How sweet the name of Jesus sounds
In a believer's ear;
It soothes his sorrows, heals his wounds
And drives away his fear.

Must Jesus bear the cross alone
And all the world go free?
No, there's a cross for ev'ryone,
And there's a cross for me.

273

Down in the Valley

An American folk song

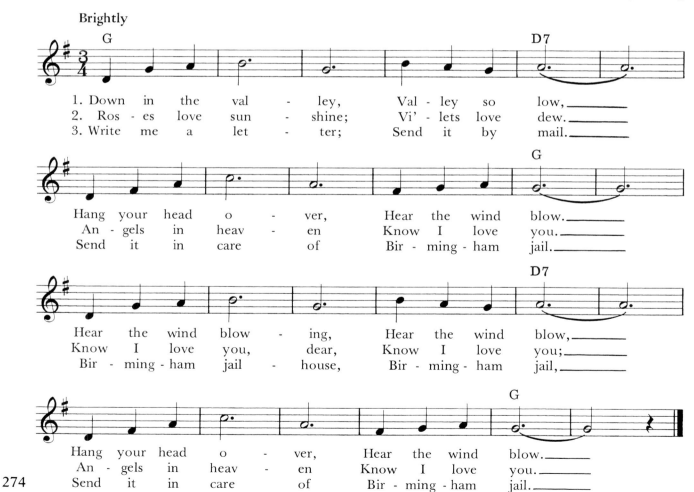

Brightly

G   D7

1. Down in the val - ley, Val - ley so low,_____
2. Ros - es love sun - shine; Vi' - lets love dew._____
3. Write me a let - ter; Send it by mail._____

G

Hang your head o - ver, Hear the wind blow._____
An - gels in heav - en Know I love you._____
Send it in care of Bir - ming - ham jail._____

D7

Hear the wind blow - ing, Hear the wind blow,_____
Know I love you, dear, Know I love you;_____
Bir - ming - ham jail - house, Bir - ming - ham jail,_____

G

Hang your head o - ver, Hear the wind blow._____
An - gels in heav - en Know I love you._____
Send it in care of Bir - ming - ham jail._____

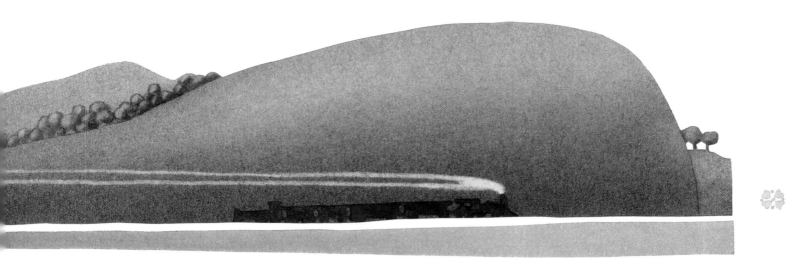

The Wabash Cannonball

A celebration of the railroad

Rolling along, in 2 (♩ = 1 beat)

G

From the great At - lan - tic O - cean To the wide Pa - cif - ic's
Oh,___ lis - ten to the jin - gle, The___ rum - ble and the

C   D7

shore, From the queen of flow - ing riv - ers To the South - land's ver - dant
roar, As she glides a - long the wood - land And___ down___ by the

G

door;____ ⎱
shore.____ ⎰   She's tall and dark and hand - some And

C   D7

known quite well by all; She's the reg - 'lar com - bi -

G   *D. C.*

na - tion Called The Wa - bash Can - non - ball._____

275

You Are My Sunshine

Words and music by Jimmie Davis and Charles Mitchell

1. The oth - er night, dear, _____ as I lay sleep - ing, _____
2. I'll al - ways love you _____ and make you hap - py, _____
3. You told me once, dear, _____ you real - ly loved me _____

_____ I dreamed I held you in my arms. _____ When I a -
_____ If you will on - ly say the same. _____ But if you
_____ And no one else could come be - tween. _____ But now you've

woke, dear, _____ I was mis - tak - en, _____ And I
leave me _____ to love an - oth - er, _____ You'll re -
left me _____ and love an - oth - er; _____ You have

hung my head and cried. _____ } You are my
gret it all some day. _____
shat - tered all my dreams. _____

sun - shine, _____ my on - ly sun - shine; _____ You make me hap - py _____

_____ when skies are gray. _____ You'll nev - er know, dear, _____ how much I

love you; _____ Please don't take my sun - shine a - way. _____

276

Wildwood Flower

Bright and snappy

An Appalachian mountain song

1. I will twine with your tress - es of ra - ven black
2. Oh, he prom - ised to love me, he prom - ised to
3. Oh, he taught me to love him; he called me his

hair,_____ With the ros - es so red and the
love_____ And to cher - ish me al - ways all
flow'r,_____ A_____ blos - som to cheer him through

lil - ies so fair,_____ With the myr - tle as
oth - ers a - bove._____ I a - woke from my
life's wear - y hour,_____ But_____ now he is

bright as the em - er - ald dew, A pale wild - wood
dream and my i - dol was clay; My pas - sion for
gone; he's_____ left me a - lone, The wild flow'rs to

flow - er with pet - als light blue._____
lov - ing had van - ished a - way._____
weep and the wild birds to mourn._____

4. I'll dance and I'll sing, and my life shall be gay.
   I'll charm every heart in the crowd I survey.
   Though my heart now is breaking, he never will know
   How his name makes me tremble, my pale cheeks to glow.

5. I'll dance and I'll sing, and my heart will be gay.
   I'll banish this weeping, drive troubles away.
   I'll live yet to see that he'll rue this dark hour
   When he won and neglected this frail wildwood flower.

Put On Your Old Grey Bonnet

Words by Stanley Murphy
Music by Percy Wenrich

With spirit

Put on your old grey bon - net With the blue rib - bon on it While I hitch old Dob - bin to the shay, ___ ___ And through the fields of clo - ver, We'll drive up to Do - ver On our gold - en wed - ding day. ___

The Little Brown Church in the Vale

A nostalgic favorite written in Iowa in 1864
Words and music by William S. Pitts

Moderately and very steady

1. There's a church in the val - ley by the wild - wood, No lov - li - er place in the dale; No spot is so dear to my child - hood As the lit - tle brown church in the vale.

2. How sweet on a clear Sab - bath morn - ing To list to the clear ring - ing bell; Its tones so sweet - ly are call - ing, O come to the church in the vale.

3. From the church in the val - ley by the wild - wood When day fades a - way in - to night, I would fain from this spot of my child - hood Wing my way to the man - sions of light.

Chorus

O, come, come, come, come,* come to the church in the wild - wood, O come to the church in the dale. No spot is so dear to my child - hood As the lit - tle brown church in the vale.

D. C.

* *Basses may continue to sing the word "come" on the lowest note of each chord.*

279

Old Blue

An American folk song

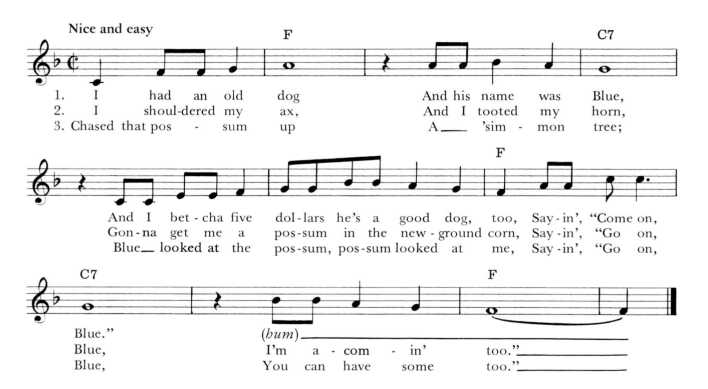

Nice and easy

1. I had an old dog And his name was Blue,
2. I shoul-dered my ax, And I tooted my horn,
3. Chased that pos - sum up A__ 'sim - mon tree;

And I bet - cha five dol - lars he's a good dog, too, Say - in', "Come on,
Gon - na get me a pos-sum in the new - ground corn, Say - in', "Go on,
Blue__ looked at the pos-sum, pos-sum looked at me, Say - in', "Go on,

Blue." (hum)____
Blue, I'm a - com - in' too."____
Blue, You can have some too."____

4. Baked that possum good and brown,
   Laid them sweet potatoes round and round,
   Sayin', "Come on, Blue, you can have some too."

5. "Blue, what makes your eyes so red?"
   "I've run them possums till I'm almost dead."
   "Go on, Blue, I'm comin' too."

6. Old Blue died, and he died so hard
   That he jarred the ground in my backyard,
   Sayin', "Go on, Blue, I'm comin' too."

7. When I get to heaven, first thing I'll do,
   Grab my horn and I'll blow for old Blue,
   Sayin', "Come on, Blue, finally got here too."

280

In the Garden

A gospel song written in 1912
Words and music by C. Austin Miles

Slowly

1. I come to the gar - den a - lone, While the
2. He speaks, and the sound of His voice Is so
3. I'd stay in the gar - den with Him Though the

dew is still on the ros - es; And the voice I hear fall - ing
sweet the birds hush their sing - ing, And the mel - o - dy that He
night a - round me be fall - ing, But He bids me go; through the

on my ear, The Son of God dis - clos - es.
gave to me With - in my heart is ring - ing.
voice of woe, His voice to me is call - ing.

Chorus

And He walks with me, and He talks with me, And He

tells me I am His own; And the joy we share as we

slower ..... *in tempo* ..... *D. C.*

tar - ry there None oth - er has ev - er known.

282

Can the Circle Be Unbroken?

An American gospel song

Moderately

1. I was stand - ing_____ by the win - dow_____ On a
2. Yes, I fol - lowed____ close be - hind her,_____ Tried to
3. Went back home, Lord,_____ cold and lone - some,_____ Since my

cold and cloud - y day,_____ When I saw the_____ hearse come
cheer up and be brave,____ But my sor - rows____ I could not
moth - er she was gone,____ All my broth - ers____ and sis - ters

roll - ing_____ For to car - ry my moth-er a - way._____
hide them____ When they laid____ her in____ the grave._____ Can the
cry - ing,____ What a home,__ so sad__ and lone._____

Chorus

cir - cle _____ be un - bro - ken,_____ By and by, Lord,

by and by?_____ There's a bet - ter_____ home a -

wait - ing_____ In the sky, Lord, in the sky._____

283

On Top of Old Smoky

A Southern mountain song

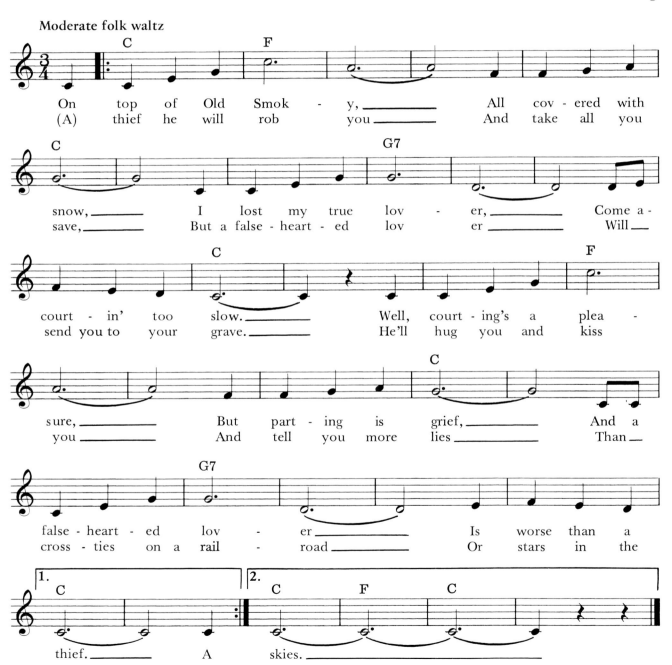

Moderate folk waltz

On top of Old Smok - y, _____ All cov - ered with
(A) thief he will rob you _____ And take all you

snow, _____ I lost my true lov - er, _____ Come a -
save, _____ But a false - heart - ed lov er _____ Will __

court - in' too slow. _____ Well, court - ing's a plea -
send you to your grave. _____ He'll hug you and kiss

sure, _____ But part - ing is grief, _____ And a
you _____ And tell you more lies _____ Than __

false - heart - ed lov - er _____ Is worse than a
cross - ties on a rail - road _____ Or stars in the

1.
thief. _____ A

2.
skies. _____

Shenandoah

*An American folk song—once a work song
for lumberjacks and sailing men*

1. Oh, Shen-an-doah,____ I long to hear you, A-
2. Oh, Shen-an-doah,____ I love your daugh-ter, A-
3. Oh, Shen-an-doah,____ I'm goin' to leave you, A-

way,____ you roll-ing riv-er.__ Oh, Shen-an-doah,__ just to be
way,____ you roll-ing riv-er.__ Oh, Shen-an-doah,__ a-cross the
way,____ you roll-ing riv-er.__ Oh, Shen-an-doah,__ I won't de-

near you,
wa-ter,   } A - way, we're bound a-way, Cross the wide Mis-sou-ri.
ceive you,

The Old Rugged Cross

A gospel hymn written in 1913
Words and music by George Bennard

286

change it some day for a crown. _____

Additional Verses

In the old rugged cross stained with blood so divine,
A wondrous beauty I see.
For 'twas on that old cross Jesus suffered and died
To pardon and sanctify me.

Chorus

To the old rugged cross I will ever be true;
Its shame and reproach gladly bear.
Then He'll call me some day to my home far away,
Where His glory forever I'll share.

Chorus

Rock of Ages

A hymn often heard at country funerals
Words by Augustus M. Toplady
Music by Thomas Hastings

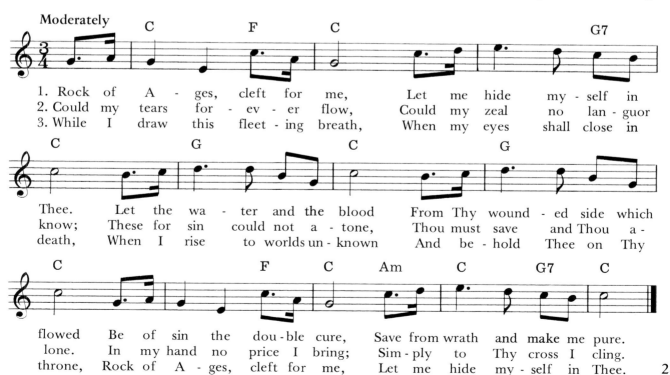

Moderately

1. Rock of A - ges, cleft for me, Let me hide my - self in
2. Could my tears for - ev - er flow, Could my zeal no lan - guor
3. While I draw this fleet - ing breath, When my eyes shall close in

Thee. Let the wa - ter and the blood From Thy wound - ed side which
know; These for sin could not a - tone, Thou must save and Thou a -
death, When I rise to worlds un - known And be - hold Thee on Thy

flowed Be of sin the dou - ble cure, Save from wrath and make me pure.
lone. In my hand no price I bring; Sim - ply to Thy cross I cling.
throne, Rock of A - ges, cleft for me, Let me hide my - self in Thee.

287

Tennessee Waltz

Words and music by Redd Stewart and Pee Wee King

I was waltz-ing__ with my dar-lin'__ To the Ten-nes-see__ Waltz__ When an old friend I hap-pened to see.__ In-tro-duced him__ to my loved one__ And__ while they__ were__ waltz-ing, My friend stole my sweet-heart from me.__ I re-mem-ber the night and the Ten-nes-see Waltz; Now I know just how much I have lost.__ Yes, I lost my__ lit-tle dar-lin'__ The__ night they__ were play-ing The beau-ti-ful Ten-nes-see Waltz.

288

Your Cheatin' Heart

Words and music by Hank Williams

Moderately, with a swing

Your cheat - in'__ heart____ Will make you weep;____ You'll cry and__
Your cheat - in'__ heart____ Will pine some - day____ And crave the__

cry____ And try to sleep.____ But sleep won't_ come____ The whole night
love____ You threw a - way.____ The time will_ come____ When you'll be

through;__
blue;__ } Your cheat - in'__ heart____ Will tell on you.____ When tears come

down____ Like fall - in' rain,____ You'll toss a - round____

__ And call my name.____ You'll walk the_ floor____ The way I

290   do;____ Your cheat - in'__ heart____ Will tell on you.____

She'll Be Comin' Round the Mountain

An American railroad song, derived from a black spiritual

1. She'll be com - in' round the moun - tain when she comes; (When she comes!) She'll be com - in' round the moun - tain when she comes. (When she comes!) She'll be com - in' round the moun - tain; She'll be com - in' round the moun - tain; She'll be com - in' round the moun - tain when she comes. (When she comes!)

2. She'll be driv - in' six white hors - es when she comes; (When she comes!) She'll be driv - in' six white hors - es when she comes. (When she comes!) She'll be driv - in' six white hors - es; She'll be driv - in' six white hors - es; She'll be driv - in' six white hors - es when she comes. (When she comes!)

3. Oh, we'll all come out to greet her when she comes; (When she comes!) Oh, we'll all come out to greet her when she comes. (When she comes!) Yes, we'll all come out to greet her; Oh, we'll all come out to greet her; all come out to greet her when she comes. (When she comes!)

Swing Low, Sweet Chariot

An American black spiritual

That Old-Time Religion

A Southern revival song

With that old-time spirit

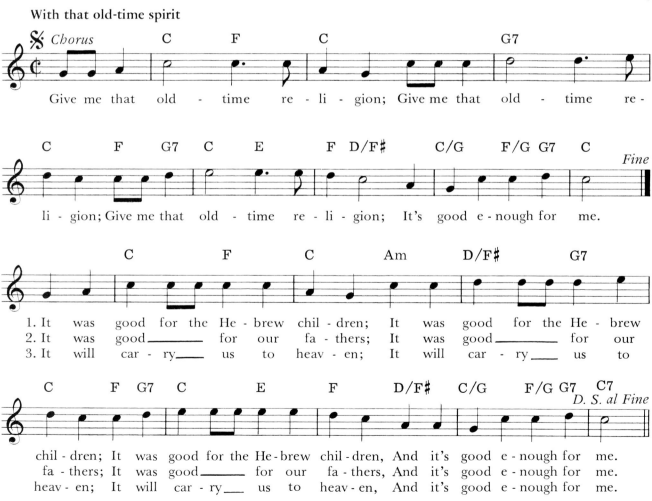

Give me that old - time re - li - gion; Give me that old - time re -

li - gion; Give me that old - time re - li - gion; It's good e - nough for me.

1. It was good for the He - brew chil - dren; It was good for the He - brew
2. It was good_____ for our fa - thers; It was good_____ for our
3. It will car - ry___ us to heav - en; It will car - ry___ us to

chil - dren; It was good for the He - brew chil - dren, And it's good e - nough for me.
fa - thers; It was good_____ for our fa - thers, And it's good e - nough for me.
heav - en; It will car - ry___ us to heav - en, And it's good e - nough for me.

294

Bringing In the Sheaves

A revival-meeting favorite
Words by Knowles Shaw
Music by George A. Minor

Moderately, with a beat

1. Sow - ing in the morn - ing, sow - ing seeds of kind - ness,
2. Sow - ing in the sun - shine, sow - ing in the shad - ows,
3. Go - ing forth with weep - ing, sow - ing for the Mas - ter,

Sow - ing in the noon - tide and the dew - y eve, Wait - ing for the har - vest
Fear - ing nei - ther clouds nor win - ter's chill-ing breeze, By and by the har - vest
Though the loss sus - tained, our spir - it of - ten grieves. When our weep - ing's o - ver,

and the time of reap - ing, We shall come re-joic - ing, bring - ing in the sheaves.
and the la - bor end - ed. We shall come re-joic - ing, bring - ing in the sheaves.
He will bid us wel - come. We shall come re-joic - ing, bring - ing in the sheaves.

Chorus

Bring - ing in the sheaves, bring - ing in the sheaves, We shall come re - joic - ing,

bring - ing in the sheaves. Bring - ing in the sheaves, bring - ing in the sheaves,

We shall come re - joic - ing, bring - ing in the sheaves.

295

Green, Green Grass of Home

Words and music by Curly Putman

1. The old home-town looks the same As I step down from the
2. (The) old house is still standing Though the paint is cracked and
3. *(Recitation) Then I awake and look around me At four gray walls*

train, And there to meet me is my ma-ma and
dry, And there's that old oak tree that I used to
that surround me, And I realize that I was only

pa-pa. Down the road I look and there runs Mar-y,
play on. Down the lane I walk with my sweet Mar-y,
dreaming. For there's a guard and there's a sad old padre,

Hair of gold and lips like cher-ries. It's good to touch the
Hair of gold and lips like cher-ries. It's good to touch the
Arm in arm we'll walk at daybreak; Again I'll touch the

green, green grass of home. Yes, they'll
green, green grass of home. Yes, they'll
green, green grass of home. (sing) Yes, they'll

all come to meet me, Arms reach-ing, smil-ing sweet-ly. It's
all come to meet me, Arms reach-ing, smil-ing sweet-ly.
all come to see me In the

296

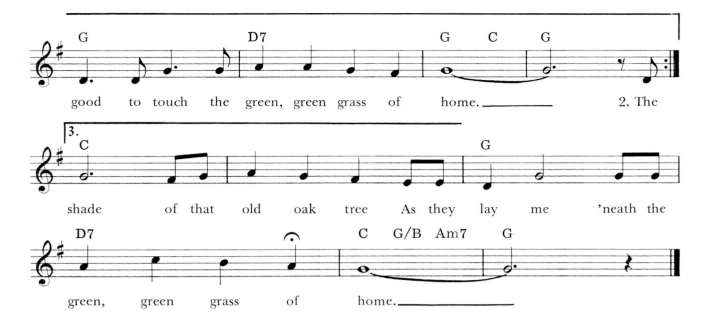

good to touch the green, green grass of home._____ 2. The

3.
shade of that old oak tree As they lay me 'neath the

green, green grass of home._____

ACKNOWLEDGMENTS

TEXT CREDITS

Pages 11–24: "Country Roads" by Paul Engle. Pages 15–16: "Country Bridges" by John R. Roberson. Page 19: "Burma-Shave Signs" by John R. Roberson. Burma Shave jingles used by permission of American Safety Razor Company, Staunton, VA 24401. Pages 21–22: "Roadside Stands" by Herbert H. Lieberman. Pages 27–44: "The Home Place" by Paul Engle. Pages 29–30: "Porches" by John R. Roberson. Page 36: "Presidents' Birthplaces" by Catherine T. Brown. Pages 47–65: "Farming" by Paul Engle. Page 48 (quote): "We Are American Farmers," by Wheeler McMllen, copyright © 1952 by Farm Journal Inc., is from the February 1952 issue of Farm Journal, used by permission of Farm Journal Inc. Page 50: "The Old Farmer's Almanac" by Herbert H. Lieberman. Recession quote from The Old Farmer's Almanac, copyright © 1942 by Yankee Publishing, Inc., used by permission of Yankee Publishing, Inc. Page 57: "Hex Signs" by Catherine T. Brown. Page 60: "Horse Trading" by John R. Roberson. Pages 67–82: "Crafts" by Paul Engle. Page 69 (quote): A People and Their Quilts, copyright © 1984 by John Rice Irwin, used by permission of Schiffer Publishing Ltd. Pages 71–72: "Baskets" by John R. Roberson. Page 72 (quotes): Baskets and Basket Makers in Southern Appalachia, copyright © 1982 by John Rice Irwin, used by permission of Schiffer Publishing Ltd. Pages 76–78: "The Quilter's Art" by Catherine T. Brown. Page 77 (poetry quote): "Mother's Patchwork Quilt" by Winnie Wilcox Garner, from A Garden of Quilts by Mary Elizabeth Johnson, copyright © 1984 by Oxmoor House, Inc., used by permission of Oxmoor House, Inc. Page 80 (quote): from "Threads of Happiness and Stitches of Love," by Susan Ramey Wright, copyright © 1984 by Southern Living Inc., appeared in the August 1984 issue of Southern Living, used by permission of Southern Living, Inc. Pages 85–101: "Country Towns" by Paul Engle. Pages 89–90: "Town Squares" by John R. Roberson. Page 91 (quote): The Old Farmer's Almanac, copyright © 1943 by Yankee Publishing, Inc., used by permission of Yankee Publishing, Inc. Pages 97–98: "The Little Red Schoolhouse" by Herbert H. Lieberman. Pages 103–119: "Gatherings" by Paul Engle. Pages 107–108: "Country Fairs" by Catherine T. Brown. Pages 113–114: "Rural Cemeteries" by Herbert H. Lieberman. Pages 123–127: "Company's Coming" by Celestine Sibley. Pages 128, 148 (quotes): Under A Buttermilk Moon: A Country Memoir, copyright © 1984 by Roy Webster, used by permission of August House Inc. Pages 129, 135, 141 (quotes): A Place Called Sweet Apple, copyright © 1967, 1985 by Celestine Sibley, used by permission of Peachtree Publishers Ltd. Page 129 (recipe): Miss Mary's Down-Home Cooking: Traditional Recipes from Lynchburg, Tennessee, copyright © 1984 by Diana Dalsass, used by permission of NAL Penguin Inc. and the author. Page 129 (quote), pages 139, 141, 147 (recipes): New Southern Cooking, copyright © 1986 by Nathalie Dupree, used by permission of Alfred A. Knopf, Inc. Pages 129, 135 (recipes), page 141 (quote), page 148 (recipe): The Heritage of Southern Cooking, copyright © 1986 by Camille Glenn, used by permission of Workman Publishing Co., Inc. Pages 130, 134 (recipes), page 134 (quote), pages 140, 141, 142 (recipes): American Home Cooking, copyright © 1980 by Nika Hazelton, used by permission of Viking Penguin Inc. and Elaine Markson Literary Agency Inc. Page 130 (quote): White Trash Cooking, copyright © 1986 by Ernest Matthew Mickler, is published by The Jargon Society/10 Speed Press, used by permission of the author. Page 130 (recipe), page 133 (quote): The Taste of Country Cooking, copyright © 1976 by Edna Lewis, used by permission of Alfred A. Knopf, Inc. Page 131 (quote): Real American Food, copyright © 1986 by Jane and Michael Stern, used by permission of Alfred A. Knopf, Inc., and Robert Cornfield Literary Agency. Page 131 (recipes), pages 132, 138 (quotes), pages 138, 143 (recipes): The American Heritage Cookbook, copyright © 1964 by American Heritage Publishing Co., Inc., used by permission of American Heritage Publishing Co., Inc. Pages 132, 138, 142, 143 (recipes), page 146 (quote), page 147 (recipe): James Beard's American Cookery, copyright © 1972 by James A. Beard, used by permission of Little, Brown & Co. Pages 132, 136, 137, 143 (recipes): The Grass Roots Cookbook, copyright © 1977 by Jean Anderson, used by permission of McIntosh & Otis, Inc. Pages 133, 136 (recipes), page 145 (quote): Country Kitchens Remembered, copyright © 1986 by Marilyn Kluger, used by permission of Dodd, Mead & Co. Page 134 (recipe): America's Cook Book, compiled by The Home Institute of The New York Herald Tribune, copyright © 1937 by Charles Scribner's Sons, renewed © 1965 by The New York Herald Tribune, used by permission of Charles Scribner's Sons. Page 135 (recipe): The New York Times Cookbook edited by Craig Claiborne, copyright © 1961 by Craig Claiborne, used by permission of Harper & Row, Publishers, Inc., and Schaffner Agency. Page 135 (recipe): The New York Times Heritage Cookbook by Jean Hewitt, copyright © 1972 by The New York Times Company, used by permission of The Putnam Publishing Group. Page 135 (quote): Red Hills and Cotton, copyright © 1942 by Ben Robertson, used by permission of University of South Carolina Press. Pages 136, 137, 139, 145 (recipes): Famous American Recipes by John and Marie Roberson, copyright © 1965 by Marie Roberson Hamm, used by permission of Mrs. Marie Ketcham. Page 138 (recipe): Old Fashioned Recipe Book, copyright © 1977 by Carla Emery, used by permission of Bantam Books, Inc. Pages 139, 140 (recipes): The New James Beard, copyright © 1981 by James Beard, used by permission of Alfred A. Knopf, Inc., and Schaffner Agency. Page 141 (recipe): The Victory Garden Cookbook, copyright © 1982 by Marian Morash and WGBH Educational Foundation, used by permission of Alfred A. Knopf, Inc., and The Sterling Lord Agency Inc. Page 141 (quote): The Member of the Wedding, copyright © 1946 by Carson McCullers, renewed © 1974 by Floria V. Lasky, used by permission of Houghton Mifflin Company and Barrie & Jenkins, Ltd., Century Hutchinson Ltd. Page 141 (recipe): Manna: Foods of the Frontier, copyright © 1972 by Gertrude Harris, used by permission of 101 Productions. Pages 142, 143 (quotes): Cross Creek, copyright 1942 by Marjorie Kinnan Rawlings, renewed © 1970 by Norton Baskin. First appeared in Scribner's Magazine in 1933, used by permission of Charles Scribner's Sons and Brandt & Brandt, Literary Agents Inc. Page 142 (quote): Soul Food Cookbook, copyright © 1969 by Bob Jeffries, used by permission of Macmillan Publishing Company. Page 145 (quote): The Country Kitchen, copyright © 1935, 1936 by Della T. Lutes, used by permission of Little, Brown and Company. Pages 145, 146, 147 (recipes): The Doubleday Cookbook, copyright © 1975 by Jean Anderson, used by permission of Doubleday & Co., Inc. Page 149 (recipe): Cross Creek Cookery, copyright © 1942 by Marjorie Kinnan Rawlings, renewed © 1970 by Norton Baskin, used by permission of Charles Scribner's Sons and Brandt & Brandt Literary Agents Inc. Pages 152–167: "A Time of Learning," copyright © 1946, renewed © 1974 by Jessamyn West, used by permission of Harcourt Brace Jovanovich Inc. and Russell & Volkening Inc. Page

173: "The Pasture" and "The Birthplace," copyright © 1928, 1939, © 1967, 1969 by Holt, Rinehart and Winston. Copyright © 1956 by Robert Frost, from *The Poetry of Robert Frost*, edited by Edward Connery Lathem, used by permission of Henry Holt & Company, Jonathan Cape Ltd. and the Estate of Robert Frost. Pages 175–183: "Lily Daw and the Three Ladies" by Eudora Welty, copyright © 1937 by University of Nebraska, renewed © 1965 by Eudora Welty, used by permission of Russell & Volkening Inc. Pages 185–192: "Reverend Black Douglas," copyright © 1985 by Alex Haley. From *Henning* by Alex Haley, to be published by Doubleday & Co., New York, used by permission of John Hawkins & Associates, Inc. Pages 193–199: "Clearing in the Sky," from *Clearing in the Sky & Other Stories*, copyright © 1950, renewed © 1978 by Jesse Stuart, used by permission of the Jesse Stuart Foundation, Judy B. Thomas, Chair, P.O. Box 391, Ashland, KY 41114. Pages 201–215: "Two Soldiers," copyright © 1942 by William Faulkner, renewed © 1970 by Estelle Faulkner and Jill Faulkner Summer, used by permission of Random House Inc. and Curtis Brown. Pages 225–233: "Hot-Collared Mule," from *Clearing in the Sky & Other Stories*, copyright © 1950, renewed © 1978 by Jesse Stuart. Reprinted by permission of the Jesse Stuart Foundation, Judy B. Thomas, Chair, P.O. Box 391, Ashland, KY 41114. Pages 235–249: "Cocks Must Crow," copyright © 1940 by Marjorie Kinnan Rawlings, renewed © 1968 by Norton Baskin, used by permission of Charles Scribner's Sons and Brandt & Brandt Literary Agents Inc. Pages 251–258: "Invisible Boy," copyright © 1945, renewed © 1973 by Ray Bradbury, used by permission of Don Congdon Associates, Inc. Pages 259–263: "The Corn-Planting" by Sherwood Anderson, copyright © 1934 by Eleanor Anderson, renewed © 1961 by Eleanor Copenhaver Anderson, used by permission of Harold Ober Associates Inc. Pages 267–271: "A Time to Keep" by Burl Ives.

Additional thanks to the following: William L. Simon and Dan Fox, music consultants; Katherine G. Ness and Dorothy G. Flynn, copyediting; Mary Lynn Maiscott, research; Sydney Wolfe Cohen, index; Lisa Garrett, Beth Caudell and Alfredo Santana, rights clearance; Doris B. Cypher, administrative assistant.

ILLUSTRATION CREDITS

Dust jacket, front cover: photograph by Tom Kelley Studio. Front flap (top): Joe Rossi/St. Paul Pioneer Press and Dispatch. Front flap (bottom): Deborah Chabrian. Back flap (top): Mario Mercado. Back flap (bottom): Leo and Diane Dillon. Binding, front cover embossing: photograph by Joe Rossi/St. Paul Pioneer Press and Dispatch. Pages 3, 9, 121, 151, 173, 194, 265: David Frampton. Pages 10, 52, 72 (top left), 77 (bottom): Lyntha Scott Eiler/The American Folklife Center at The Library of Congress. Pages 12, 23, 28 (bottom), 32, 38–39, 40, 48 (bottom), 53, 62, 64–65: photos by Joe Rossi/St. Paul Pioneer Press and Dispatch. Pages 13, 56, 95: © Mark Chester. Pages 14, 42 (top): courtesy of The Jesse Stuart Foundation, P.O. Box 391, Ashland, Kentucky 41114. Page 15: *Stone City* by Grant Wood, reproduced by permission of the Joslyn Art Museum, Omaha, Nebraska. Pages 15, 37: © Christopher Gallo. Pages 16 (top), 19, 21 (center), 22 (top right), 30 (left): John Bowdren. Pages 16 (bottom), 29 (top), 43 (bottom), 59, 71 (top), 74 (bottom), 76: © Robin Hood. Page 17: © Lud Munchmeyer. Page 18: © Marion Davis. Pages 20, 21 (bottom), 22 (bottom), 24, 26, 28 (top), 29 (bottom), 30 (bottom), 41, 42 (bottom), 43 (top), 44–45, 61, 87, 96, 105, 107 (top), 112: © William A. Bake. Pages 21 (top), 48 (top), 51 (bottom left), 69, 77 (top), 77 (center right), 78 (bottom), 109, 117: Terry Eiler/The American Folklife Center at The Library of Congress. Page 22 (top left): © Robert Essel/Manhattan Views Inc. Page 25: © Bullaty Lomeo. Page 31: *Harvest Meal*, appliqué tapestry, 51½ by 69 inches; © 1984 Arlette Rose Gosieski; collection of the artist. Pages 33, 66: from *A People and Their Quilts* by John Rice Irwin; photo © Robin Hood. Page 35: *Spring in Town* by Grant Wood, reproduced by permission of The Sheldon Swope Art Gallery, Terre Haute, Indiana. Page 36 (center): © V. W. Lamar/courtesy of Department of Natural Resources, Division of Parks, Recreation, and Historic Preservation, Jefferson City, Missouri. Page 36 (bottom): photo by W. L. McCoy, Hodgenville, Kentucky/Chicago Historical Society, Neg. no. ICHi–11483. Page 46: *July Hay* by Thomas Hart Benton, reproduced by permission of The Metropolitan Museum of Art, George A. Hearn Fund, 1943. Page 49: photo © by Blair Seitz, 1985/Seitz & Seitz, Harrisburg, Pennsylvania. Page 50: courtesy of Yankee Publishing Incorporated, Dublin, New Hampshire. Page 5l (top right): © Charles Klamkin. Page 54 (top left): courtesy of The Estate of Eric Sloane. Pages 54–55: A. Upitis/FPG. Page 57 (center): photography by Ernest Coppolino and Robert Milazzo; collection of Angelo Perrone. Pages 57 (top right), 73, 75, 77 (left center): photography by Ernest Coppolino and Robert Milazzo; The Cousley Collections. Page 57 (bottom right): Pennsylvania Dutch Visitors Bureau. Pages 60, 68: Jim Phelan, calligraphy by Angelo Perrone. Page 63: © Dan Guravich. Page 70: © Jeaninne S. Lamb. Pages 71 (bottom), 72 (top right, center, bottom left and right), 216, 221: Deborah Chabrian. Page 74 (top): photo courtesy of Berea College, Broomcraft; The Cousley Collections. Page 79: photograph from *Country Samplers*, copyright 1984 by Oxmoor House, Inc. Reproduced by permission of the publisher. Page 80: crewelwork by Joanne Perrone; photography by Ernest Coppolino and Robert Milazzo. Page 81: from *Decorated Tinware*, Index of American Design, National Gallery of Art, Washington. Page 82: photographs © Schecter Lee/ESTO. Page 83: photo by Jack Disbrow, Wilton, Connecticut. Page 84: © James Quick. Page 86: © Ralph Morang. Page 88: © 1987, Zigy Kaluzny. Pages 89, 99: © Chase McNiss, Hudson, New Hampshire. Page 90: © D. W. Roberts. Pages 91, 97, 113 (top right): © Angelo Perrone. Page 92: *Doctor and Doll* by Norman Rockwell, reprinted from *The Saturday Evening Post* © 1929 The Curtis Publishing Co. Pages 93, 100–101, 115: © Annie Griffiths. Page 94: Steve Dunwell/The Image Bank. Page 98: *Last Day of School* by John Falter, reprinted from *The Saturday Evening Post* © 1945 The Curtis Publishing Co. Pages 102–103: Gerri Johnson/The American Folklife Center at The Library of Congress. Page 106: Grandma Moses: *Country Fair*; copyright © 1985, Grandma Moses Properties Co., New York. Page 107 (bottom): photo by A. C. Haralson/Arkansas Department of Parks & Tourism. Page 108: Carl Fleischauer/The American Folklife Center at The Library of Congress. Page 110: Bruce Kliewe/H. Armstrong Roberts. Page 113 (bottom): stone rubbing by Don Hedin, photography by Ernest Coppolino and Robert Milazzo; collection of Marion Davis. Page 114: *All-Day Dinner on the Grounds of the Grove Level Baptist Church*, from *From the Hills of Georgia* by Mattie Lou O'Kelley; copyright © 1983 by Mattie Lou O'Kelley; by permission of Little, Brown and Company, in association with The Atlantic Monthly Press. Page 116: Norman Rockwell, *The County Agricultural Agent*, oil on canvas 36½″ x 70″, University Collection, Sheldon Memorial Art Gallery, University of Nebraska–Lincoln, gift of Nathan Gold. Pages 118–119: Grant Wood, American, 1891–1942, *Dinner for Threshers*, 1934, oil on masonite, 20″ x 81″; reproduced by permission of The Fine Arts Museum of San Francisco. Page 122: © Charles Harbutt/Archive Pictures Inc. Pages 128–129, 130–132, 134–139, 141–143, 146–149: Paul Blakey. Pages 133, 140, 144: Mario Mercado. Pages 153, 156, 161, 165: Robert Baxter. Page 168: Ben Wohlberg. Pages 174, 177, 182: Susi Kilgore. Pages 184, 189: Richard Williams. Pages 200–201, 208, 215: Bernie Fuchs. Pages 225, 229: Ted Co-Conis. Pages 234, 241, 247, 249: William Low. Page 250: Winslow P. Pels. Page 263: Herb Tauss. Page 266: photo by Peter Leach-Lewis, Foundation for Higher Spiritual Learning, Centreville, Virginia; courtesy of Mr. and Mrs. Burl Ives. Pages 267, 268, 269, 271: courtesy of Mr. and Mrs. Burl Ives. Page 270: photo by Claude Harta, San Carlos, Mexico; courtesy of Mr. and Mrs. Burl Ives. Pages 272–273, 274–275, 276–277, 278–279, 280–281, 282–283, 284–285, 287, 288–289, 290–291, 292, 294–295, 297: Leo and Diane Dillon.

INDEX

300

302